D0225373

Florissant Valley Library
St. Louis Community College
3400 Pershall Road
Ferguson, MO  63135-1499
314-513-4514

# The Welfare Debate

**Recent Titles in**
**Historical Guides to Controversial Issues in America**

# The Welfare Debate

Greg M. Shaw

Historical Guides to Controversial Issues in America

GREENWOOD PRESS
Westport, Connecticut • London

**Library of Congress Cataloging-in-Publication Data**

Shaw, Greg M.
   The welfare debate / Greg M. Shaw.
      p.  cm. — (Historical guides to controversial issues in
America, ISSN 1541–0021)
   Includes bibliographical references and index.
   ISBN-13: 978–0–313–33892–2 (alk. paper)
  1.  Public welfare—United States.   2.  United States—Social policy—History.   I. Title.
   HV91.S47   2007
   362.5'560973—dc22        2007026484

British Library Cataloguing in Publication Data is available.

Copyright © 2007 by Greg M. Shaw

All rights reserved. No portion of this book may be
reproduced, by any process or technique, without the
express written consent of the publisher.

Library of Congress Catalog Card Number: 2007026484
ISBN-13: 978–0–313–33892–2
ISSN: 1541–0021

First published in 2007

Greenwood Press, 88 Post Road West, Westport, CT 06881
An imprint of Greenwood Publishing Group, Inc.
www.greenwood.com

Printed in the United States of America

The paper used in this book complies with the
Permanent Paper Standard issued by the National
Information Standards Organization (Z39.48–1984).

10  9  8  7  6  5  4  3  2  1

*To Fiona and Ian,*
*who teach me about justice every day,*
*and to Mollie*
*for all her love and support*

Poverty is an anomaly to rich people. It is very difficult to make out why people who want dinner do not ring the bell.

—Walter Bagehot (*The Waverly Novels*, 1858)

# Contents

# Illustrations

# Preface

To survey the history of the debate over poverty relief in America is to confront a pair of important continuities spanning more than three centuries. First, since colonial days, some version of the arguments that the poor deserve at least a minimal subsistence and that some of them are not entirely at fault for their condition have clashed with an insistence that aid corrupts recipients' work ethic. A second dimension of the debate over relief has involved the question of public versus private assistance to the needy; both forms of aid have coexisted over a very long period of time. This second question raises issues of supervision of the poor, program funding, and Americans' interpretations of the rights of citizenship. Of course, these debates have not remained static through time. The changing nature of the labor market, the growth of the federal government, and evolving understandings of motherhood and of the role of women more generally have contributed to shifting perspectives on when and how to address poverty using community resources. Specifically, these long-term shifts in the political-social-economic context have prompted significant changes in how Americans think about poverty: as a moral status versus a more purely structural economic condition. Thus, to review the history of welfare is to uncover not only the continuities but also important changes in poverty relief and the debates over it. This book tracks both from colonial times to the present.

A challenge in crafting this history of the American welfare debate has been the need to trace the terrain of subjective perceptions of welfare provision and the arguments these perceptions drive while not getting lost in a complicated discussion of objective policy developments across states, time, and levels of government. I have sought to strike a balance, treating both the practices and the debates about them. Space limitations have dictated a focus on significant themes rather than on detailed examinations of numerous events along the way, for poverty relief efforts have come a very long way indeed since Europeans arrived on America's shores in the opening decade of the seventeenth century. Synthesizing existing scholarship with historical primary sources and materials from research and advocacy organizations, governments, the elite media, and general news reports hopefully has rendered an account of the American welfare debate that is at once interesting to both the specialist and the generalist and that is permeated with the flavor of the heated discourse on welfare over time. A list of suggested further readings is provided for those whose curiosity leads them to learn more.

Along the way I have incurred many debts. These begin at home with my wonderful wife and two children. They have endured a too-busy dad at times and more talk of poverty policy than they care to recall. Several students at Illinois Wesleyan University also provided very helpful research assistance, including Anne Bostrom, Liz Chandler, Sarah Keister, Sarah Mysiewicz, and Bailee Soltys. Gita Bazarauskaite's contributions as research assistant, proofreader, and critic were invaluable. Kristen Vogel and Sarah George lent their excellent librarianship. Mollie Ward, Bob Shapiro, and Jim Simeone reviewed the manuscript and gave me considerable good advice. Thanks also to Paul Bushnell, Matt Pursell, and Stewart Winger for enlightening conversations about early America. I am also grateful to Sandy Towers at Greenwood Press for her expert guidance. Jim Plath helped with the Ernest Hemingway observation that begins chapter 5. Of course, I remain responsible for any remaining faults in the work. Lastly, I gratefully acknowledge a grant from Illinois Wesleyan University that supported the 2001 survey of state policy makers discussed in chapter 7.

# Introduction

To loosely paraphrase the late British political theorist Isaiah Berlin, when Americans discuss welfare, they disagree on many small things, but they agree on one big thing.[1] Since the early seventeenth century, Americans have widely believed in a collective obligation to provide for the welfare of the very poor. Libertarians at various times have dissented from this position, and while they have exerted some influence over the debate, theirs has ultimately been an unsuccessful argument. From the earliest settlements in Jamestown and Plymouth to the current era of mandated workfare, collective provision for the poor has marked the entirety of American history. These efforts have at times been privately financed instead of relying entirely on public funds. Further, relief has come with conditions, with time limits, and with varying levels of generosity and miserliness, and often it has come with a mixture of resentfulness and sanctimoniousness. But these efforts *have* come. They have persisted in one form or another through boom times and economic depressions; across rural and urban communities; through eras when Americans privileged motherhood and a more recent era when quite the opposite was true; and from preindustrial years to times of rapid urbanization, total war, periods marked by illusions of near-universal affluence, and, of course, grand declarations of "war on poverty." Through all these times, Americans have funded programs, either publicly or privately, to provide a way through for the desperately poor among us, sometimes grudgingly or resignedly, sometimes piously, and, on rare occasions, even ambitiously. A basic obligation to extend some help to the poor has marked the American experience throughout.

Beyond this very general understanding, however, Americans have disagreed widely on the particulars of provision for the poor. The main points of friction have turned on a series of related issues that hearken back to the question of deservingness. Debates over public versus private funding for relief, of local versus state versus federal organization of welfare programs, and of the scope and generosity of assistance at some point all have come down to questions of who deserves help, how much, and under what circumstances. Behind these core questions lies a wariness—indeed, among many, a conviction—that open-ended welfare provision fosters dependency and the erosion of personal initiative. Much of the debate over welfare boils down to the thorny question of how to balance the widely consensual urge to help the poor with a fear of dependency building. To the extent that Americans have disagreed on this balance, communities have historically extended more or less help to their poorest members. Varying degrees of endorsement of the dependency-building thesis led many nineteenth-century cities and towns to construct poorhouses, but others to rely heavily instead on alternative methods of more autonomy-preserving poor relief. Arguments over the efficiency and morality of cash assistance during the third quarter of the 1800s led to a retrenchment of relief during those years in some, but certainly not all, eastern cities. In the twentieth century, disagreements over the efficacy of labor markets in meeting poor people's needs led some southern states to withdraw welfare during planting and harvest seasons, while northern states maintained greater continuity in their care for the poor. Also, the predisposition toward surveillance and supervision of the poor—in part to ferret out presumptively less worthy aid recipients—catalyzed involuntary *binding out* of children from desperately poor families during the 1800s, surprise nighttime inspections of welfare recipients' homes through the middle part of the twentieth century, and fingerprinting initiatives at welfare agencies beginning in the 1990s.

To the very great extent that Americans disagree on the proper balance between meeting the basic needs of poor people and undermining individual initiative, the debate over welfare has touched repeatedly on some common themes while also changing as it has passed over a shifting social, political, and economic terrain. Evolving understandings of markets, motherhood, race, federalism, and the extent to which the poor constitute a deviant class have guided many of the most important changes in this protracted debate. Other issues enter at various points but arguably pale in comparison to these five themes. Fundamental disagreements related to these key issues make welfare policy decisions not quite politically intractable, but certainly very difficult. In recent decades, many politicians have been loath to confront the issue, despite objective developments on the ground that call for action. The late 1970s, with its perception of the growth of an urban *underclass* (as contentious as that term has been) was such a moment, prompting Joseph A. Califano Jr., President Jimmy Carter's secretary of Health, Education, and Welfare, to dub welfare reform "the Mideast of domestic politics."[2] In his view and that of many other observers, people on all sides of welfare hated the program, but for different reasons. That impasse finally was broken in the mid-1990s. Nevertheless, if history is any guide, another wave of welfare-related problems almost certainly will wash over the stage of American politics within a generation, and many of the same issues will likely challenge citizens, policy makers, and the poor all over again.

The welfare debate in the United States does not tend to run along tracks defined by clear economic class divisions. America's relative freedom from class consciousness, usually attributed to the absence of any recognized history of feudalism (notwithstanding the widespread use of indentured and slave labor up until the Civil War), denies most Americans a default class-based way to think about the conditions of the poor and instead encourages thinking about rugged individuals who advance in the world in an up-by-the-bootstraps fashion. This, in turn, tempts many Americans to label the poor as deviant. Such labeling serves certain social, economic, and political functions. In particular, it sets the poor apart from the rest of our economically stable society, lending to the majority population a measure of psychic peace and providing a justification for only minimally addressing structural poverty—that is, poverty due not to personal moral failings but rather to systemic obstacles to advancement.[3] Insofar as it focuses instead on the so-called deviance of poor people, the welfare debate maintains the element of fear of dependency building, precisely because, in many quarters, it is premised on the idea that poverty lends itself primarily to an individual explanation instead of a structural one. According to this conservative school of thought, poor people are poor due mostly to their own failings instead of any dearth of opportunities in the market. Liberals, on the other hand, point to a steady growth in the gross domestic product through the latter half of the twentieth century but also to stagnating progress in reducing the poverty rate after 1970. Overall wealth has grown, but so has economic inequality. Liberal and conservative arguments over these perspectives have been, and certainly remain, powerful, but neither of the two sides has ever quite managed to best the other. Hence the purpose of this book: to trace the changes but also the continuities in the debate over welfare in the United States.

The following chapters attempt a limited project. The book's sharp focus on welfare necessarily means that many related topics go underdiscussed. Health care and food assistance, child care, job creation, housing assistance, trends in economic inequality, and the broader network of social insurance programs—primarily Social Security, disability, and survivors' and retirement benefits—receive very little attention here, despite their close connections to the larger question of economic provision for poor people. Attentive readers will recognize the points at which those other policies relate to welfare. Suggestions for further reading appear in Appendix 2.

## THE PLAN OF THE BOOK

Chapter 1 surveys some major themes in provision for the poor from the earliest English settlements up through the end of the eighteenth century. The English roots of American welfare policies lie in the Elizabethan Poor Law of 1601. In its two-pronged approach to pauperism, the state acknowledged some responsibility for the poor while simultaneously binding them with rules—indeed, severe punishments for persistent panhandling and the like. Early American poor laws—first colonial, then state practices—echoed their English source. Local communities adopted various methods for treating their poor, from auctioning them into the care of townspeople for a few months at a time to running them off under threat. Chapter 2 picks up at 1800 and traces the ways in which nineteenth-century Americans designed poor relief to control a growing poor population and to mitigate the specter of civil unrest in the newly developing urban centers of the mid-Atlantic and New England regions. The poorhouse was a primary expression of the perceived imperative to rule the poor, and that method competed with prisons, hospitals, indenture, and auctions of the poor as ways to achieve both surveillance over and shelter for the needy. These asylums sometimes combined the destitute, the mentally ill, orphans, criminals, and unmarried pregnant women under one roof. Though ultimately recognized as failures during the second half of the nineteenth century, poorhouses captured the theme of treating the poor as a deviant group.

Chapter 3 explores the early social-work movement, which, despite its often patronizing methods, began to recognize poor people as individuals instead of anonymous members of an amorphous class. By 1910 the private social-work movement clashed with calls for state-sponsored mothers' pensions. The pension movement expanded through the second decade of the twentieth century as rapidly as any social-provision movement ever has, which, in turn, set the stage for a federal response, mainly for poor widows and their children, under the Social Security Act of 1935. Under this federal legislation, the new Aid to Dependent Children (ADC) program served small numbers of women and children with modest monthly stipends. The ADC program represented a rejection of the intensive casework tradition that social workers had developed over the four previous decades. In time, that population of ADC recipients would grow and change into one that many white

Americans came to resent: never-married mothers, of whom a growing number were African American. State responses to the changing face of the welfare caseload led to conflicts between state governments and federal authorities and, in time, caught the attention of the general public and the Kennedy administration. Chapter 4 examines the War on Poverty, a high-water mark in America's long struggle against economic and social privation. The War on Poverty left in its wake, by the early 1970s, a political Left fragmented on questions of welfare, as well as a growing unease with aggressive government efforts to bring relief to poor families and neighborhoods in particular, and with the New Deal project more generally.

Chapter 5 examines this emerging conservative consensus and the rise of concepts such as the *urban underclass* and a *culture of poverty*, two notions that served as obstacles to concerted efforts to fight persistent poverty. During the 1970s and 1980s, critics of the War on Poverty called for an end to what they saw as wasteful and counterproductive spending on welfare, while welfare supporters criticized conservatives for what the political Left saw as a war on the poor. By the mid-to-late 1980s, several pieces were in place, politically speaking, for a major push toward comprehensive welfare reform. Chapter 6 discusses the coalescence of a neoconservative alliance that would enact sweeping state and federal welfare reforms in the 1990s, effectively ending the welfare contract agreed to in 1935. Welfare policy making devolved even more to state governments, and welfare's entitlement-funding basis, up to that point an open-ended financial commitment from Congress, ended. Chapter 7 summarizes what has become of the welfare debate since the 1996 legislation and what has become of welfare itself and the people who still rely on it. Chapter 8 looks back over four centuries of rhetoric and policy on public assistance in America to draw conclusions about the continuities, evolutions of thought, and ideological disjunctions that have characterized the welfare debate.

## NOTES

1. Berlin 1953. According to Berlin's formulation, there are two dominant types of thinkers: the fox, who knows many small things, and the hedgehog, who knows one big thing.
2. Califano 1981, p. 321.
3. Gans 1995, chap. 4.

# 1

# The Early American Roots of Welfare

Early Americans did not invent poor relief; they borrowed it from England. A mere six years after Parliament's famous consolidation of England's poor laws in 1601, English émigrés founded the American settlement they named Jamestown, Virginia. They and those who followed not only brought with them the broad principles of the Elizabethan Poor Law but also applied to their new communities many of the specifics of that legislation, sometimes in slightly amended form and sometimes as exact copies. These English ideas that crossed the Atlantic in the early 1600s have echoed throughout four centuries of American welfare policy making. Some practices, such as debtors' prisons and the stripping and whipping of unrepentant beggars, disappeared from the landscape during the first two and a half centuries. Others, such as residency requirements for assistance, persisted as late as the 1960s when, in this particular example, the U.S. Supreme Court ruled against state residency requirements for welfare eligibility.[1] Though early American efforts to provide for the desperately poor varied across time and place, they repeatedly harkened back to the dual principles of the Elizabethan Poor Law: public responsibility for the poor, combined with often-strict controls on those who sought assistance. By the 1730s, as the population passed the 750,000 mark and the largest towns began to assume the trappings of cities, poor-relief efforts evidenced an overt imperative of maintaining social control.[2] Colonial and local poverty policies—an explicit and formal federal role would have to wait until 1935—reflected an enduring arrangement of priorities: protecting society mattered more than protecting the poor.[3]

At the opening of the seventeenth century, poverty as a political problem had only existed for a short time. Prior to this, privation was seen as a natural by-product of the economy. Those who suffered it did not necessarily also suffer the social disconnectedness that goes with the modern understanding of poverty, and, largely for this reason, governments did not generally recognize a need to ameliorate it. Due to the decline of ecclesiastical sources of poor relief in the mid-to-late 1500s and a gradual shift to a mercantilist economy, England experienced a sharp rise in the number of vagrants and beggars, a phenomenon that at least one informed observer referred to as "a chronic plague."[4] The social disorganization caused by "valiant beggars and sturdy vagabonds" led some to conclude that paupers were, literally, the cause of all evil.[5] Parliamentary legislation in 1551 compelled citizens to contribute to local church boards that used the funds for poor relief in their respective cities and towns. Parishes were to appoint collectors who "shall gently ask and demand of every man and woman what they of their charity will give weekly towards the relief of the poor."[6] Anyone refusing to serve as a collector was obliged to pay 20 shillings to the alms box for the poor.[7] Knitting this law together with other fragmented poverty statues in 1601, Parliament created a legal framework that turned church vestrymen into overseers of and providers for the poor, prescribed severe punishments for able-bodied beggars, arranged foster care for orphans, helped direct funds to provide wages or work materials for the able-bodied poor and to care for the elderly and infirm, and authorized justices of the peace to commit to prison poor people who declined work. The goal was to impose discipline on "rogues, vagabonds, and sturdy beggars, and other lewd and idle persons."[8] Preserving social order was paramount during this time of unsettling social and economic change.

To minimize wandering vagrancy, Parliament created settlement laws as early as 1503. While these settlement laws were modified over time, they usually prescribed a period of residency in a particular place before a person became eligible for poor relief. The 1503 law set the requirement at three years. Under later versions of the statute, persons could establish residency by purchasing property, paying rent of at least 10 pounds per year, or serving for one year in a parish position.[9] Local overseers of the poor held considerable power in these matters. During the sixteenth and seventeenth centuries, overseers' actions were not subject to appeal by the poor people under their supervision. An appeals process was finally introduced in England during the early eighteenth century.[10]

To institutionalize poor relief under a merger of local parishes and a growing state seemed a logical move for English lawmakers in that this gave central roles to the two dominant political forces of the era. The extent of relief efforts and the conditions under which those efforts could occur evolved with changes in the economy and residential patterns. The English model of parish-based assistance to the poor under state strictures provided a widely copied pattern for American colonial treatment of the needy. The influential Puritan settlers, despite being religious dissenters, substantially borrowed English practices regarding the poor. Perhaps ironically, this pattern of poor relief stuck more firmly in America than it did in England. Throughout the second half of the nineteenth century, the English Parliament gradually repealed the old poor law in favor of greater state provision for the needy, recognizing the harm done by inhibiting the movement of labor under the settlement laws.[11] In 1834, England nationalized responsibility for the poor; in the United States, however, local and state responsibility dominated well into the early twentieth century.[12] The lag in American adoption of more centralized authority and uniform provision in this area not only marks a stark difference between American poor relief and its more comprehensive counterparts in other developed nations, but also embodies a long-enduring characteristic of American welfare provision more generally.

## WHAT EARLY AMERICANS SAID: THE COLONIAL DEBATE OVER POVERTY

The most thoroughly documented history of colonial American poor relief comes from the mid-Atlantic and Northeast regions, due primarily to the three largest cities of that era—Boston, New York, and Philadelphia—being located there. Further, poor-relief patterns from these areas influenced broader American thinking about poverty for generations, and hence those areas deserve special attention.

Two dominant streams of thinking marked colonial notions about poverty. First, many viewed helping poor people as a Christian obligation and thus an opportunity to extend grace to one's fellow man or woman. Others, however, went on to distinguish between the inadvertently poor and those guilty of idleness, with the latter experiencing poverty as divine punishment for their lack of self-application. Expressing the first perspective, John Winthrop saw the presence of the poor as a "God-given opportunity for men to do good, to serve society, and their Creator."[13] In his widely circulated essay on Christian charity, penned shortly before he left England for America in the spring of 1630, Winthrop argued that God made some people strong and others weak, some rich and some poor to enhance human diversity, provide alms-giving opportunities to others, and foster interpersonal reliance with the goal of building stronger bonds of humanity.[14] Winthrop's discourse on this point was very much in line with the biblical account of the Good Samaritan. From this view, settlers in the New World would be each other's keepers.

On the other hand, many later colonial thinkers, including the Reverend Cotton Mather, argued that those who insist on idleness should be allowed to starve if that was their apparent choice.[15] Since human beings were endowed by God with skills and initiative, each faced an obligation for self-help to the greatest extent possible. This theme of self-help was subsequently incorporated in a variety of secular and religious arguments about the poor throughout the colonial period and beyond.

Despite the tension between these two views, a significant number of early Americans believed sufficiently in charity that the perceived obligation to help one's fellow citizen persisted in the face of the terrible difficulties Europeans confronted in the New World. In this spirit, John Winthrop's 1630 "City upon a Hill" sermon stood as a statement of collective responsibility, envisioning that the community would look out for the good of its members. Winthrop's call for people to "knit together in this work as one" and to bear in mind their moral obligations not only to delight in each others' successes but to labor for each others' good meant that community well-being was foremost.[16] In light of the more stringent outlook advocated by Mather and others, it is almost certainly an exaggeration to point to Winthrop's famous homily as indicative of how the Puritans generally thought about collective responsibility to assist the poor, despite the many affirmations of collective responsibility in the historical literature. Yet Winthrop indeed captured an important line of thinking in early New England, even if these two themes played greater or lesser roles across rural versus more urban communities through time and even across congregations.

Although caring for one's neighbors proved a spiritual and material challenge, even under good conditions, this difficulty did not dissuade many early Americans from trying. Especially in New England, the 1600s was an era when Americans were intently focused on religious matters and specifically on the nature of their godly obligations to humanity in the material realm. Seventeenth-century New Englanders generally believed their obligations to unfortunate neighbors were substantial, and they offered significant generosity toward the needy, even to strangers. For example, church records from Dorchester and Roxbury, Massachusetts, from 1650 and 1683, reveal that better than two-thirds of all church collections benefited causes beyond the community, including those in places as distant as Dublin, London, and the Bahamas.[17]

This broad generosity began to trail off in the last quarter of the 1600s as emotional attachments to Europe wore thin and the prosperity of the New World contracted, due in part to an unfavorable shift in the ratio of population to useful land in the settled areas.[18] Despite these dwindling resources, in 1710 Cotton Mather elaborated, in a 200-page tract entitled "Bonifacius: An Essay upon the Good," the gravity of personal relationships and the duty to help one's neighbor.[19] Assisting one's neighbor despite limited resources, in the context of economic strains in the early 1700s, led many thinkers to circumscribe this notion of collective obligation to the poor. Giving should be prioritized, with nearby neighbors ranking above more distant ones. The Reverend Samuel Cooper of Boston noted in the early 1700s that a Christian man tries to do good but also realizes that "his abilities are limited . . . he chiefly exerts himself for that society in particular, to which he is most nearly related, in which his influence will be most felt, and his benevolent designs are most likely to take effect."[20] Almost certainly, this urge to favor those in closest proximity prompted the settlement laws that proliferated at the beginning of the eighteenth century, restricting poor people's migration from community to community. Efforts to help the poor could feasibly extend only so far.

The partial retrenchment of beneficence toward the poor throughout the early years of the eighteenth century was partially a product of the softening of Calvinism, which, in turn, was partly attributable to the religious revival known as the Great Awakening.[21] In this period, the idea gradually spread that individuals could indeed induce their own salvation, as opposed to it being predetermined. By extension, Americans also began to believe more in the power, and thus the responsibility, of individuals to effect their own economic well-being.[22] Divine determinism died hard, however, in some quarters. Speaking to a group of indigent residents of Boston near the turn of the eighteenth century, Cotton Mather explained that what they lacked had been given to others: "'Tis the Lord who has taken away from you what he has given to others . . . 'Tis the God of heaven who has ordered your being found among the poor of the earth . . . [God] has made you to be what you are and will have you to be a vessel not guilded with some of the shining dust that he has allowed unto others."[23] Despite these fatalistic tones, even Mather dedicated substantial energy to caring for the downtrodden, with frequent visits to the poor during his 43-year career at Boston's Second Congregational Church.[24] Mather's predeterminism lost credibility through time, for as Newtonian thought began to offer an explanation of the physics of the universe, people came to believe that God was not so much involved in the minute movements of the physical world but instead acted as a largely hands-off monitor of them.

As a corollary to this rising primacy of self-help throughout the first half of the 1700s, some Boston ministers articulated a belief that God provided the market as a means to obtain desired goods and that the burden for prosperity lay with the individual. This encomium to the marketplace, especially the version offered by Reverend Benjamin Colman in 1719, not only struck many Christians as idolatrous of the market but also missed the point that some portion of the needy were victims of circumstance. A less belabored version of the pro-market argument came in 1752 from the Reverend Charles Chauncy of Boston, who preached that God did not create poverty, but rather, poverty resulted from a failure of individuals' work effort. Chauncy believed that God provided for humankind by granting men and women a willingness to work, and that failure to avail one's self of that gift was a sin. The argument captured the imagination of Boston clergy and of the public more generally because of three qualities of the message. First, it indicated that Providence was distributed impartially. Everyone could enjoy it if they were willing to work. Second, the message was grounded in biblical text, legitimizing it in the eyes of the faithful. And most importantly, this perspective delegated human well-being to humans themselves. Just as God in a Newtonian universe was no longer responsible for holding up the planets once they were created and set in motion, God was not responsible for providing manna for people. God had shown them a way to provide for themselves. It was up to them to use it.[25]

The growing subjective recognition of poverty as the artifact of personal failings was almost certainly driven by the expansion of an objectively larger displaced and poor population throughout the late 1600s and early 1700s. Boston's shipbuilding businesses faced competition from other northeastern towns during this time, and this, combined with notable price inflation and an influx of widows and other displaced persons resulting from the Anglo-French wars, led to the dramatic expansion of the ranks of the very poor. The problem grew in ways that caught the attention of a wide range of observers of the period. These developments fostered a view of the poor as a separate class, as the very poor came to consist of more than widows, children, and the sick. Throughout the early 1700s, war veterans, new immigrants from Europe, migrants from inland areas fleeing conflicts that Europeans had provoked with native peoples, and the seasonally unemployed joined the ranks of the new urban poor.[26] Growing relief needs burdened community resources, both public and private, further straining belief in the power of private charity and encouraging Americans to place greater stock in the practical aspects of publicly funded relief efforts. Historian Gary Nash estimates that typical municipal poor-relief expenses amounted to between 10 and 35 percent of all expenditures during the late colonial period.[27] Boston's overseers of the poor spent some 25 to 30 pounds sterling per thousand inhabitants during the 1720s and 1730s, but that figure more than doubled by the 1740s and then doubled again by the 1770s. Similar patterns were seen in Philadelphia and New York.[28] Up until this time, poverty had been generally thought of as the exception rather than the rule in America, with an expanding frontier encouraging European Americans to think in terms of greater opportunity.

As intuitive as equality of opportunity might have seemed, radical inequality was, in fact, the norm by the early 1700s. Tax records and probate court documents from the eighteenth century reveal dramatic wealth disparities during this period. Historians James Lemon and Gary Nash, working from tax and probate records, found that typically the upper 10 percent of adult white males owned approximately one-third of the wealth.[29] In Chester County, Pennsylvania, records document that between 1748 and 1800, the poorest 30 percent of landowners saw their portion of taxable property fall from just over 13 percent of the total to less than 4 percent, while during the same period the upper 10 percent saw their wealth grow from 29 percent to 38 percent.[30] If colonial America did not promise wealth to all—and it did not—it at least offered the opportunity to achieve what was referred to as *competency*. That competency, however, was subject to a significant skew across classes. With poverty rates growing apace—they quadrupled in New York between 1750 and 1775, and similarly elsewhere—economic stresses of the late colonial era prompted Americans to think about poor relief in new ways.[31]

Institutionalization of the poor in sick hospitals and poorhouses had gained some credibility during the 1730s, and that response would come to seem even more reasonable throughout the late 1700s and early 1800s as Americans came to envision the desperately poor as not only largely at fault for their own situations but also as a threat to social order. The emergence of a truly wealthy class during the latter half of the eighteenth century certainly led to some civil unrest and cross-class resentments, even violence, but it also prompted political elites to believe in America as a place where individuals could prosper, even if a substantial portion of that affluence was earned on the backs of indentured and slave labor.[32]

## WHAT EARLY AMERICANS DID: ENGLISH POOR LAW PRACTICES TRANSPLANTED TO AMERICA

The rhetoric surrounding poverty in seventeenth-century America included considerable talk of communal obligation for the poor. Yet the complexion of American laws included punitive elements as well, echoing the English model. The earliest poor laws, extant in fragments, mandated labor, as in Virginia's 1619 statute requiring idle able-bodied persons to be placed into compulsory work.[33] Similarly, in 1633 the Massachusetts General Court set harsh punishments for those who spent their time "idly or unprofitably."[34] In time, comprehensive poor laws arose, governing town and city obligations, punishments for unruly poor people, settlement provisions, and funding mechanisms. These took effect in the Plymouth Colony in 1642, in Virginia in 1646, in Connecticut in 1673, in Massachusetts in 1692, and in Pennsylvania in 1706. Some of these laws copied English practices directly. When the Rhode Island legislature adopted its poor law, it prescribed an explicit borrowing, calling for engagement of the poor "according to the provisions of the law of England."[35]

From the very earliest years of European settlement in America, significant collective responsibility was acknowledged. From the beginning, the Virginia Company required all employees to contribute to a common storehouse of goods to be distributed to all according to their needs.[36] Early on, Massachusetts also established a precedent of caring for the poor. In 1624 James Sherley, secretary for the Merchant Adventurers, shipped a heifer to Plymouth Colony to initiate a breeding stock to benefit the needy. Five years later, the Massachusetts Bay Company directed the resident governor of the Salem settlement, John Endecott, "to raise a general stock for community purposes, including the relief of the poor."[37] Further, Plymouth Colony adopted a law in 1642 declaring that each township was to provide for its needy as it found "most convenient and suitable for themselves by an order and general agreement in a public town meeting."[38] Publicly supported poor relief was central to the Massachusetts experience. It represented for many colonists a religiously and civically grounded part of well-ordered community life. This idea of sharing portions of the collective wealth with needy members of the community was embraced by many of the leaders of the Plymouth Colony, including William Bradford, Edward Winslow, Robert Cushman, John Winthrop, and others during the early to mid-1600s. This represented an exercise in community building, articulated in the language of the Mayflower Compact and enacted throughout Massachusetts and across the Northeast more generally.[39] Throughout the first half of the seventeenth century, town meetings in Plymouth collectively decided how best to help the poor among the community, though in 1649, as the population expanded, townspeople delegated this authority to selectmen. The number of poor people assisted during this time remained small: only 57 beneficiaries appear in Plymouth records spanning 1630 to 1645, and a mere 11 individuals are listed between 1660 and 1675.[40] In this latter period, Plymouth records show that most people who received relief did so for only a year or two at a time. A few individuals appeared on the roles for up to five years. In one highly unusual case, Plymouth Colony assisted Sarah Lambert from 1660 to 1675.[41] Livestock owned collectively in Plymouth helped raise some of the funds used to assist the poor. More formal methods of helping the needy emerged in Boston during the 1640s, particularly the practice of the town paying home owners to take in destitute roomers in exchange for cash payments. This led in time to pauper auctions, at which the needy were sent to live with other community members, who were compensated by the city or town for their services for as much as a year at a time.

In keeping with English practices, local arrangements to care for the poor were the norm throughout the 1600s and beyond in most places. Lagging behind the English tradition of formalizing these local obligations, legal grounding for poor relief nevertheless was slow to develop in the colonies. Instead, ad hoc arrangements typically prevailed. Numerous examples exist in community records of town councils paying expenses to help poor people, determined on a case-by-case basis. Support for pregnant women during their so-called times of laying-in was common. Gifts of firewood were also frequently extended, as were burial services. Local overseers of the poor took responsibility for scrutinizing the lives of petitioners for assistance, carrying on liaison between those would-be beneficiaries and the local town council and mentoring individuals who received relief. Under William Penn's poor law of 1693, justices of the peace were made responsible for the administration of relief in Pennsylvania.[42] In 1691, Massachusetts created its first office of overseer of the poor[43] in response to the growing burden of reviewing requests for assistance, a chore that had outstripped the abilities of local selectmen. The funds spent by Boston on care for the poor grew dramatically throughout the late 1600s into the early 1700s. In 1700 the sum amounted to approximately 500 pounds; by 1715 it had reached four times that amount.[44]

Boston was particularly hard pressed throughout this period due to a worsening economy, but other cities, too, were strained by the growth in the poor population during the late 1600s and early to mid-1700s. Local discretion remained the rule, though in a first-of-its-kind move, the General Court in Plymouth decided in 1675 that people who could demonstrate established residency were due relief to be paid from the public treasury.[45]

This question of legal residency became an important concern for the colonies within the first century of European colonization of America. Colonial legislatures and city and town councils enacted settlement laws with the goal of preserving local funds to assist only local residents. Existing records suggest that most cities and towns spent at least a large minority of their relief funds transporting nonresident poor persons out of their jurisdictions in the hope of avoiding long-term public charges. Fear of outsiders overstaying their welcome extended even to economically stable families that sheltered visitors. As early as 1636, Boston's selectmen adopted an ordinance prohibiting townspeople from hosting visitors for more than two weeks at a time in their homes without first securing the city government's permission.[46] This practice was solidly grounded in the English poor law, which understood that a visitor who stayed three nights became a legal responsibility of the host family.[47] Settlement laws spread throughout many of the colonies in the late 1600s.

Strengthening its existing settlement law, Massachusetts increased its residency requirement in 1701 so that a person seeking aid had to show that they had lived in a given place for one year.[48] Nonresidents were routinely expelled, or warned out, from towns throughout the colonies. According to the *Warning Out Book* of the Boston overseers, an average of 25 persons was warned out from Boston annually between 1721 and 1742. The growing burden of poor new arrivals led the Boston selectmen in 1735 to allow for nonresident poor people to be removed from the city without review by the county court.[49] Fear of being expelled seemed to do little to inhibit migration, however. The annual number warned out from Boston rose to 65 by 1750 and tripled to some 200 persons per year through the period 1753 to 1764. By the 1770s, Boston warned out more than 450 people annually.[50] New Hampshire followed Massachusetts's example by enacting its first settlement law in 1719, and Rhode Island did the same in 1748.[51] Acknowledging a mobile population, cities and towns developed legal means by which a person could establish residency. Typical was the payment of rent or the purchase of property. New York's 1784 law required five pounds rent per year or purchasing property worth at least 30 pounds. This echoed back to the 1660s settlement law in England, which prescribed rent of 10 pounds per year.[52]

Concern over migration extended, of course, to those arriving from across the Atlantic. By the beginning of the eighteenth century, many coastal cities compelled ship captains to post cash bonds for persons they brought to America who appeared likely to become destitute. New York enacted such a bonding rule in 1721.[53] By the end of the 1700s, New York bore a disproportionate burden in this respect, and city officials convinced the legislature to require a bond of $300 per passenger, refundable if the person did not become a public charge within two years, and to create fines of $500 per nonbonded passenger. Despite the rigor of this law, critics still charged that the $500 fine provided an inexpensive means for foreign nations to unload their paupers and criminals in America.[54]

Struggling local governments would generally have to wait until the late 1700s before states began taking financial responsibility for poor relief. In the meantime, the economic trauma of the mid-eighteenth century prompted private charities to lend support to local governments' efforts. These early public-private partnerships were instrumental in Philadelphia. There, approximately one-quarter of all relief expenditures in 1765 came from private charity sources, and when the city workhouse was built in 1767, the colonial legislature formalized its funding through public and private sources.[55] Private charities were not limited to Philadelphia during the 1600s and 1700s. A variety of them sprang up as ethnically based mutual aid societies. The Scots' Charitable Society, formed in 1644, provided assistance to those of Scottish origin on both a cash basis and by supporting home-based thread-spinning operations.[56] A privately funded home for widows and their children was founded in New Orleans in 1729. The Massachusetts Charitable Fire Society was formed in 1794, and the New York Society for the Relief of Poor

Widows with Small Children in 1798. Mutual aid societies were also created by free blacks, including a Masonic lodge in Boston that commenced in 1784. Similar groups for African Americans were formed later in Newport, Boston, Charleston, and New York.[57] Various trade-based mutual aid societies also sprang up, including the Society of House Carpenters in New York in 1767 and the Marine Society in 1769.[58] The same economic instability that had prompted the early construction of poorhouses and a shift toward a more punitive mentality toward the poor also gave rise to self-help initiatives such as these mutual aid societies that flourished during the eighteenth century.

## THE EMERGENCE OF URBAN POVERTY IN THE LATE COLONIAL PERIOD

The economic dislocation visited upon many colonial cities during the second and third quarters of the eighteenth century prompted several changes in poverty relief tactics that would prove enduring. It was during this period that poverty came to be clearly identified as a distinct problem that government was obliged to confront and that was associated with social dislocation. In response came the move toward institutionalizing the poor in the 1730s, a practice that would stretch into the late 1800s. The dramatic growth in the number of destitute people prompted Americans to think of many of the poor not so much as victims of circumstance—either in the Calvinistic sense or in the fashion of widows, orphans, and injured workers—but as debauched subjects of intemperance and laziness. This period also witnessed tentative steps toward more centralized responsibility for funding poor relief, with colonial, and later state, governments stepping into more significant roles. Carving cities out of the wilderness would prove to be a tormented exercise and one that saw only halting progress made in provision for the poor. In absorbing the lessons of the early 1700s, Americans began to think in terms of an important distinction between the so-called worthy and unworthy poor, which, in turn, set in motion two very different modes of response: charity for the former and punishment for the latter.

The variety of methods that had been attempted to allow poor families to live in their own homes, including granting them permission to cut firewood from the town woodlot or to grow vegetables on land owned by the village, eventually gave way to more systematic relief efforts. In-kind benefits were commonly extended, but in time, the auctioning of paupers to live in the homes of those willing to take them on in return for a cash payment spread. The preference, of course, was that extended family members would shelter their kin, but, failing that, town councils sent the person to live with another family, typically to the lowest bidder. These arrangements usually were of short duration, only a few months at a time.[59] Auctions promised financial efficiency for the town or city government. In 1766 in Exeter, Rhode Island, town authorities found a lower bid to care for Hannah Remick, one that reduced by 50 percent the expenses it had been paying Remick's former caretaker.[60] Those who were auctioned were promised little in the bargain. When, in 1794, the Glocester, Rhode Island, council extended help to the widow Elisabeth Smith and her children, the council paid Seth Hunt, a townsperson, 8 pounds per year to provide this shelter. The contract specified provision of a house, "firewood, privilege of sauce [garden produce] and fruit, and reasonable pay at the direction of the council for all other necessaries and trouble."[61]

New England towns commonly auctioned children. The process was usually referred to as *orphan apprenticeship* or *pauper apprenticeship*. Destitute children, including both orphans and children of destitute families, were often sent to be raised in more respectable homes. These children became indentured servants, obliged to obey and work for their new masters, who, in turn, assumed a responsibility to care for them and to teach them a trade or skill. Children were often removed from their homes at an early age, despite protests from parents. During the late 1700s, the average age of this so-called binding of children was seven years.[62] The removal of children from destitute homes had begun at least as early as 1656. In that year, the Boston council ordered that Goodwife Samon's son, who was living without any reliable means, was to be put to work by his mother before the time of the next town meeting, or the townspeople would themselves press him into service.[63] Binding out children endured in place of more formal arrangements throughout the eighteenth century. For instance, not until well into the nineteenth century did Rhode Island authorities begin sending children to live in orphanages instead of with other families.[64]

As the eighteenth century wore on and the number of poor people overwhelmed the auction system, communities began, throughout the second quarter of the 1800s, to turn to a more aggressive response: the poorhouse. The dual rationale behind the movement toward institutionalizing the poor was to isolate them from mainstream society and to shelter them less expensively than was achieved through assistance given to poor families living in their own homes, or by way of what was called *outdoor relief*. By contrast, *indoor relief* promised not only financial savings for cash-strapped cities but also a great measure of social control over the poor. Intense frustration among city leaders in New York led them in 1732 to commission a poorhouse to be built. New York's was not the first—Boston had opened its poorhouse in 1664, and Philadelphia erected its in 1732—but the argument behind the New York city council's decision clearly captured one important part of the rationale for institutionalizing the poor. The council's resolution read, in part, that the

"continual increase of the poor within this city is very great an exceeding bur-
densome to the inhabitants . . . [and that] . . . provision be made for the relief
and setting on work of poor needy persons and idle wandering vagabonds,
sturdy beggars and others, who frequently commit divers misdemeanors, . . .
[and] become debauched."[65] The new building was completed in 1736. The
number of inmates, as poorhouse residents were called, steadily grew, reaching 425 by the spring of 1772.[66] Throughout the remainder of the eighteenth
century, almshouses appeared in many other New England towns and cities.
They were established in eight cities in Rhode Island alone between 1779 and
1790.[67] The poorhouse would, by the second quarter of the nineteenth century, become a chief tool of confronting poverty. Boston's poorhouse hosted
nearly 90 people at a time during most of the 1730s, and more than 100 by
the time of its 1742 census. By 1756 that figure would reach 148.[68]

Beyond controlling the poor, almshouses and workhouses were expected
to provide relief more economically than by housing poor people in their
own homes. In many places, however, they proved less efficient than their
proponents had hoped. Because of this realization, by the early 1800s, most
Rhode Island towns had returned to their earlier practice of housing the poor
in the homes of townspeople.[69] This second period of auctioning the poor in
Rhode Island differed from the first in that during these later years, poor people
were grouped together in a single home or in a small cluster of homes rather
than being sheltered as individuals. Several towns adopted the practice of
contracting with a single, economically stable person to take over care of all
of the town's poor people. In 1794, South Kingston voters agreed that Samuel
Stanton would "take, keep and maintain all and every of the poor of this
town" for $400.[70]

The urge to institutionalize the poor also led to the creation of orphanages. The first was established by a Catholic convent in New Orleans in 1727.
This facility also hosted a day school and a hospital. Another privately funded
orphanage began in Savannah, Georgia, in 1738.[71] In 1790, Charleston,
South Carolina, opened the first municipal, publicly funded orphanage in the
nation. This particular facility had operated for decades as a project of a pair
of Anglican Church congregations. In its pre-Revolutionary incarnation, the
Charleston Orphan House had enjoyed legal authority to collect taxes for its
support, in the English fashion. The Charleston Orphan House's church war-
dens bound out many teenage orphans to apprenticeships, helping to defray
the cost of the children's care.[72]

Institutionalization affected men and women differently. Records from
Philadelphia during the 1760s and 1770s indicate that men were commonly
sent to the workhouse, where they were expected to contribute to the cost of

their care, while women were typically sheltered in the Bettering House. The cross-gender differences appear far beyond what could be explained by the frequency of pregnancy, an understandable reason to shelter women without requiring them to work.[73] In line with this assumption that men were more suitable for the workforce than were women, spaces in Philadelphia's public hospital, which opened in 1752, show that in its first decade of operation, male patients outnumbered female patients by approximately two to one. The rationale, articulated in the hospital's annual report of 1764, was that nursing ill men back to health allowed them to reenter the workforce more quickly than they otherwise would.[74] When not offered help, women were warned out from New England towns at very high rates. Between 1750 and 1800, women made up two-thirds of those adults warned out from Rhode Island towns.[75]

Beyond gender differences in treatment of the poor during the late 1700s, there existed, of course, dramatic racial disparities as well. Records from Rhode Island indicate that in the late eighteenth century, black and Native American women were the least likely poor people to receive help. Rhode Island town officials expressed concern over cases of black women living without their husbands, some of whom appeared to be employed elsewhere. Cultural norms seemed to be at stake in these evaluations of the poor, as town officials openly disapproved of this exception to the patriarchal household that was the New England norm of the time.[76] Women of color were warned out of Rhode Island towns at more than twice their portion of the population. Between 1750 and 1800, they made up 13 percent of those warned out, while comprising less than 5 percent of Rhode Island's population.[77] For those women lucky enough to receive public assistance in Rhode Island in the second half of the eighteenth century, few spent more than one year on public relief. No woman of color ever did, at least not in any of the 15 cities studied by historian Ruth Herndon.[78] African Americans also made up a disproportionate number of those persons warned out from New York during the late 1700s.[79]

Beyond the move toward institutionalizing the poor throughout the mid-1700s, the emergence of widespread poverty produced a growing cross-class animosity. The massive economic dislocation of the 1750s to 1770s created a noticeable rise in the number of transient vagrants and requests for aid. It also prompted a raft of pamphlets and newspaper editorials criticizing the wealthy for enriching themselves on the backs of the poor. One pamphleteer in Boston in 1750 observed bitterly that the rich could manage to "build ships, houses, buy farms, set up their coaches, chariots, live very splendidly, purchase fame, [and] posts of honor" while such a large and growing portion of the population suffered.[80] A writer in the *New York Gazette* in 1765 wondered if it was right that "999 should suffer for the extravagance or grandeur of one, especially when it is considered that men frequently owe their wealth to the impoverishment of their neighbours."[81] Another writer in New York in 1769 admonished his readers to recall that "it is to the meaner class of mankind, the industrious poor, that so many of us are indebted for those goodly dwellings we inhabit, for that comfortable substance we enjoy, while others are languishing under the disagreeable sensations of penury and want."[82] Wealth inequality throughout this pre-Revolutionary period was dramatic. In short, the wealthiest became wealthier, and the poor gained ground only very slowly. In both Boston and Philadelphia on the eve of the Revolution, the most well off 5 percent of the population held half the wealth, while the poorest half of the population could claim only about 5 percent of it.[83]

These disparities led to class-based tensions over who should be empowered to influence town meetings. Massachusetts governor William Shirley touched on a central issue in 1747 when he complained about the power of the commoners so-called mob at town meetings. He protested the "mobbish turn . . . in their town meetings . . . where the meanest inhabitants . . . by their constant attendance there generally are the majority and outvote the gentlemen, merchants, substantial traders and all the better part of the inhabitants, to whom it is irksome to attend."[84] Almost certainly the wealthy realized their privileged situation and feared the growing frustrations of those who had much less. Even James Madison made clear in his contributions to the *Federalist Papers*, during the late 1780s debate over the proposed Constitution, that the chief divide in American society lay between the haves and the have-nots.[85]

Most historians believe that these class tensions of the late eighteenth century did not substantially spill over into a widespread call for the American Revolution to involve also a wiping clean of debts.[86] In fact, many people of modest station seemed to view early America as, in the words of William Moraley, an indentured servant in Pennsylvania, the "best poor man's country in the world." Alexis de Tocqueville, the famous French commentator on America during the Jacksonian period, would echo this sentiment. Despite being popularized by various historians, and comporting with Adam Smith's thinking on supply and demand and how efficient markets would provide adequately for those willing to work, this assertion defies much of the evidence of widespread poverty and social dislocation in early America, particularly after 1730.[87] As comforting as this image of an early America that gave a fair shake to even its least prosperous inhabitants might seem, it strains to square itself with the evidence. It is not surprising that in a land where most of those arriving in the first two centuries of European settlement came under some form of indentured or slave labor, widespread privation was an important feature of early American life. Despite the purported opportunities for economic advancement, a sizeable minority remained poor. Notwithstanding overt structural impediments to advancement, many early Americans viewed the new continent as a place where, in the words of the historian Michael Katz, "opportunity awaited anyone with energy and talent, [and] poverty signaled personal failure." Nevertheless, Katz continues, the "ubiquity of work and opportunity, of course, were myths, even in the early Republic. The transformation in economic relations, the growth of cities, immigration, the seasonality of labor, fluctuations in consumer demand, periodic depressions, low wages, restricted opportunities for women, industrial accidents, high mortality, and the absence of any social insurance: together these chiseled chronic poverty and dependence into American social life."[88] Nineteenth-century America, reconfigured by urbanization and immigration, would witness these themes magnified and debated, in particular over an evolving terrain of religious thinking about poverty and charity and questions of public versus private sources of relief.

## NOTES

1. *Shapiro v. Thompson,* 1969.
2. Nash 1979; Alexander 1980.
3. Mohl 1971; Marshall 1981.
4. Mohl 1971, p. 38; Marshall 1981, p. 30.
5. Nicholls 1899, vol. 1, p. 187; Bridenbaugh 1968, pp. 78–79.
6. Nicholls 1899, vol. 1, p. 133.
7. Nicholls 1899, vol. 1, pp. 133–34.
8. Ibid., vol. 1, pp. 188–92, 228.
9. Poynter 1969; Taylor 1976.
10. Bartkowski and Regis 2003, p. 29.
11. Nicholls 1899, vol. 2, chap. 18; Grace Abbott 1966, p. 6.
12. Creech 1936, p. xi (Edith Abbott, Introduction).
13. Bartkowski and Regis 2003, p. 30.
14. Winthrop 1630 (reprinted in Hall 2004).
15. Trattner 1999, p. 22.
16. Winthrop 1630 (reprinted in Hall 2004, p. 169; spelling updated by editor).
17. Wright 1992, p. 23.
18. Ibid.
19. Ibid., p. 26.
20. Ibid., p. 28.
21. Nash 1976c, p. 17; Rosenberg 1971.
22. Olivas 2004, p. 262.
23. Ibid., p. 266.

24. Ibid., p. 268.
25. Olivas 2004.
26. Nash 1976b, pp. 576–77; Nash 1976c, p. 8; Heisterman and Keener 1934; Edith Abbott 1940, pp. 150–54; Bridenbaugh 1968, p. 233.
27. Nash 1976b.
28. Nash 1976c, p. 8.
29. Lemon and Nash 1970.
30. Ibid., p. 177.
31. Nash 1976c, p. 9.
32. van der Zee 1985, p. 33; Bailyn 1986.
33. Iceland 2003, p. 11.
34. Ibid., pp. 11–12.
35. Trattner 1999, p. 17; Wulf 2004, pp. 166–67.
36. Scott 1977, p. 6.
37. Lee 1982, p. 564.
38. Kelso 1969, p. 95.
39. Lee 1982, pp. 564–67.
40. Ibid., pp. 569, 578.
41. Ibid., pp. 576–77.
42. Notes on the history of Delaware's overseers of the poor, available online at http://www.state.de.us/sos/dpa/collections/aghist/2230.shtml. (accessed June 18, 2007)
43. Sanborn 1868, p. 493.
44. Trattner 1999, p. 30.
45. Sanborn 1868, p. 490.
46. Bridenbaugh 1968, p. 79.
47. Taylor 1976.
48. Sanborn 1868, p. 492.
49. Dolgoff and Feldstein 2003, p. 64.
50. Nash 1976b, pp. 562–63.
51. Sanborn 1868, p. 492.
52. Mohl 1971, pp. 55–56.
53. Trattner 1999, p. 21.
54. Mohl 1971, pp. 60–61.
55. Alexander 1983, pp. 19–25; Bridenbaugh 1968, p. 395.
56. Mohl 1971, p. 49; Bridenbaugh 1968, pp. 81, 235.
57. Dolgoff and Feldstein 2003, pp. 66–67.
58. Mohl 1971, p. 50.
59. Herndon 2004, pp. 138–40.
60. Ibid., p. 140.
61. Ibid.
62. Ibid., pp. 140–41.
63. Trattner 1999, p. 24.
64. Herndon 2004, p. 141.
65. Mohl 1971, pp. 44–45.

66. Mohl 1971, p. 44.
67. Herndon 2004, p. 150.
68. Nash 1976b, pp. 558–60.
69. Herndon 2004, pp. 150–51.
70. Ibid., p. 151.
71. Folks 1971 [1900], p. 10.
72. John Murray 2004, p. 214.
73. Wulf 2004, p. 178.
74. Ibid., pp. 173–74.
75. Herndon 2004, p. 146.
76. Ibid., p. 145–46.
77. Ibid., p. 146.
78. Ibid., p. 147.
79. Hodges 1999, p. 208.
80. Nash 1976b, p. 580.
81. Ibid.
82. Ibid.
83. Ibid., p. 550.
84. Nash 1976c, p. 22.
85. See especially *Federalist Paper #10* in Hamilton et al. 1961.
86. Nash 1979; Wood 1969.
87. See Lemon 1972.
88. Katz 1989, p. 14.

# 2

# Controlling the Poor in Nineteenth-Century America

By the beginning of the nineteenth century, government-based assistance, while it would wax and wane over the next hundred years, had become an enduring feature of the landscape. New York formalized a local government obligation to care for the poor through legislation adopted in 1784. Other states following suit shortly thereafter.[1] The nineteenth century would witness growing urban poverty and evolving secular and religious debates over how that problem should be addressed. These tensions were aggravated by an influx of poor immigrants arriving in what seemed like waves during this century. The 1800s witnessed a transformed public discourse on poverty and the poor, owing to an emerging understanding of deep poverty as a chronic condition for some, an awareness of intermittent poverty for many as an artifact of the new urban life, and finally a shift from thinking about the poor as a class to a consideration of impoverished individuals as a focus of the new field of social work late in the century.

Like its colonial-era predecessors, nineteenth-century American poor relief was shaped significantly by English practices. Massachusetts and Rhode Island explicitly modeled their efforts on those in England.[2] Two central tenets of the poor law in particular made the transition across the Atlantic. Local administration of relief efforts and the primacy of community norms regarding work and deservingness prevailed. Second, fiscal pressures on communities catalyzed fears of migrating poor people and efforts to restrict eligibility for local assistance. These concerns intensified as industrialization and the growth of cities throughout the mid-nineteenth century led to large populations of wage laborers

who were both vulnerable to the vicissitudes of urban life and highly visible to
the middle class. These pressures, combined with the long-standing belief in
the corrupting effects of relief, led to more systematic programs to control the
poor, or, as they came to be called during this era, the dangerous classes.[3]

Drawing on notions of the necessity to supervise the poor, local communities on both sides of the Atlantic appointed overseers of the poor, who took
responsibility for ensuring that public funds were not wasted on individuals
deemed unworthy of assistance and acted as liaisons between the poor and the
city and town councils that funded assistance. In their capacity as overseers,
these individuals typically adopted a directive approach to their charges. While
so-called outdoor relief—assistance provided to the poor living in their own
homes—was widely used, it often came in the form of in-kind benefits. Provision of food, coal, and firewood was common. Cash aid represented a moral
danger, so the thinking went, though it was still granted in many places. Boston mayor Josiah Quincy, who chaired the Commonwealth's Committee on
the Pauper Laws, complained in 1821 that public outdoor relief was, of any
method of helping the poor, the "most wasteful, the most expensive, and the
most injurious to their morals and destructive to their industrious habits."[4]
Beyond outdoor relief, a few other methods of care accounted for nearly all
modes of help offered throughout the nineteenth century, all with a heavy
dose of social control: auctioning the poor to local families or to a group home
operated by an individual in the community, almshouse care, and indenture.
Little distinction was made early on between relief for adults and that for
children, with the exception that indenture applied more often to children
than to adults. These methods captured the dual nature of the English poor
law transplanted to America: government responsibility for limited assistance,
combined with at times heavy-handed controls on the behavior of the poor.

Despite myths of a laissez-faire early America, there very much existed a
spirit of collective obligation to help the poor. This spirit found both public
and private expressions, largely religious in the latter case. As the historian
William Novak documents in considerable detail, from 1787 forward, significant governmental efforts strove to create a well-regulated society, involving the passage and enforcement of laws designed to regulate the market in
many respects.[5] Further, Conrad Wright argues that up through the mid-
1800s, "almost all colonial New Englanders shared a common understanding
of the true believer's charitable responsibilities. At its center was an apologetic
tradition, an intricate and enduring set of explanations for the individual
Christian's natural ability to fulfill the Bible's injunctions to emulate the
purity of Jesus, the universal love of the good Samaritan."[6] This sentiment
indeed appears in much of the literature of the period and was evidenced
by the extensive urban missionary outreach undertaken by religious groups,

especially in eastern cities. During the early decades of the 1800s, a variety of Quaker, Calvinist, and other pietistic groups in New York, animated by the Second Great Awakening, enthusiastically launched assistance programs extending both material and spiritual help to the poor. Groups such as the New York City Tract Society, the New York Female Moral Reform Society, and the New York Protestant Episcopal City Mission Society offered privately funded outdoor relief, mentoring, education, friendly visits (a forerunner of social work), food, and clothing to the city's growing poor population. In time, religious groups' efforts would come to vie with public aid for foremost prominence.[7] These widespread charity efforts led some observers to characterize the mid-1800s as evidencing a "kinder, more generous spirit" toward the poor, based on Christian principles.[8] However prevalent this sense of Christian duty was, though, the perceived obligation toward the poor certainly did not preclude paternalistic approaches borrowed from England and adapted to the American context. So-called tough love (to coin a phrase that did not appear for nearly another two centuries) clearly enjoyed substantial currency during this period.

As extensive as these public and private relief efforts were, a significant part of their impetus still involved a striving to control the poor. One primary expression of the urge to control involved limiting the mobility of poor people. Settlement laws establishing residency requirements for assistance attempted to prevent migrant poor people from soliciting aid in towns beyond their own. The Massachusetts settlement law of 1794 not only required established residency in the commonwealth but also American citizenship of those receiving assistance.[9] Rhode Island's law allowed local governments to whip vagabonds who appeared in towns from which they had previously been run off or warned out. These New England settlement laws remained substantially in place throughout the nineteenth century.[10]

Immigration from Europe chafed American relief officials. As early as the second decade of the century, leaders in eastern cities bemoaned immigration as a principle cause of poverty.[11] This sentiment persisted into the early twentieth century. The British author Rudyard Kipling wrote in 1892 of New York City's government that it was a "despotism of the alien, by the alien, for the alien, tempered with occasional insurrections of decent folk."[12]

Beyond settlement laws, another way of effecting supervision of the poor was the pauper auction. Under this system, needy individuals were taken into private homes where they were sheltered by those willing to accept a stipend from the town or city for their service. Most communities let out the poor to the lowest bidder, inviting at best neglect and at worst outright abuse of the poor by their erstwhile caretakers.[13] Pauper auctions were used from before the American Revolution through the 1850s. They were most widely employed

in New England, though every Atlantic seaboard state except Maryland and
Delaware experienced them. The 1799 Poor Law for the Northwest Territory
explicitly allowed for them. Pauper auctions took place in Illinois as late as
the 1820s and in Missouri into the 1850s.[14] The auction system also applied
to destitute infants. New York City placed infants in homes at the rate of $1
per week during 1823, 129 of them during April of that year.[15] Defenders of
the practice of auctioning the poor supported the practice by pointing to its
efficiency and moral supervision. Boston's Josiah Quincy, in his 1821 report
to the legislature, noted that auctions met both the need to supervise the poor
and the imperative to meet the needs of the desperately poor on fiscally sound
terms.[16] William Plumer, former governor of New Hampshire, wrote in 1827
that auctions were the "most eligible and cheapest method" for dispensing of
paupers. Two New York towns reported savings of between one-third and two-
thirds of the previous costs of outdoor relief once they shifted to an auction
system.[17] From an exclusively financial perspective, if the alternative was the
expensive proposition of paying people to live in their own homes or institutionalizing them in poorhouses, auctioning arguably made some sense.

The financial aspects of pauper auctions, however, were not the whole of
the conversation. The 1824 Yates Commission report in New York State (over-
seen by New York's secretary of state) concluded that the auction system was
counterproductive in that it had resulted in the death of several persons com-
mitted to negligent caretakers.[18] The Yates report detailed the major poor-
relief mechanisms and concluded that the systems then in place, despite their
founding rationales, were detrimental to poor people's morals, especially those
of children. By modern standards, pauper auctions represented the complete
objectification of the individuals who were auctioned. Beyond being let out to
the lowest bidder, they were often described in terms similar to those of a stock
animal or a slave. In order to heighten interest in the auction as an event, local
governments sometimes provided liquor to those in attendance. New Jersey, in
a progressive move in 1797, banned alcohol distribution at pauper auctions,
except those conducted by civil officers. Once under the roof of the successful bidder, the pauper was subject to whatever meanness his or her purchaser
might offer. Many accounts reveal that some of the people who bid were desperately poor themselves and saw auctioned paupers as an income and labor
source. Until 1809 paupers in West Greenwich, Rhode Island, were auctioned
month by month. Later auctions were for a year at a time. Auctioned persons
were often separated from their family members. Despite the widespread use
of the pauper auction system, the Yates report proved to be an influential
document and prompted a drumbeat of opposition to this practice. Studies
in other eastern cities during this period arrived at similar conclusions. As a
result, pauper auctions began to disappear in the 1820s.[19]

A further step toward the goal of controlling the poor came in the form of involuntary indenture, a common practice throughout the first half of the 1800s. Indenture was economically efficient in that it placed labor resources where labor was needed, particularly on the opening frontier. From 1735 forward, children of neglectful parents in Boston were subject to being bound out, as it was called, by local overseers of the poor. Similarly, children of beggars in Maryland were subject to indenture beginning in 1797.[20] Critics charged that indenture amounted to "private enterprise in human stock."[21] Its defenders nevertheless insisted that indenture provided to the children in question both a moral upbringing and the acquisition of a trade by the time of their release, typically at age 18 for girls and 21 for boys.[22] The laws of several states led to the widespread indenture of children, especially, though not exclusively, in the Northeast. During 1839 officials in New York City indentured 349 children to work on Long Island farms. Idle or vagrant poor adults in New York could be involuntarily indentured for one year.[23] In its 1865 annual report, the Massachusetts Board of State Charities noted that over the years, more than 4,000 children of the commonwealth had been bound out. The board noted approvingly that "it will be seen at once what a relief to the state, and what an advantage to them it would prove, if they could be placed in suitable families."[24]

The most prominent form of controlling the poor during the 1800s was the poorhouse. These institutions, which often housed not only the poor but also the insane and infirm, provided a mechanism to segregate and supervise the very poor in an era of growing class consciousness.[25] As we have seen, poorhouses traced their history back to 1664 in Boston, and Philadelphia built its first poorhouse in 1732. By the 1820s, the poorhouse flourished as a model of maintenance of the desperately needy. New York's 1824 County Poorhouse Act called for the consolidation of almshouses at the county level instead of operating them in local communities, in the hope this would provide both greater control of the poor and more uniformity in their treatment. Massachusetts, too, saw a rapid spread of poorhouses during the first half of the nineteenth century. In 1824, Massachusetts had 83 poorhouses. By 1839 it hosted 180, and by 1860 the number had risen to 219. By the mid-1860s, 80 percent of individuals receiving long-term aid in Massachusetts resided in an institution.[26] Poorhouses were not so numerous in all the states, but by the middle of the 1800s, they were a dominant method of handling those unable to support themselves. Unfortunately, state agencies, particularly in the mid-nineteenth century, substantially conflated care for the impoverished with that for the mentally ill, the infirm, and criminals. In numerous states, throughout most of the nineteenth century, a single state agency held responsibility for overseeing all these classes of persons. This merger in the governmental sector reflected the ways private agencies treated these populations as well. For example, the National Conference of Charities and Corrections, which existed during the last two decades of the 1800s, addressed these very different groups under a common organizational umbrella.

In the mid-1800s, debates over the wisdom of the poorhouse as a tool for poverty relief hinged substantially on their presumed economy. The conversation would shift after about 1870 to one of effectiveness and humane treatment of the inmates, as they were called, but for over a half-century, institutionalization was a standard response to poverty. F. B. Sanborn, writing in 1872, argued that while institutionalizing the poor was "more economical" than housing them in their own homes, he lamented that it was easier to enter than break free from an almshouse and that internment there tended to be lengthened by its tragically perverse qualities.[27] Seeing poorhouses as dependency-building traps, as intuitive as that may seem from a twenty-first-century perspective, was a viewpoint that was slow to evolve in the 1800s.

Institutionalization was common in the northern and mid-Atlantic states but was less used in the South. Slaves, comprising over one-third of the southern population, were, of course, excluded from poor relief. Even free African Americans were probably excluded in nearly every location, though historical records are not definitive on this point.[28] Orphaned children of free blacks were categorically excluded from the Charleston, South Carolina, Orphan House, the first such publicly funded institution in the nation, opened in 1790.[29] Experiences in the South varied, but the poor law was a common model. One exception was in Louisiana, which, having been previously governed by the French and the Spanish, evidenced resistance to American ways. In 1817 the Louisiana legislature considered a bill to provide for the poor, but it failed, with opponents arguing that such laws were "calculated to encourage laziness and make the state of Louisiana a receptacle for the poor of other states."[30] Not until 1880 would Louisiana compel its parishes to care for their own needy citizens. In other southern states throughout the early 1800s, poor laws were widely adopted, requiring counties to maintain their own poor and for grandparents to care for grandchildren in the absence of the middle generation, and establishing settlement laws.[31]

Even though poor laws were common in the South, not all states in that region implemented them with alacrity. Many counties in North Carolina were unable to secure overseers of the poor on a regular basis during the 1830s. In Georgia the practice of providing public aid was so disapproved of and underdeveloped that in 1830 Governor George Gilmer asserted, in a way that challenges the imagination, that begging was virtually unknown in his state and that pauperism did not exist. There the poor simply struggled along the best they could in the absence of any institutionalized help.[32] Any notion of a continuity of care was decades off in the antebellum South and would continue to be so after the Civil War. Local records abound with disagreements over local or state government obligation to support the poor or even whether, instead, private individuals might be pressed into volunteer service as overseers. In Jefferson County, Alabama, the county commissioners grew so frustrated with the finances of their almshouse that in 1897 they ordered it closed and mandated that all the residents be sent to a poor farm. Exceptions were made for minor children, who were sent to a convent.[33]

The imperative throughout the 1800s to control the poor would persist into the next century, though notions of exactly how that was to be accomplished shifted over time. Urbanization and its accompanying economic insecurity heightened fears of the so-called dangerous classes. Toward the latter part of the century, a more individualized treatment of the poor emerged from the "friendly visitor" movement, the roots of which can be traced to the urban missionaries of the 1820s and 1830s. This focus on the individual marked the beginnings of modern social work, but an overriding preoccupation with surveillance and supervision of the poor would persist,[34] helping to ensure that relief efforts continued to focus on short-term maintenance of the poor. Hence these efforts would do little to improve the lot of the poor.

## AN ENDURING DISTINCTION: THE WORTHY VERSUS UNWORTHY POOR

Running through much of the nineteenth century debate over the poor was the crucial distinction between the very poor—such as widows, orphans, and the handicapped—who were viewed largely as victims of circumstance, and, on the other hand, paupers, who were seen as chronically irresponsible and thus much less deserving of assistance. Claims differ as to when this distinction between the so-called worthy and unworthy poor arose. Social-policy scholar Herbert Gans places its genesis in England in the 1830s.[35] This was a period when revisions of the English poor law represented a major effort to distinguish between chronic, norm-violating paupers and persons who were merely poor.[36] Yet in his 1821 report on the conditions of almshouses in Massachusetts, Josiah Quincy clearly identified two broad classes of the poor: those who were completely infirm and unable to work, and those capable of labor but who typically chose not to work. Going still further back, historian Charles Lee places the origin of the worthy versus unworthy distinction in fourteenth-century Europe.[37] Drawing this contrast between classes was not merely an academic exercise. Given that a large portion of the money communities spent on poor relief went toward transporting the poor out of their own community only to foist them onto another, poor-relief money was scarce. Thus the decision as to where and how to spend it mattered a great deal.[38] Having limited funds, Michigan's poorhouse commissioners in their 1873 annual report drew a sharp distinction between, on the one hand, the "helpless and dependent" poor who deserved care, and, on the other hand, the "vagrants, idlers, and dissolute paupers, who often times are not only lazy but criminal." The commissioners continued, "They are generally the very worst class of paupers: low, vile, and miserable, contaminating the whole establishment, and creating disorder and trouble [and are] . . . often dangerous. . . . It is no charity to admit such paupers to the poor-house, and they have no business there."[39] The Michigan report went on to lament that one-third of the Wayne County (Detroit) poorhouse population was of this undeserving type.

Regarding the able-bodied poor, the dominant assumption throughout the early nineteenth century was that poverty was a function of individual failings rather than a structurally induced phenomenon. Speaking at the dedication of a new chapel for the almshouse in Portsmouth, New Hampshire, in 1834, Reverend Charles Burroughs articulated the difference between poverty and pauperism: "The former is an unavoidable evil, to which many are brought from necessity, and in the wide and gracious Providence of God. It is the result, not of our faults, but of our misfortunes. . . . [In contrast] pauperism is the consequence of willful error, of shameful indolence, or vicious habit."[40] Burroughs was not alone in his assessment that many of the poor, and by definition all paupers, were responsible for their own plight. Walter Channing articulated in 1843 a common sentiment regarding poverty as "solely . . . the product of him or of her who has entered its dreadful . . . service. Let me repeat it, the causes of poverty are looked for, and found in him or her who suffers it."[41] The 1827 report by the Philadelphia Board of Guardians noted that "the poor in consequence of vice constitute here and everywhere, by far the greater part of the poor."[42] Overseers of the poor in Beverly, Massachusetts, noted that "the idle will beg in preference to working; relief is extended to them without suitable discrimination. They are not left to feel the just consequences of their idleness."[43] The 1824 Yates Report in New York expressed a similar sentiment, noting that the industrious poor would be corrupted by witnessing other poor people living off relief. Even after urban poverty developed as a distinct phenomenon throughout during the 1850s, a shift that lent credibility to the idea of the poor as victims of forces beyond their control, the political economist Herbert Spencer would write in 1872 that "the poverty of the incapable, the distresses that come upon the imprudent, the starvation of the idle, and those shoulderings aside of the weak by the strong . . . are the decrees of a large, far-seeing benevolence."[44] For Spencer and the Social Darwinists later, competition ruled the social world, and hard work and self-help provided the sole path out of poverty. For these observers, protecting the weak only encouraged them to breed and pollute the social pool.[45]

## THE INDUSTRIAL REVOLUTION AND THE RISE OF URBAN POVERTY

The second quarter of the 1800s saw a marked increase in anxiety over poverty. The rising cost of the care of the poor combined with religious pietism and apprehension over class tensions prompted considerable concern about what to do with an increasingly visible urban poor population. The period witnessed significant attempts to determine the causes of poverty and reduce its prevalence, marking a clear departure from colonial practices.[46] These efforts, however, only minimally attempted to use public authority to effect ameliorative ends, such as through offering apprenticeships for youths. Arguments from economists Adam Smith, David Ricardo, Thomas Malthus, and others throughout the late eighteenth century advanced the notion that the poor law was not only expensive but actually depressed wages by offering an incentive for the poor to avoid the labor market. From this perspective, public assistance lowered the standard of living instead of raising it. Despite this rhetoric about a minimalist state and homage to a free market, government regulations and subsidies were, and are, very real parts of the economic landscape, meaning in turn that a market populated by rugged individuals was, and is, far more illusory than real.[47]

As the mid-nineteenth century progressed, city life was increasingly troubled by poverty issues. Often unrewarding labor markets aggravated the condition of urban wage workers. Between 1750 and 1850, the percentage of adults in New York who were listed in census records as laborers rose from 6 percent to 27 percent.[48] Much of the piecework labor that low-skilled workers performed did not provide an adequate living. An 1844 study by Boston clergyman R. C. Waterston calculated the impossible number of hours a shirt maker would have to work in order to support herself, with shirts valued at six or seven cents each, and pants at a quarter.[49] The economic depression of 1857–1858 saw dramatically rising levels of unemployment, especially in large eastern cities. At this time, Philadelphia experienced layoffs of an estimated 20,000 to 30,000 workers, and in New York, the number was between 30,000 and 40,000.[50] By the 1870s, displaced workers who became wandering vagrants would become so numerous that they inspired a new term in the American lexicon: *tramp*.[51]

The convergence of massive immigration from Europe during the 1840s and 1850s, due to the Irish potato famine and political unrest on the continent, and the growing trend of wage labor in the cities meant that by the mid-1850s grinding poverty had become a fact of life in many urban centers, a development not easily ignored by the economically well off. Perspectives on poverty were aggravated by the lack of urban planning in many places; the desperately poor often lived in close proximity to thriving commercial districts and upscale neighborhoods. The realization by the middle and upper classes that so many poor people lived nearby in filthy slums grabbed attention in very concrete ways. It was during this time that Charles Brace, the organizer of the Children's Aid Society in New York, labeled these slum dwellers as the "dangerous classes," an epithet that stuck.[52] While fear of crime and threats of class warfare likely motivated most of the concern about the poor, a dominant public expression about this concern adopted the language of protecting public health. The prospect of communicable diseases spreading from slum dwellers to the more affluent figured prominently in the thinking of reformers and the middle class more generally. In New York, earlier panics of yellow fever in 1822 and cholera in 1832 had alarmed not only public health officials but also charitable organizations working with the city's poor.[53] Focusing on the utter lack of clean air, water, and decent housing in impoverished neighborhoods, Dr. John Griscom, a prominent sanitary reformer of the 1840s, complained that "one half of the world does not know how the other half lives."[54] By the 1860s, the more prosperous portion of the population had indeed learned something about the relationship between disease and the unsanitary conditions in the overcrowded tenements, as smallpox, typhoid, cholera, and other epidemics came to be more or less well recognized.[55]

Although poverty proved a widespread and pressing problem by the 1850s, poor relief continued to be thought of as a local function despite the financial stress it placed on city governments, which in turn led to intermittent funding of relief programs. Emblematic of this belief in a minimal federal role in poor relief and related matters, President Franklin Pierce vetoed an 1854 act that would have been the nation's first mental illness assistance law, claiming that he could not find authority in the Constitution to support a federal role in this area. That same year, President Pierce vetoed a bill that would have granted public land for use by states to help them care for the indigent. The president argued that the government could not become "the great almoner of public charity throughout the United States."[56] A campaign by reformer Dorothea Dix beginning in the 1840s had raised awareness of terrible conditions in asylums, not only in her native Massachusetts but around the nation.[57] Dix was ahead of her time in recognizing the links between mental illness and poverty. She critiqued what she thought was a mistaken belief in local control and instead argued for greater state and federal roles, but federal aid was still decades off.

With immigration continuing apace, tensions rose over the cost of providing relief to new arrivals on America's shores. Some critics claimed that European nations were dumping their poor on the United States. Just how systematic this trend was is probably impossible to determine, though various accounts lend it significant credibility. In 1839 a group of immigrants, many still clad in the uniform of the Edinburgh almshouse, arrived in New York. Their passage had been arranged by the overseers of the poor in Edinburgh.[58]

## THE RISE AND DECLINE OF THE POORHOUSE

In keeping with the firm belief on both sides of the Atlantic in the corrupting effects of unsupervised living among those on relief, the 1835 report of the English Poor Law Commissioners noted that relief for the able-bodied should be given only in the poorhouse. Many in America agreed. By the 1870s, poorhouses would be recognized by many for what they were: costly, dangerous to their inhabitants, and thoroughly unsuited for children. But before that realization took hold, hundreds of thousands of poor people were housed in these institutions, more throughout the middle part of the nineteenth century than during any other time.

The logic of poorhouses was straightforward. Sheltering people in large facilities under one roof promised both extensive control over their behavior and an economical means of providing poor relief. Given the local burden for funding the vast majority of poorhouses during this period, cost was a chief concern. Perhaps more important, the stringent living standards in most poorhouses provided their own fail-safe mechanism for sorting the worthy from the unworthy poor. Presumably, only those persons who were truly desperate would consent to live in such deplorable, oftentimes abusive conditions. Those able to work would surely choose to reside elsewhere. A well-run poorhouse would not be a temptation to those able, even if only barely, to care for themselves.[59]

Poorhouses existed as early as the 1600s, though they did not become common until the first couple of decades of the 1800s. These early institutions appeared predominantly in large cities: Boston in 1664; Salem, Massachusetts, in 1719; Portsmouth, New Hampshire, in 1716; Newport, Rhode Island, in 1723; Philadelphia in 1732; New York City in 1736; Charleston, South Carolina, in 1736; Providence in 1753; and Baltimore in 1773.[60] Poorhouses were later built in numerous communities around the country. Institutionalization was premised on the assumption that the vast majority of poor people were poor owing to irresponsible lifestyles and economic decisions; thus, housing them would provide a measure of control over otherwise self-destructive lives. To remediate them, and to defray the cost of running the institution, residents routinely were put to work. In some places, the residents provided cheap labor to fulfill commercial orders.[61] Yet this principle should not be overstated. It was important that the industrial production of the poorhouses not compete with that of local factories, lest the former undermine the latter. For this reason, much of the work done by inmates in poorhouses was menial and sometimes little more than make-work, such as washing laundry, breaking stone, and moving piles of wood.[62] Of chief importance, the work was seen as therapeutic, and that aspect of poorhouse life often trumped all others. In 1820 the managers of Philadelphia's poorhouse replaced the horses that turned the treadmills with poorhouse residents. A review commission critiqued the economic inefficiency of this new arrangement, but the managers opted to retain the residents as power sources precisely because of the drudgery involved. Residents in the poorhouse in Providence during the 1850s were routinely required to move piles of wood from one corner of the yard to the other and then back again. The 1851 rules for the Philadelphia poorhouse noted that idleness by able-bodied men was an affront to social norms. As late as 1882, in Buffalo, New York, Reverend S. Humphrey Gurteen suggested that all poorhouses operate a stone-breaking or wood-splitting yard or a laundry in order to provide a test of poor people's willingness to work.[63]

These arguments for the moral strengthening afforded by poorhouse life increasingly conflicted with indictments of such institutions during the third quarter of the nineteenth century. During the 1850s and 1860s, some of the more progressive states created government agencies responsible for overseeing asylums and almshouses. This surveillance resulted in much more focused criticism than had occurred before.[64] A select committee of the New York state senate visited a series of poorhouses in 1856 and issued a highly critical report citing terrible hygiene, overcrowding, bad medical care, and an inexcusably high death rate from communicable diseases among the residents.[65] A subsequent report on New York almshouses decried housing of boys in the laundry of one facility, noting that "they were intermingled with the inmates of the wash-house around the cauldrons where the dirty clothes were being boiled. Here was an insane woman raving and uttering wild gibberings, a half-crazy man was sardonically grinning, and an overgrown idiotic boy of malicious disposition was . . . torturing one of the little boys," all this under the dirty, dripping water from an overzealous floor mopping being conducted on the level above.[66] The previous year in Charleston, South Carolina, a similar report had emerged from a review of that city's poorhouse.[67] Deplorable conditions were found not only in the major cities of the East but also in the Midwest. Evaluating their own poorhouses in 1873, Michigan's Board of State Commissioners overseeing charitable, penal, pauper, and reformatory institutions wrote in their annual report that, "of all the inmates in these poorhouses there are none in a more deplorable condition that the insane paupers. About one-third of the whole number of them are kept closely confined in cells, most of which are small, dark and filthy in the extreme. . . . They are a constant source of annoyance and trouble to those who have them in charge, who, being unskilled in the management of crazy persons, frequently become vexed with them and treat them with harshness and severity. Many of them have no bedding and no clothing . . . They are regarded as beyond cure, and they receive no treatment whatever for the ill that afflicts them. Thus they remain, often for years, until death comes to relieve them."[68]

These reports incited a cascade of investigations of poorhouses and, in turn, a move away from sheltering children in them. As one historian later wrote, "from that time on the conviction spread that the collection of children in almshouses had been a terrible mistake."[69] State laws severely limiting the sheltering of children in poorhouses ensued: Ohio in 1866, Michigan and Massachusetts in the early 1870s, and Wisconsin in 1878. Seven other states, mainly in the North, followed suit throughout the 1890s. By 1900 one-fourth of the states had passed such laws.[70] Despite these changes in many states, the census of 1890 found nearly 5,000 children living in poorhouses nationwide.[71] The realization of the dysfunction of poorhouses during the latter half of the 1800s led to their gradual decline, especially after 1880, but the transition away from them required decades. In 1880, Pennsylvania sheltered some 20,000 people in poorhouses, Massachusetts nearly 14,000, and New York nearly 58,000.[72]

Between the 1870s and 1890s, indentured labor by children in the frontier West likewise fell out of favor. The practice of foster care gained momentum. Proponents of boarding out children to live with families who might bring them up as their own praised what they called the obvious advantages of this mode of care, even though they also realized the limited number of suitable homes for such children.[73] The move toward foster care was supported by the founding of children's home societies in 28 states during the last two decades of the nineteenth century.[74] Both the foster care movement and the closure of poorhouses more generally represented a gradual shift away from treatment of the very poor as an amorphous class and toward the recognition of these people as individuals with unique needs. This shift in thinking would contribute both to the social work movement of the late 1800s and, in time, to the state-operated relief programs of the early twentieth century. But first, the poor would be confronted with a wave of attacks on outdoor relief, which in many cases offered their only means of living in their own homes.

## THE ATTACK ON OUTDOOR RELIEF

Despite being criticized for fostering undisciplined living among its recipients, outdoor relief continued throughout the 1800s as a common form of assistance. Records from the period show that hundreds of thousands of people were assisted in their own homes through public and private (mainly religious) efforts. In his study of outdoor relief in New York State, historian Michael Katz found that the population receiving outdoor relief in that state rose from 11,937 in 1840 to 63,764 in 1850, and to 174,403 by 1860.[75] Despite claims to the contrary, supplying part of the rationale for the poor-house, some evidence indicates that outdoor relief allowed communities to support their poor more efficiently than did institutionalization. In the year 1870, New York spent an average of $109 on each poorhouse resident, com-pared with an average of $8.96 on each outdoor relief recipient.[76] The more than 10-fold difference in annual costs likely reflects that outdoor relief was not only fundamentally less expensive but also tended to be of shorter duration; that is, poorhouse residents likely remained there for significantly longer periods of time than families found it necessary to rely on outdoor relief. Scholarship on this point is mixed. In any case, poorhouses were quite expensive. Near their peak of use in the late 1870s, states spent substantial sums on their operations. In 1879, New York expended $1.6 million on its almshouses; Pennsylvania, $1.5 million; and Massachusetts, $1.7 million.[77]

The broad use of outdoor relief occurred not only in the Northeast, which established a tradition of aid to the poor well before nationhood, but also in some parts of the South. Throughout the late 1800s and into the early 1900s, Kentucky saw most of its poor relief provided in cash to people living in their own homes. Practically none of the counties in southeastern Kentucky maintained their own asylums, making outdoor relief a natural alternative.[78] Despite the endurance of outdoor relief as a common tool throughout most of the nineteenth century, it came under severe attack in many places during the second half of the 1800s.

Arguments against public outdoor relief arose primarily from private charity organizations and took to task city programs on the basis of cost to taxpayers and presumed ill effects on recipients' morals. The New York State Board of Charities, striking a tone much like that of charity organizations elsewhere, pronounced that outdoor relief is "injurious and hurtful to the unfortunate and worthy poor, demoralizing in its tendencies, a prolific source of pau-perism and official corruption, and an unjust burden upon the public."[79] Charity-based opponents of outdoor relief in Brooklyn stepped up their criti-cism of that program in the 1870s when Brooklyn's food package expanded to include such luxuries as sugar and tea. (Prior to that, the package was limited to staples: rice, wheat flour, or potatoes.) A Brooklyn family might expect to receive either food or fuel, but not both in the same week. The food allowance in the 1870s typically averaged about $1 per week, the equivalent of one-fifth of an unskilled worker's weekly pay.[80]

Later during this period, Frederic Almy, secretary of the New York Charity Organization Society in Buffalo, offered an argument against outdoor relief in 1899 that resonated with those articulated around the country during that time.[81] Almy's report showed that by the close of the nineteenth century, 10 of the nation's 40 largest cities no longer operated publicly funded outdoor relief programs. He proposed that even in large cities, private agencies could do a better job of relief than could governments, insisting that provision of open-ended aid depressed the work effort of the poor. Almy insisted that having received public outdoor relief, "more than twenty thousand persons were degraded to the condition of public paupers, deprived of their feelings of honourable independence and self-respect, and . . . were exposed to a powerful temptation to practice deception and fraud, had their fears of the consequences of idleness, . . . at least greatly lessened, and were many of them undoubtedly prepared to become ultimately, inmates of the alms-house or the penitentiary."[82]

Looking back through history, welfare-policy scholars Frances Fox Piven and Richard Cloward conclude that the retrenchment of public relief was part of an effort by factory owners and railroad companies to ensure an ample supply of workers willing to accept low wages during this period of dramatic industrialization. Public outdoor relief was suspended temporarily in New York in 1874, except for coal, and it was eliminated outright in Philadelphia in 1879. Funding was also significantly reduced in Providence in 1879 and in Cleveland the same year.[83] Despite the belief in many quarters during this time that there were enough jobs to go around for anyone who applied him- or herself, the very real demand for relief continued. Outdoor relief across the country was curtailed but not completely eliminated. Private charities simply could not handle the load by themselves, especially during periods of economic depression.[84]

## PUBLIC VERSUS PRIVATE RELIEF SOURCES

Throughout the nineteenth century, private charities played an important role in augmenting public aid—and often arguing vigorously against it. Their prominence in the field of poverty policy, however, rose and fell with Americans' evolving understandings of poverty. As the century progressed, particularly after the 1840s, more Americans came to understand poverty, especially urban poverty, as partly a product of structural problems in the economy and not simply as the result of individual moral failures. In a changing economy, more wage laborers remained vulnerable to fluctuations of the market. In the 1870s and 1880s, the political economist Henry George articulated a strong statement of this perspective, diagnosing poverty as primarily the result of an unjust concentration of unearned wealth in the hands of landowners. Based on the proposition that the value of land is a product of society, not of any single property owner, George elaborated a proposal to tax away the rent, or the excess value produced by land, in order to remove an incentive for speculators and to encourage more productive use of land. This was to be the single tax. George's ideas, presented in *Progress and Poverty* (1879), won him a considerable following, but also some critics. Felix Alder, a contemporary of George, described the single tax as "a single draught of socialism with unstinted individualism thereafter."[85] The significance of George's thinking lay in his view of poverty as abnormal, not as inevitable.[86] George's framing of poverty as largely due to structural explanations was not entirely novel. Jacksonians in the 1820s and 1830s had argued as much. Nonetheless, George's formulation was important.

Arguments about structural impediments to well-being, however, did not dominate the period. Relief continued to be ungenerous, irregular, and in the case of aid from private charities, couched in scrutiny of the recipient. Large private charities operated parallel to public relief agencies in many cities. They included Boston's Society for the Prevention of Pauperism, established 1835; the Baltimore-based Association for the Improvement of the Condition of the Poor, begun in 1849; Philadelphia's Union Benevolent Association, founded in the early 1830s; and the New York Association for Improving the Condition of the Poor, dating from 1843. Some of these agencies grew out of frustration with publicly funded relief. The New York Association for Improving the Condition of the Poor, an offshoot of the New York City Tract Society, arose particularly due to perceived government incompetence during the depression of 1837, but it also very much pursued religious goals.[87] The rise of large, private charities created tension between those entities and public agencies. That tension would endure until the passage of the Social Security Act in 1935. At the core of the debate was a concern that handouts without close supervision of the poor did more harm than good in that they undermined the work ethic and fostered licentiousness. Typical of the period was the criticism of the New York Association for Improving the Condition of the Poor, in its 1855 annual report, that "soup kitchens have been tried over and over again, until their mischiefs have been so fully ascertained that they now find favor nowhere. It is now a recognized principle among sound social economists and philanthropists, that the poor should not be aided in promiscuous masses at soup kitchens, but by personal visits at their homes."[88] Despite these concerns, cities indeed spent significant sums on poor relief. Brooklyn spent an average of nearly $115,000 annually on outdoor relief during the mid-1870s.[89]

A second important part of the debate turned on the fear that publicly funded relief was susceptible to political corruption. Seth Low, mayor of Brooklyn during the 1880s and later of New York City after its consolidation, complained to the sixth annual conference on charities in 1879 that outdoor relief in Brooklyn during the 1870s had served particularly political purposes. Low proposed that "families with voters were the first served. The 'out-door' relief appropriations became a vast political corruption fund."[90] Further, favoritism emerged as politically well-connected vendors of goods and materials given in kind to the poor experienced more demand for the services than did less-well-connected merchants.[91]

Supporters of private philanthropies further decried the existence of public aid agencies as undermining contributions to private charities.[92] President Franklin Pierce, in the message accompanying his 1854 veto of federal aid to poor asylums, noted that the "foundations of charity will be dried up at home, and the several states, instead of bestowing their own means on the social wants of their own people, may themselves . . . become humble suppliants for the bounty of the Federal Government, reversing their true relation to this Union."[93] Variations on this particular argument would extend well into the 1930s.

A conflict of fundamental beliefs about the nature of poverty complicated these concerns over public versus private charity. Throughout the 1800s, Americans' attitudes toward poverty were torn between two contradictory beliefs. The first was that poverty was part of a divine plan, even if not understood by human beings. In the lament of the biblical Job, God has given and God has taken away without troubling to explain those decisions to mortals. While Americans were not as Calvinistic during this period as they had been in the early 1700s, this notion of heavenly dispensation still carried considerable weight.[94] This perspective recognized that poverty elicited charity from the well-to-do, prompting beneficence, which rewarded their souls. Poverty also taught the poor humility and gratitude, benefiting their souls, if not necessarily their bodies. A competing belief was that in an expanding America, there should be no reason for poverty to exist, given infinite opportunities for making one's way.[95] The weight given to one perspective or the other shifted with changes in the economy. During good times, most middle-class people probably believed in the existence of broadly spread opportunity and saw little reason for chronic poverty. This belief was an important driver of the private charity movement and its paternalistic methods of supervision of the poor. During times of economic depression, however, the awareness of a more worthy poor increased. This was certainly the case during the late 1830s and again in the 1850s.

Charity organizations played another important role late in the nineteenth century in fostering a changed thinking about poverty. During the 1880s and 1890s, an important perspective arose that viewed the poor less as a formless, anonymous mass and more as individuals with their own needs. The movement involving what were called friendly visitors, typically middle-class women who visited poor families, that had sprung up during the Second Great Awakening of the early 1800s became prominent throughout the 1870s and 1880s. These so-called visitors were not, however, simply making social calls. The central idea was to mentor poor people toward more constructive lifestyles. Visitors were part detective, part mentor, and part religious evangelist. Their visits involved efforts to determine the causes of the family's poverty and to suggest ways to overcome it through material and spiritual lifestyle changes. Their goal was certainly not to steer poor families toward greater reliance on charity.[96] During the late 1800s, this Social Gospel movement was advanced by the belief, part of the Third Great Awakening, that all people could be saved religiously, and by extension, economically and socially. Visitors generally opposed public outdoor relief programs, instead favoring limited, private relief only where necessary.

The most prominent voice of this nascent social-work movement of the late 1880s was Josephine Shaw Lowell, founder of the New York Charity Organization Society and member of the New York State Board of Charities. As a matter of strict doctrine, Lowell believed that no gift of charity could be liberally given without undermining the morality of the recipient. Gifts, if offered at all, must be couched in a mentoring relationship, such as that embodied by the friendly visitors or professional social workers. But her objection extended beyond what she understood to be detrimental effects on recipients. Lowell's blend of libertarianism and utilitarianism led her to endorse the principle that the only reason money (such as taxes) should be taken from one and given to another is that both—the giver and the receiver—are better as a result. Further, she believed strongly that the fear of starvation served as a highly effective incentive to work. A staunch opponent of outdoor relief, Lowell argued that all the members of a community suffer when aid is given too liberally, such as under what she believed to be the corrupt system of publicly funded assistance to families living in their own homes. If relief must be given, it should come from private charities, which she believed were equipped to give aid in a supervisory context. In keeping with this outlook, Lowell supported the idea of public funding of otherwise private charities. She supported a role for government in inspecting private institutions that house the poor and, further, public funding of those private institutions.[97] Lowell's support for public funding to support private charity work should not be misinterpreted as support for dole giving, for she firmly believed in the presumed spirit-destroying quality of relief. Exhibiting a near fetish with the work ethic of poor persons, she endorsed what by her own description were radical interventions, insisting that "the cause of the want and suffering are to be removed if possible even if the process be as painful as plucking out an eye or cutting off a limb."[98] In line with the scrutiny advocated for would-be residents of poorhouses, Lowell believed that solicitors of aid should be tested with overtly difficult, unpleasant, and badly remunerated chores. After all, she wrote, if the chores are not sufficiently onerous or if they pay too well, they will not provide a valid test of need.

If Lowell was a hard-nosed, rule-bound social worker, others of her generation took a more subtle case-by-case approach. Chicago-based social worker Jane Addams saw the story of a young man who approached her at Hull House as illustrative of a crucial lesson. The young man was seeking assistance for his family. Addams declined to give him money but instead suggested he go to work digging a nearby drainage canal. The young man said he had always been accustomed to indoor work and that he did not readily tolerate outdoor work in the winter. Despite this, he went to work digging, promptly contracted pneumonia, and died two days later. This episode taught Addams that hard-and-fast rules often fail, and that social workers must evaluate petitioners individually in order to understand their life circumstances, personal abilities, and limitations.[99]

## CIVIL WAR PENSIONS AS A COUNTERPOINT TO TRADITIONAL POVERTY RELIEF

If much of nineteenth century poverty relief was characterized by strong efforts to control the poor and to provide them only enough to survive—without simultaneously undermining their work effort—Civil War veteran pensions for Union soldiers stand as a dramatic exception on both counts. This pension program deserves some consideration due the important role it played as a precursor to federal welfare efforts beginning in the twentieth century. Civil War veterans' pensions were very widely distributed in the North and became more generous through time. They provided a precedent that helped smooth the way for the Social Security Act in the midst of the Great Depression, for these pensions demonstrated that publicly funded social insurance could be provided without sending the United States down a slippery slope toward full-blown socialism and without fundamentally undermining the economy or laborers' participation in it. While the Civil War pensions were not conceived explicitly as an antipoverty program, they served that purpose and eventually advanced a more expansive welfare state in America.[100]

Civil War pensions initially benefited veterans and war widows. After some shrinkage in the program due to human attrition in the early 1870s, Congress legislated a series of changes to ease benefit claims under the program. In 1873 approximately 250,000 veterans drew pensions, but by the end of the 1880s, that number had reached some one-half million. Despite being tainted by fraud, the program grew so much that by the mid-1890s, pension expenditures consumed 40 percent of federal government spending. By 1910 fully 28 percent of men aged 65 or over received a pension, better than one-half million of them, with benefits averaging $189 per year.[101] These benefits were generous by contemporary standards and became more so over time. In 1890 Congress severed the link between disability and pension eligibility, meaning that any Union veteran or his survivor could claim a pension. Veterans came to constitute a well-organized pressure group, and the federal budget surplus created by the tariffs provided the funds. By the 1890s, so many old soldiers filed claims for pensions that members of Congress spent a significant portion of their time helping investigate claims, and Friday evenings in Congress often became pension night. Despite the frequent absence of a quorum, many private bills were passed in Congress making these old soldiers eligible for the pension. Even some old soldiers who had been classified as deserters were legislatively made eligible for pensions. The last of these pensions were paid to surviving spouses in the early 1940s.[102]

As broad as the Civil War pension program was, it led only indirectly to a larger federally coordinated social-insurance program. That would require a few more decades and a nationwide depression. In the meantime, states filled some of the gaps, creating mothers' pensions and workers' compensation programs throughout the second decade of the twentieth century and unemployment insurance beginning in the early 1930s. The rapid expansion and permissiveness of the war pensions did, however, contribute to a broader sense that publicly funded relief and social insurance programs were politically viable in the American context, an idea that had been quite controversial up to this point. The nineteenth century ended with this question not quite settled, though the private charity movement would never fully recover the prominent position it held during the retrenchment of outdoor relief in the 1870s and 1880s. The other contribution of the private charity movement, the insight to treat poor people as individuals instead of merely members of a class, would endure beyond the debate over funding sources. Neither of these changes, however, would fundamentally alter the tradition of social control over the poor, a tradition that was solidified during the nineteenth century.

## NOTES

1. Folks 1971 [1900], p. 6; Mohl 1971, p. 53.
2. Quincy 1821; Katz 1996, p. 14.
3. Bourque 2004.
4. Quincy 1821.
5  Novak 1996.
6. Wright 1992, p. 6.
7. Rosenberg 1971.
8. *North Atlantic Review* 74 (April 1852): 464–65.
9. Sanborn 1872, p. 7.
10. Sanborn 1868, p. 495.
11. Bremner 1956, p. 8.
12. Ibid., p. 10.
13. Katz 1996, p. 15.
14. Klebaner 1955, p. 203.
15. Folks 1971 [1900], p. 8.

16. Quincy 1821.
17. Klebaner 1955, pp. 195–96.
18. Katz 1996, p. 20; Mohl 1971, pp. 63–64.
19. Klebaner 1955, p. 195.
20. Folks 1971 [1900], chap. 1.
21. Bremner 1956, p. 47.
22. John Murray 2004, p. 226–27.
23. Folks 1971 [1900], pp. 6, 15.
24. *First Annual Report of the Board of State Charities (Massachusetts) 1865.*
Boston: Wright and Potter. Quote at p. xxi.
25. Rothman 1971.
26. Trattner 1999, pp. 58–59.
27. Sanborn 1872, p. 19.
28. Wisner 1970, p. 23–24.
29. John Murray 2004, p. 228.
30. Wisner 1970, p. 26.
31. Ibid., pp. 27–28.
32. Ibid., p. 37.
33. Ibid., p. 46.
34. Gilliom 2001.
35. Gans 1995, p. 2.
36. Himmelfarb 1983, p. 160.
37. Lee 1982, p. 572.
38. Katz 1989, pp. 11–12.
39. *1873 Report of the Board of State Commissioners for the General Supervision of Charitable, Penal, Pauper, and Reformatory Institutions (Michigan),* pp. 71–72.
Lansing: W.S. George and Co.
40. Iceland 2003, p. 12.
41. Katz 1989, p. 14.
42. Katz 1993, p. 6.
43. Katz 1996, p. 170.
44. McCarthy 1962, p. 37.
45. Bremner 1956, pp. 18–19.
46. Trattner 1999, p. 47.
47. Himmelfarb 1983; Novak 1996.
48. Katz 1996, p. 4.
49. Bremner 1956, p. 75.
50. Feder 1936, pp. 18–19.
51. Katz 1993, p. 11.
52. Bremner 1956, chap. 1.
53. Rosenberg 1971, p. 263.
54. Bremner 1956, p. 4.
55. Ibid., p. 7.
56. Jacobs 1968, p. 41.
57. Grace Abbott 1966 [1941], p. 13; Trattner 1999, pp. 63–67.

58. Bremner 1956, p. 9.
59. Katz 1993, pp. 6–7; Marshall 1981, p. 36.
60. Katz 1996, p. 15.
61. Bourque 2004, p. 193.
62. Block et al. 1987, chap. 1.
63. Katz 1993, chap. 1.
64. Bremner 1956, pp. 48–49.
65. Katz 1996, p. 26.
66. Bremner 1956, p. 49.
67. Katz 1996, pp. 26–27.
68. *1873 Report of the Board of State Commissioners for the General Supervision of Charitable, Penal, Pauper, and Reformatory Institutions (Michigan)*, pp. 68–69.
69. Folks 1971 [1900], p. 47.
70. Bremner 1956, p. 50.
71. Folks 1971 [1900], pp. 47–51.
72. Thanet 1881.
73. Bosanquet 1899, p. 187.
74. Leff 1973, p. 398.
75. Piven and Cloward 1987.
76. Katz 1996, chap. 2.
77. Thanet 1881.
78. Estabrook 1929, p. 224.
79. Mohl 1983, p. 45.
80. Katz 1996, p. 49.
81. Ibid., p. 43–44.
82. Ibid., p. 41.
83. Block et al. 1987, p. 15; Mohl 1983, pp. 41–42.
84. Katz 1996, p. 54.
85. Bremner 1956, p. 25
86. Bremner 1956, pp. 23–27.
87. Feder 1936, p. 20; Rosenberg 1971, chap. 9.
88. Feder 1936, p. 21.
89. Feder 1936, pp. 21–23; Low 1879, p. 202.
90. Low 1879, p. 208.
91. Edith Abbott 1936.
92. Trattner 1999, pp. 56–57.
93. Grace Abbott 1966 [1941], pp. 16–17.
94. Olivas 2004, pp. 262–63; Rosenberg 1971.
95. Bremner 1956, p. 16; Olivas 2004, p. 262.
96. Bremner 1956, pp. 52–53.
97. Lowell 1884, p. 85.
98. Ibid., p. 94.
99. Jacobs 1968, p. 43.
100. Skocpol 1992.
101. Ibid., p. 65.
102. Amenta 1998; Skocpol 1992.

# 3

# From Mothers' Pensions to a Troubled Aid to Dependent Children Program

Almsgiving to street beggars, or to those who apply at the door, is another method—however reprehensible—of giving aid . . . since [this] money is given outright, and no attempt is made to control the action of its recipients, it must be classed, like that distributed by public officials, with aid given to the poor in their homes. . . . The pauper type, whether in receipt of beggarly alms or of generous income, is a shameless and insolvent social debtor.

—Edward Devine, general secretary of the Charity Organization
Society of the City of New York (1914)[1]

Continued dependence upon relief induces a spiritual and moral disintegration fundamentally destructive to the national fiber. To dole out relief in this way is to administer a narcotic, a subtle destroyer of the human spirit . . . work must be found for able-bodied but destitute workers.

—Franklin Roosevelt in his January 1935
State of the Union address to Congress[2]

The sharp distinction between poor persons and paupers that prevailed throughout most of the nineteenth century continued well into the twentieth century. Even among those observers who were sympathetic to the poor, such as the socialist settlement house worker Robert Hunter, sought to document the "evils" of poverty "among the dependent and vicious classes, which constitute the social wreckage in the abysses of our cities."[3] Hunter, like many others of his generation, distinguished between the poor, who lack necessary resources, and paupers, who live by charity or public aid. In adopting this tone, Hunter hued to a tradition begun in the mid-1800s, one characterizing London newspaper writings by Henry Mayhew, and later the work of Jacob Riis, a turn-of-the-century photo chronicler of New York City's poor.[4]

The percentage of people living in poverty from the latter half of the nineteenth century through the early 1960s was estimated by various analysts as approximately one-fifth of the population. Various studies found that approximately 19 percent of New York's population received assistance during the period 1897–1899, either as an in-patient in an institution or in the form of outdoor relief. Comparable figures for Boston from 1903 show that more than 20 percent of the city's population received aid. In 1893 some 14 percent of the families living in Manhattan were evicted.[5] Hunter blamed labor market slowdowns as a primary reason for poverty, citing figures from the late 1800s showing that up to one-third of workers in a many cities lacked year-round employment. In synthesizing these diverse reports, Hunter contributed significantly to the development of poverty thresholds that later analysts would refine.[6]

Despite this context of widespread poverty, due at least in part to structural causes, early twentieth-century writers differentiated among the poor, separating those perceived to have brought poverty on themselves through imprudence from those who were victims of a troubled labor market. Over both cases, a certain laissez-faire attitude prevailed. Hunter wrote in 1904 that "the sins of men should bring their own punishment, and the poverty which punishes the vicious and the sinful is good and necessary. . . . It would be unwise to legislate out of existence, even were it possible to do so, that poverty which penalizes the voluntary idle and vicious."[7] Hunter flatly condemned the giving of doles, calling it not "true charity" but rather "brutality."[8] He systematized what people a century later would consider tough love in terms shown in Table 3.1.

Others, including Edward Devine, general secretary of the Charity Organization Society of the City of New York, echoed the revulsion at almsgiving, expressing doubt that handouts can ever be tailored to a beggar's true needs, given what he saw as the penchant for mendacity among that class.[9] Disdain for the poor was expressed not only in the way assistance was delivered but also in overt political disenfranchisement. As of 1934, 14 states still deprived paupers of suffrage.[10]

Even if many observers rejected the prospect of constructively tailoring relief work to the individual, a growing school of thought—scientific social work—increasingly relied on Sigmund Freud's insights regarding early childhood influences on later parenting skills, combined with the flowering of the social sciences more generally throughout the late nineteenth and early twentieth centuries. The maturation of the social sciences led social workers

**Table 3.1.**
**Dependents and Robert Hunter's recommended treatment.**

| Group | Treatment |
| --- | --- |
| Absolute dependents: the aged, children, crippled, incurable, blind, deaf and dumb, insane, epileptic, imbecile, idiots, feeble-minded | Proper care continued as long as may be necessary in institutions or elsewhere |
| Dependents capable of self-support: the professional vagrant, beggar, morally insane | Industrial education, repression, confinement for protection of society |
| Temporary dependents likely to become chronic: the sick, the inebriate, those addicted to drugs | Complete cure in proper institutions to prevent infirmity of a permanent character |
| Temporary dependents: the unemployed, widows with children | Supply an economic existence free from any taint of pauperism |

*Source:* Adapted from Robert Hunter, *Poverty* (New York: Macmillan, 1904), 76 –77.

to display greater confidence in their ability to understand—and by extension, enhance—personality and the behavior of the poor. One important source for the accepted practices of this new scientific social work was Mary Richmond's *Social Diagnosis,* published in 1917 and expanded upon in her later book *What Is Social Casework?* in 1922. By the beginning of the 1920s, an era of professionalization was firmly taking hold in social work. As the profession developed during the first three decades of the twentieth century, the emphasis focused more intently on the individual as a target of therapy.

The individualist tradition viewed persons as largely responsible for their own betterment. This was the time of up-by-the-bootstraps Horatio Alger stories. The individualist tradition persisted even among thinkers who would be placed on the political left today. This focus on the individual rather than attempting to assist entire classes hinged on a belief that little could be done to reverse the structural causes of poverty, but that the personal failings underlying it could be usefully addressed. This approach differed from the much more anonymous treatment afforded residents of poorhouses throughout the 1800s. A central idea of scientific social work held that through intensive casework, skilled social workers could teach improved living skills. This represented a refinement of friendly visiting of the late 1800s. In time, the influence of advanced understanding of the human psyche tended to steer casework away from poverty issues and toward the mental health field; thus by the beginning of the Great Depression, casework had lost some of its focus on poverty.[11]

This shifting focus of psychologically grounded casework and persistent skepticism in many quarters regarding the efficacy of publicly funded relief programs undermined municipal efforts to help the poor during the late 1800s and very early 1900s. Programs in several large cities, including New York, Philadelphia, and Baltimore, were cancelled in the 1890s and the first decade of the twentieth century. The arguments for their elimination posited that private charities would suffer if they had to compete with public programs, and that cash assistance given without a significant casework element would corrupt recipients. Further, critics argued that governments could not be trusted to adequately fund administration, so implementation would suffer, and relief would become tied up with politics, corrupting both.[12] Critics of mothers' pensions, such as Mary Richmond in her speech to the 1912 National Conference of Social Work, argued that public funds would lead fathers to desert their families and that "no private funds for relief can successfully compete very long with a public fund, whether the latter is adequate or not. Inevitably the sources of private charitable relief dry up."[13] Arguments made in the 1880s by Josephine Shaw Lowell persisted, helping to perpetuate a strong preference for private charity over public relief in most cities. This great reluctance on the part of private charity organizations to brook the divide between public and private relief meant that the American Association for Organizing Charities did not even admit public agencies in its membership until 1921.[14]

Beginning in the second decade of the twentieth century, a very different argument came from other corners of the social-work field. Julia Lathrop, then chief of the U.S. Children's Bureau, argued instead for a competent and reliable public source of funds for poor mothers. She believed the profession was only beginning to learn how to support poor families, and that if social work was to move beyond the legacy of the poor laws, it must embrace public funding.[15] Lathrop's school of thought would ultimately win this struggle. Along the way, a recognition developed that capitalist economies naturally produce business cycles that inevitably lead to depressions and high unemployment. Slowly, more in the social-work profession, as well as policy makers, embraced this view. As Grace Abbott, professor of public welfare administration at the University of Chicago, noted in the 1930s, a large portion of poverty was due to employers' habit of laying off workers when not needed, with very little thought of the implications for those who would lose their jobs.[16]

## THE TRANSITION TO PUBLIC RELIEF

Arguments for private poverty relief lost much of their potency during the second decade of the twentieth century. That decade witnessed a string of city and state adoptions of publicly funded relief programs that would set the stage for the legislation of the Social Security Act in 1935. During this period, a handful of large cities created elaborate government agencies to handle welfare functions, including Kansas City in 1910 and Chicago in 1913. The more important developments of that time occurred at the state level, beginning with the legislation of a mothers' pension program in Illinois in 1911. This shift represented a significant break with the tradition of private charity that had dominated up to this point. By the second decade of the twentieth century, progressives viewed poverty as primarily an economic condition instead of a moral one. To the extent that this removed the pejorative label from the poor, it also meant that government-funded relief was a less-significant violation of the well-entrenched social-work tradition. Speaking in 1939, Grace Abbott reflected that she had always thought that if the needs of the poor are to be met adequately, the state must play a role. That year, four years after the passage of the Social Security Act, Abbott observed that "among social workers there is hardly more than a historic remnant of the old opposition to the state in social service."[17] Such confident talk would, however, have to wait until vigorous battles at both the federal and state levels had been fought and won. Private social-work advocates would not abandon their positions easily.

The movement toward the adoption of mothers' pensions was in part based on the outcomes of a 1909 White House conference on the care of dependent children. The attendees included luminaries of the day: Booker T. Washington, Jane Addams, and Theodore Dreiser, among others. President Theodore Roosevelt set the tone by articulating a government responsibility for orphans and children of widows, though the president was cautious about open-ended commitments to cash relief.[18] This conference helped solidify the idea of government responsibility for the poor and that children should be raised by their parents whenever possible. This assertion represented a firm rejection of the turn-of-the-century practice of children of poor parents being sent to orphanages. Forced relegation of children to orphanages distressed many in the social-work community by this time, and the 1909 conference report articulated that children ought not be separated from their mothers solely for reasons of poverty, but rather only in cases of significant unsuitability.[19] While the conference acknowledged the widespread preference for private over public aid, and Theodore Roosevelt explicitly said as much, various participants would, within a very few years, advocate for a fundamental shift on this point. Edith Abbott, Grace Abbott, Julia Lathrop, Florence Kelley, Jane Addams, and others supported publicly funded poor relief. In short order, both the General Federation of Women's Clubs and the National Congress of Mothers threw their support behind mothers' pensions. In 1911 the American Federation of Labor lent its voice to the movement as well.[20] Its president,

Samuel Gompers, held a dim view of women in the workforce, less out of charity toward women than in defense of men's jobs.[21]

Despite this growing professionalization of relief provision, the notion that cash assistance cannot be given without utterly corrupting families and inviting laxness forestalled the creation of more-extensive cash-assistance programs. Progressives were forced to move slowly on this issue, but the movement advanced significantly between 1911 and 1920, with 40 states enacting mothers' pension laws. By the end of the 1920s, four more had done so. The trend began in the North and spread later to the South.[22] This assistance, directed primarily at widows, allowed women to care for their children without the distraction of work outside the home, something in which mothers, it was said, ideally should not be engaged. A child saved from preventable illness and destitution was a citizen gained, so maternalists insisted.[23] The public was generally supportive of the idea of mother's pensions before these were legislated by states, but organizational support was required before this latent public sentiment could take on an expression as policy.

The opposition to state-funded mothers' pensions came largely from private charities, which tended to believe that public welfare programs inevitably corrupt due to their lack of a mentoring casework component. These critics perhaps need not have worried about early mothers' pensions, as the initial grants were not spread widely, and the dollar amount was modest. As of 1931 only two states—Massachusetts and New York—offered pensions exceeding $40 per month, and in several southern states, the monthly grant was less than $15. In only nine states did these programs benefit more than 15 families per 10,000 individuals as of 1931.[24]

The lack of generosity of these mothers' pensions did not assuage critics' qualms about public aid. Edward Devine, general secretary of the New York Charity Organization Society and vocal opponent of public aid, seemed to fear for his fellow social workers' turf when he asked, "Who are these brash reformers who so cheerfully impugn the motives of old-fashioned givers, of the conscientious directors of charitable institutions, of pious founders of hospitals and all manner of benefactions?"[25] Devine's fear of other people doing good and crowding his turf motivated a two-pronged argument. First, opponents reiterated the fundamental principles of scientific social work, that counseling must accompany aid to avoid an otherwise corrupting influence of giving. They argued that bureaucratized public aid would represent a step backward into the pauperism they claimed had accompanied public outdoor relief before private aid largely took over in the late 1800s. They feared this public aid would almost certainly create a new class of dependents. Further, opponents argued that cash grants represented an assault on the family, harmful to the children and sure to undermine the character of parents.[26]

The small contingent of private agency social workers was overwhelmed by the broad progressive coalition that pushed fast and hard for mothers' pensions. It wasn't a fair fight. The progressives had on their side not only a large number of allies, but also the argument that these pensions would be small, directed to widows and their children—a very worthy clientele—and morally uplifting.[27] The progressives also cast poverty as too big a problem to be left outside the sphere of government obligation. Progressives argued that social justice must involve bringing "the power of the state and national government into the economic struggle on the side of women, children, and other unprotected groups."[28] To drive home their critique of current casework practices, they described the invasive methods used by social workers as "the third degree."[29] While it was not inevitable that this line of argument was to win the debate, it certainly did, and the scientific-social-work movement never recovered its turn-of-the-century preeminence. The progressives' arguments carried the day regarding mothers' pensions, similar to how they would in the related field of workers' compensation laws during this time. In 1911 alone, 10 states enacted workers' compensation programs.[30]

Moving beyond rhetoric, one early step in the shift toward mothers' pensions occurred in New York. That state adopted a grant program for widows with children that provided cash equal to the cost of institutionalizing their children.[31] The budget-neutral quality of this would have appealed to fiscal conservatives, and the in-home care aspect would enjoy broad approval. However, in a move designed to protect their status, social-work professionals persuaded New York's governor to not sign the bill. Similar developments occurred in a few other states. Courts in California liberally interpreted laws to provide county-level aid to children living in their homes. In 1910, New Jersey's attorney general responded similarly. In 1908 the Oklahoma legislature provided scholarships to children of widows, and in 1911, Michigan did likewise.[32]

The first fully formed mothers' pension program emerged in Illinois in 1911.[33] The law was prompted by protests to the state legislature from Merritt Pinckney, a Cook County juvenile court judge. Pinckney insisted he was unwilling to continue ordering the removal of children from homes to be placed in an institution based solely on the poverty of the household.[34] At the time, public assistance in Cook County was limited to groceries and coal, plus some help from private charities.[35] The judge made his recommendation for publicly funded assistance without knowledge of exactly how many cases would fall under such a program or of the cost of such an effort. Local social workers trusted him, and Chicago charities pooled their resources to staff the program in the city.[36] Other states quickly followed suit, and the mothers' pension movement set an expansionary pace matched by no other piece of social justice legislation, with the exception of workers'

48 THE WELFARE DEBATE

compensation. Mothers' pensions were adopted by 40 states in less than a decade. These programs passed state legislatures by large margins, and in the two states—Colorado and Arizona—that held referenda on them, majorities of more than two-to-one approved them.[37]

Progressives' jubilation over the rapid expansion of these programs was tempered by the findings of how limited program aid was. These pensions ranged from $9 to $15 per month for the first child and $4 to $10 for each subsequent child. The pensions typically applied to children under age 14, one- to three-year state residency requirements were common, and moral fitness standards typically conditioned the benefits. All states required documentation of poverty and mandated the cessation of these pensions upon receipt of some other pension.[38]

These mothers' pensions were highly significant in the historical development of an American welfare state.[39] However, they were also politically fragile. When push came to shove and budgets were squeezed during the early 1930s, many municipalities ceased their cash aid. Most of the mothers' pension programs established during the 1920s received no state funds. By 1927 only 3 states had not established state-level authorities to address poverty, but in an age of patronage politics, state supervision did not necessarily translate into competent administration, and funding still fell within local or county purview.[40] By 1931 local and county welfare agencies in only 17 states received any state financial support, and only 8 states assumed any administrative responsibility for them. With the onset of the Great Depression these local, county, and state agencies failed in large numbers. In 1931 the New York Department of Public Welfare cut the food allotment of every 10th family in order to address its own budget shortfalls. In 3 states and in 69 counties around the nation, budget shortfalls led to the elimination of mothers' aid altogether between 1930 and 1932. By early 1933, nearly 1,000 municipalities had defaulted on these programs.[41] Even when up and running as designed, these early social insurance programs reflected a great degree of fiscal conservatism. As of 1929, state workers' compensation and mothers' pensions combined amounted to no more than 1 percent of the gross national product, and less than one-half of the amount the federal government spent on Civil War pensions per year during the 1870s, stingy by any measure.[42]

In the early years of these laws, most counties refused to implement them, claiming there were no eligible cases within their boundaries or that private agencies could do a better job. Prior to the passage of the Social Security Act in 1935, no more than one-half of the counties in the nation had implemented their respective state's mothers' pension program.[43] However, despite being fragile, these new efforts permanently tipped the balance of private versus public aid. By 1929 most antipoverty expenditures came from governmental, not private, sources.[44] New York, with its 1931 program of home relief, became the first state to allocate state money to its cities and counties for such purposes. Other states followed, with other northern-tier states doing much the same. Looking back on these programs, we see a case of rapid policy diffusion, but their primary legacy was to raise expectations and provide a model for welfare provision, more so than to provide welfare benefits per se. By 1934, the year before the Social Security Act was passed, only South Carolina and Georgia lacked mothers' pension programs.[45]

With the Great Depression deepening, a variety of proposals surfaced to help the poor. Senator Huey Long of Louisiana, a populist critic of the New Deal, waged a campaign to "share our wealth." His movement garnered enthusiasm in many parts of the country, though Long failed to win passage of his legislation. Long's movement echoed that of Francis Townsend in the early twentieth century. Townsend had proposed a guaranteed pension of $200 per month for those over 60, provided they left the labor force and spent the money the same month. The political left feared that the Townsend plan's transactions tax was regressive. The political right feared the plan would reduce the work incentive and that it would rob companies of profits. The Townsend bill was defeated in the House, mainly along party lines, with most Democrats voting against it. In this later proposal, begun in 1934, Senator Long's campaign overtly used the language of "soak the rich" taxation, and he called for a "share the wealth society."[46] The share-our-wealth movement tried to redistribute money from the rich to the poor by limiting personal wealth and income via the tax code. Those over 65 would receive pensions of $30 per month or more, and World War I veterans, who in the 1920s had been promised pensions to be paid in 1945, would receive them immediately. Long pitched this plan, hoping it would win him the presidency.[47] Long's movement probably accelerated Roosevelt's push for a Social Security bill. Raymond Moley, a pro-business advisor to Roosevelt, noted later that the president launched the social-welfare-oriented second New Deal in order to "steal Long's thunder."[48]

A major point of conflict that required resolution before Congress could proceed with a federally backed welfare program had to do with federalism. The traditional local basis for welfare provision persisted in the minds of many, from local agency staff to members of Congress. Many argued that politics and relief should not be mixed. A 1931 request from the then governor Franklin Roosevelt for federal aid for the poor in New York triggered an opinion letter in *The New York Times* from the former U.S. senator James Wadsworth opining that "it would be better if we should suffer a little more now and keep politics away from relief than to let politics in and suffer a great deal more in the future as a result."[49] Wadsworth was not alone in his orientation. When U.S. Senator Robert Wagner of New York questioned Grace

Abbott in 1932, he spoke for himself while making it seem that he was speaking for others when he asked, "There are some people, and even some public
men, that still contend that, if the public had not undertaken this aid at all,
private contributions would have been stimulated and would have cared for
this situation. I should like to have your views about that." Abbott attempted
to rebut the senator's concern, but she faced persistent opposition.[50] Her sis-
ter, Edith Abbott, would acknowledge in 1936 that local control of welfare
programs had, through the height of patronage politics and even somewhat
beyond, rendered relief vulnerable to political favoritism. She lamented that
even at that late date, public poor relief had its troubles, as relief services
were, she said, "drifting back to the old system of petty incompetence and are
becoming more political and more unskilled almost day by day. . . . In some
areas everything connected with poor relief . . . [and is] influenced by politics." Highlighting a case of blatant patronage, a former barkeeper was put
in charge of Social Security in a county in a Midwestern state. This instance
might not have been so bad had he at least been a good barkeeper, but he
was not even that, Abbott observed.[51] The essence of the problem was that
poor relief was prostituted to buy votes in some locales. In observing these
problems, Edith Abbott was really calling for a greater federal role in order
to overcome corrupt local governments. By this point, merit systems were
better established at the federal level than in local or state governments. Only
10 states had civil service laws in place. Roosevelt had insisted that partisan
politics be kept out of the business of relief, but fears persisted, complicating
the legislation of Social Security and its accompanying Aid to Dependent
Children (ADC). Part of the objection rested on often unstated assumptions
about federalism as a governing principle, and part relied on the well-worn
argument about casework versus help in the absence of supervision. Even
as late as 1935, many members of Congress still adhered to the argument
espoused by social-work organizations before the Great Depression. In the
report of the Committee on Economic Security issued in January 1935, the
Committee declared that states should resume providing relief in line with
the wisdom that "families that have always been partially or wholly dependent on others for support can best be assisted through the tried procedures
of social casework, with its individualized treatment."[52]

One last dimension of conflict would have to be settled before the federal
government could move ahead with a truly national welfare program: race.
Regarding African Americans, attention was given to black poverty by white
charity organizations prior to the 1930s, but that attention did not translate
into sustained help, and Congress' consideration of race certainly did not
translate into a universal program under ADC. Black mothers were widely
excluded from mothers' pensions in the states. A 1933 report by the U.S.

Children's Bureau found that only about 3 percent of recipients nationwide were black, far below the percentage of African Americans living in poverty at the time. In Mississippi and Louisiana, there were no black recipients in 1931.[53] Blacks' radical underrepresentation on relief rolls aggravated their economic precariousness during the Great Depression years. African Americans represented a majority portion of displaced tenant farmers, so they made up a large portion of the ranks of rootless people wandering the country. Other programs of the time discriminated by race as well. The Civilian Conservation Corps used racial quotas, and the Agricultural Adjustment Act distributed help based in part on a race-laden formula. The National Labor Administration also discriminated against racial minorities.[54] Just as these Great Depression programs did not protect against racial discrimination, ADC left doors very much open for selective implementation across states and communities upon its creation. Race would continue to be a point of conflict well after the passage of the Social Security Act.

In hindsight, it is perhaps tempting to ascribe inevitability to the passage of the Social Security Act. However, that would be a mistake, as there remained significant resistance to reliance on government for broad social insurance purposes throughout the mid-1930s. One example comes in how the American Federation of Labor (AFL) dealt with a request for its support for an unemployment insurance program. At its 1930 convention, AFL president William Green spoke of how "the American workman, proud of his freedom and his liberty, is not yet willing to make himself a ward of the state and a ward of the government." Even in 1931, with some seven million people unemployed, the AFL insisted that federal unemployment insurance was "unsuited to our economic and political requirements here and unsatisfactory to American working men and women."[55] Finally, in July 1932, with some 11 million unemployed, the AFL executive council reluctantly instructed Green to draft a plan for unemployment insurance to be proposed to Congress.[56] The tide was turning.

## LEGISLATING AID TO DEPENDENT CHILDREN

Considering that the Social Security Act would become one of the most important pieces of New Deal legislation, the law ironically left ambiguous a pair of important questions, one regarding federalism, the other regarding scope of eligibility. Title IV of the act, creating the ADC program, was not exactly an afterthought, though senior figures in the Roosevelt administration relegated its drafting to the U.S. Children's Bureau, a division of the Department of Labor, in part because of their belief that cash relief for poor widows and their children would wither away in time as these persons were gradually absorbed into more permanent social insurance programs.[57] The questions left unsettled by Title IV regarding political control and eligibility would remain substantially unsettled until the late 1960s. But one principle that was clear from the start was that open-ended relief to all comers was unacceptable. Roosevelt, in his oft-quoted passage about the dole being a narcotic to the soul, captured a prevalent belief of the times that long-term cash assistance must be reserved for those unable to fend for themselves. In line with this understanding, Title IV granted aid to children deprived of at least one parent but left many of the details to state and local governments. This new federal role in legislation represented a significant step in creating stable finances for welfare, but it also marked the end of more general relief, such as that extended under the Federal Emergency Relief Administration. That assistance ended in 1935. From that year forward, cash assistance would be given only to individuals in discrete categories: single mothers, children, the aged, and the like. The Social Security Act marked a turning point in welfare provision because of the new federal responsibility for certain categories of the poor, but it also ended any serious push for universal, federal welfare based on poverty alone.

The senior staff at the Children's Bureau crafted the language of what would become ADC under the assumption that the earlier mothers' pensions had been failures. They expressed this sentiment in their 1933 report, *Mothers' Aid, 1931*. Because they believed mothers' pensions offered inadequate coverage and insufficient monetary payments to allow women to remain at home with their children, their bill did not include work requirements or incentives. They also wrote provisions into their version of Title IV that would have required states to adopt certain minimum competency levels for the social workers responsible for handling ADC cases. When male members of the Roosevelt administration revised the bill, most of those provisions were removed. Harry Hopkins, Roosevelt's mentor on social policy, referred to many social workers as so-called pantry snoopers for their propensity to scrutinize the lives of their poor clients, this despite his own social-work background. He was intent that this pattern would not continue under ADC.[58] As a consequence, the first 25 years of ADC would be characterized primarily as an exercise in eligibility determination rather than service provision or individual counseling. Those services were offered only by state or local option.[59] This changed beginning in 1962.

A small number of provisions of ADC suggest the beginnings, albeit modest, of the idea of welfare as a right. The law specified money payments, not just in-kind benefits, as some states would have likely used. The law also stipulated that applicants had the opportunity for a hearing if adverse actions were taken on their applications. Third, Congress required that states implement the program by way of a single state agency with an eye to avoiding county-level fragmentation. Despite these provisions, liberal advocates in the

Roosevelt administration repeatedly highlighted the perils of turning assistance programs over to the states, a move they were sure would result in states offering niggardly cash assistance.

For their part, officials in many state governments feared ADC would provide poor people an exit option from the labor market, leading to higher prevailing wages. In response, the original language that the administration sent to Congress called for cash benefits under ADC high enough to provide "a reasonable subsistence compatible with decency and health."[60] Both the House Ways and Means Committee and the Senate Finance Committee objected. Southerners resented being told how to treat blacks. The bill was amended in Congress to require states to provide assistance "as far as practicable under the circumstances of such state."[61] Wilbur Cohen at the Committee for Economic Security noted in retrospect that the striking of the "decency and health" provision was "the bill's most significant long-range loss."[62] Not only did the legislation include this watered down language, both the House and Senate reports on the bill indicated that each state may "impose such other eligibility requirements—as to means, moral character, etc.—as it sees fit."[63] This ethos of local control over welfare was robust at the time of ADC's creation and readily persisted into the 1950s and beyond. The February 1953 newsletter of the Alabama State Department of Public Welfare captured this sentiment neatly in its front page article entitled "Community Responsibility for Welfare." It began, "Communities can decide for themselves whether they will be 'good places in which to live.' Governmental social welfare programs . . . cannot replace community endeavors for general local benefit. They were never intended to do so."[64] The tradition of states' rights, and indeed of local prerogatives, would not be eclipsed by the federal creation of the ADC program.

It is hard to say for sure how much members of Congress expected the new ADC program to intersect with race in the South. Various scholars, including Robert Lieberman in his *Shifting the Color Line* (1998), write of the ways ADC intentionally isolated African Americans by leaving them to the hands of state officials with demonstrated track records of racial discrimination. However, Edwin Witte, executive director of Roosevelt's Committee on Economic Security (the body that oversaw the drafting of the Social Security Act), recalled that it never occurred to his committee that the "Negro question" would arise in connection with welfare payments.[65] It is uncertain whether Witte was simply naïve or so cynical that he thought the southern states would so dominate welfare implementation that blacks would never be enrolled, and thus no questions would be raised as to how small their benefits would be. In either case, vast evidence chronicles states' use of race as a litmus test for eligibility and, when ADC payments were made, the level of generosity of those payments.[66]

The decentralization of ADC policy making raised concerns among advocates of racial justice outside of government at the time as well. The *Amsterdam News,* New York City's leading African American paper, opined that "most of us should be able to remember how state benefits are dispensed in the South." [67] Similar concerns came from Congress. Speaking of old age pensions but capturing a similar fear that marked ADC's legislation, Louisiana Senator Huey Long spoke plainly about the likelihood of racial discrimination when he rhetorically asked, "Who in the South is the most needful of pensions assistance? . . . Mr. President, it is the colored man. How many colored people do you think would get on one of these select lists? Let's be frank about this business. I am possibly the only Southern senator here who can be frank about it."[68] Congress could have built into the law an antidiscrimination provision to protect blacks from state or local discrimination. George Edmund Haynes, the executive secretary of the Race Relations Department of the National Council of Churches urged the Senate Finance Committee in 1935 to include a clause prohibiting race discrimination under the Social Security Act. The Senate, and ultimately the Congress, declined to include such language.[69]

Beyond eligibility determination, the generosity of benefits was also left substantially up to states. Initially, the federal share for ADC payments was set at one-third of the costs of benefits, up to $18 per month for the first child and $12 per month for each additional child.[70] No caretaker grants were created at this time. Those would be added in 1950. Cross-state variation in benefits was dramatic from the start. In 1939 the average payment was $13 per child per month, or $31 per family, nationally. In Arkansas the monthly benefit per child was $2.50, or $8.14 per family on average; in New York benefits amounted to $24.50 per child, or $47.68 per family.[71] Many states were slow to adopt ADC at all. Twenty-six states did so by 1936, and most did by the end of the decade. Rural states tended to be the laggards.

The federal sponsorship of this new welfare program did not entirely settle the anxiety of its liberal critics. Testifying before a House committee in 1938, Aubrey Williams, a Works Progress Administration (WPA) staff member, was asked if he thought turning WPA over to the states would improve its efficiency. He responded in the negative, emphatically proclaiming that "many local relief systems are cruelly inhumane. Their methods involve nailing people's names upon the doors of the town hall, publicizing them as the town's paupers, [and asking them to] forfeit their citizenship."[72] Stories of publicizing the names of welfare recipients indeed continued, but over time, what garnered more attention was the state use of the so-called suitable home provisions to exclude many never-married women and other mothers deemed morally unfit from cash assistance. While it is impossible to estimate accurately the number of potential eligible persons denied aid, tens of thousands were periodically removed from the rolls during the 1950s via these mechanisms based on the early twentieth-century shift in thinking about protecting the best interests of the children. These provisions, formalized in the states during the 1950s, would become the legal vehicle for considerable racial and other discrimination.[73]

In hindsight, the creation of ADC cut in at least two directions. It represented a significant step in solidifying a federally backed welfare program that would not suffer the fiscal cutbacks that plagued mothers' pensions prior to 1935. In time, a series of federal standards regarding eligibility evolved that made applying for welfare a more uniform experience across states. On the other hand, to the extent that states were left in a position to shape ADC to local economic conditions and political preferences, there would not be a single, national welfare program, but rather as many different programs as there were states. Many social policy historians have referred to this decision to subject welfare to the full force of federalism—with all of the fragmentation that entails—as a mistake. At the time, however, anxiety over what was to become of ADC was lessened considerably by the belief that in the foreseeable future, welfare for poor mothers and their children would fade away, meaning that what Congress created in 1935 need only be temporary. Looking back on that time from the perspective of the early 1960s, Alabama Senator Lister Hill commented that members of Congress assumed ADC would not last for many years, and that instead the poor would be folded into the larger social insurance programs under the Social Security Act. Social Security Administrator Arthur Altmeyer also voiced his confident opinion in 1949 that eventually ADC would whither away due to the poor being absorbed under other assistance programs, or that state or local governments would absorb the few uncovered persons who remained. In 1954, the Secretary of the Department of Health, Education, and Welfare expressed similar optimism that this absorption would happen quickly.[74] A step was taken toward this in 1939 with the addition of survivors' benefits, targeted at widows and their children, but that step actually bifurcated the poor into politically strong versus weak programs. Of course, this bifurcation still troubles the debate over welfare today.

Importantly, the Great Depression fundamentally altered Americans' thinking about the causes of poverty. Structural explanations came to the fore, and the idea of individuals at risk due to economic forces beyond their control became a legitimate part of the repertoire when seeking to explain why people became poor and why they either recovered from or remained stuck in that position. This would perhaps be one of the most important changes of the era regarding welfare provision.

## STATE RESPONSES TO AID TO DEPENDENT CHILDREN, 1930s–1950s

States were slow to adopt ADC, and even in those places that did, administration unfolded unevenly. Arizona provided an egregious example of neglect in initially declining to enroll Native Americans. The federal government refused for a time to fund Arizona's ADC program because of this exclusion.[75] By November 1936, only 26 states had received federal grants for ADC.[76] Kentucky, in 1943, was among the last. Kentucky's program began small, servicing not quite 13,000 children in 1945. Racial figures for Kentucky's early ADC caseload are not available, though the implication of the 1945 report of the Kentucky Department of Welfare makes clear that servicing "colored" people was not a priority for the commonwealth. That year, the department spent $4.7 million on old-age assistance, $75,000 for its "pauper idiot program," $15,000 on its home for incurables, $8,000 for "conveyance of lunatics," but only $4,000 to operate the Colored Red Cross Hospital.[77] Further, that report noted that all white patients at the state hospital were housed in a modern facility but that no such building existed for black patients.[78]

Out of concern about not upsetting state economies, southerners insisted on ADC being more modest than old-age insurance so that working-age people would have fewer exit options from the labor market. One way to achieve this was to assign a one-half federal reimbursement rate to the old-age program (meaning for every dollar a state contributed to its program, the federal government would match it with another dollar, up to a certain point) but only a one-third federal reimbursement rate for ADC. This virtually guaranteed modest welfare benefits to poor children.[79]

Modest benefits did little to hold down use of the new program by the poor. The ADC caseload grew quickly. By 1940, 760,000 children were enrolled, some three times the number enrolled in mothers' pensions during their peak years in the early 1930s. If one counts ADC caretaker parents (caretaker grants were not added until 1950), more than one million people relied on ADC by 1940. Sixteen percent of female-headed households were on ADC by 1940, three times the proportion on mothers' pensions in 1931.[80] Enrollment was further encouraged by new federal regulations in 1947. These rules required states to process applications promptly and to extend aid to "all eligible individuals."[81] The federal match also rose from $18 to $24 for a first child, and from $12 to $15 each for subsequent children. The prompt processing regulation was directed at states that used a waiting-list system, a method states employed in order to pick and choose among applicants. ADC caseloads rose dramatically during the 1950s, with the national enrollment increasing 50 percent during Eisenhower's term alone. By 1960 payments would exceed $1 billion per year.[82]

The other major change in the face of the ADC caseload was its demographic makeup. The initial clientele was, as anticipated, substantially composed of children of widows. During 1938 fully one-half of beneficiaries were this type. By the early 1940s, however, only 20 percent were. By 1950, children of widows made up only 18 percent of the national welfare caseload, and by 1961 that figure would drop to 7 percent.[83] The changing characteristics of the welfare caseload led states to institute exclusionary policies over which they would argue with federal authorities until well into the 1960s.

The metamorphosis of the ADC clientele during the 1940s occurred at a time when states were tending to settle into a routine administration of this new program. Certainly, racial and other dimensions of discrimination occurred on a widespread basis throughout that decade, but there was also a significant emphasis on routine eligibility determination. Charges of partisan favoritism in welfare administration were much less frequently heard than they had been during the 1930s, social work grew increasingly professionalized, and federal regulations began to give the new program a sheen of even-handedness. The gradual change was noted in a 1950 column in *Public Welfare,* the journal of the American Public Welfare Association, by an author who approvingly commented on the near disappearance of state legal exclusions of mothers who gave birth out of wedlock, while acknowledging a continuing social stigma surrounding such births.[84] As the 1950s began, however, the changed demographic makeup of the welfare caseload and its expansion led states to assume a more aggressive posture in screening women whom policy makers deemed unworthy.

The imputed unworthiness of never-married mothers ran afoul of a logic in place since the early twentieth century. The purpose of home relief during the progressive period was to afford children the best possible environment to escape poverty. ADC replaced earlier programs with the goal of providing wholesome homes for poor children. Many believed these never-married mothers were only marginally providing wholesome environments for their children, as sexually promiscuous mothers defeated the purpose of providing aid to keep children at home. As a result, many states sought to disqualify women based on their perceived moral character and discriminated against them by race. Many agricultural states in the South routinely disqualified able-bodied welfare recipients during harvest and planting times on the assumption that there was enough work for everyone who wanted it. Some in the social-work community protested these tactics, but the policies continued.

Broadly, they assumed two forms: so-called suitable home and substitute parent provisions.

Between 1950 and 1960, nine states formally adopted suitable home provisions. Women with boyfriends or untidy homes were often excluded. In 1960, Louisiana adopted a particularly harsh policy, ending aid to all homes containing a child born out of wedlock.[85] Surprise home visits were a common tactic to ferret out unsuitable mothers. These were often conducted at night, and it was not uncommon for two social workers to work in tandem, one approaching the front door, the other guarding the back for elusive men. The presence of a man in the home was sufficient to disqualify recipients in many places. A 1957 survey of these jurisdictions found that all except one (Maine) attributed improved casework to these surprise visits.[86] In the late 1950s, the city manager of Newburgh, New York, declared that any unwed woman on ADC who birthed another child would be removed from the rolls. Because this type of restriction went against federal law, New York state officials, fearful of losing federal funds, prevented the city manager from implementing this proposed policy.[87]

In a related approach, states also employed substitute parent provisions during the 1950s. States considered live-in boyfriends as substitutes for missing biological fathers and, in turn, deemed the children no longer deprived of parental support. This particular argument would come to a head in 1960, as Arthur Flemming, the outgoing secretary of the Department of Health, Education, and Welfare, ruled that states that remove children from welfare under substitute parent provisions must also provide alternative housing for them. In 1961 Congress delayed the implementation of the Flemming rule until 1962 and instructed the department to go no further in attacking suitable home provisions.[88]

One side of the debate over how to deal with women who birthed children out of wedlock relied on the assumption that poor women routinely conceived children in order to win welfare eligibility or to increase their cash benefits by enlarging their families. The fact that fertility rates throughout this period remained lower among women on welfare than among women not on welfare did little to abate the conversation. Cultural explanations were offered for child bearing outside of marriage. As regards African Americans, these explanations included an assumption that black people tend to undervalue two-parent families as a holdover from the days of slavery.[89] Cultural explanations were gingerly, and sometimes not so gingerly, offered as explanations for higher rates of out-of-wedlock births among African Americans, even by those who were well aware of racial discrimination and a deficit of opportunities for black workers at the time.[90] Others would go so far as, in blanket fashion, to characterize unmarried mothers on ADC as cases of purported character disorders and individuals in need of psychological therapy.[91]

In addition to the impact of changing racial characteristics of the ADC case-load, Americans' perspective on poor women shifted in response to the continued entry of women into the workforce throughout the 1950s. This trend implied, for many policy makers, that women, even single women with children, should be given what they seemed to be asking for: an opportunity to participate in the labor force. Not until 1967 would Congress legislate the first work require-ments for welfare parents, but the tide was gradually turning on this point. This movement, combined with the fact that most women on welfare were divorced, separated, or had never married, opened welfare recipients as a class to charges of poverty by choice. Though the general public paid scant attention to welfare issues during the 1950s, policy makers' frustrations grew, and they reached for a variety of tools to control welfare expansion. Beyond legal exclusions such as suitable home and substitute parent provisions, shaming—a nineteenth cen-tury approach—was revisited. By the mid-1950s, 21 states had legislated that welfare rolls be open for public inspection in an effort to let welfare recipients know they were under scrutiny. This had no discernable effect on the percent-age of eligible people who applied for welfare, but it certainly evidenced the frustration of state policy makers at a time when welfare recipients appeared stuck in dependency, despite rising general affluence across the nation.[92]

## POVERTY AND WELFARE DEPENDENCY AS (NON)ISSUES IN THE 1950s

With the postwar economic boom increasing wages and rates of home ownership, poverty and welfare receded as issues for the general public, at least the white public, throughout the 1950s. Given racial segregation in both the North and the South, most white Americans had limited opportunities to learn about how black people coped with their disproportionately high rates of poverty. Also, rates of welfare use raised few hackles throughout this decade. The number of families on ADC rose by only about 110,000 between 1950 and 1960.[93] Shame, discrimination, and a lack of information about how to apply for welfare depressed enrollment. All that would change in the 1960s.

For its part, the social-work community focused most of its efforts on refin-ing best practices of their trade rather than hashing out fundamental or exis-tential questions of public versus private aid or economic rights. A perusal of the social work journals *Public Welfare* and *The Social Service Review* through-out the 1940s and 1950s uncovers only scarce discussion over underlying value questions of welfare provision. The argument over the very existence of the program had ceased. Even from the Deep South came columns such as one by Blanche Saunders, case supervisor in the Mobile, Alabama, Depart-ment of Public Welfare in 1950 titled "ADC—A Good Investment." The crux of the essay was that

ADC . . . is an investment of public money to reduce and offset the costs the community otherwise might pay because of family break-downs. In other words, ADC is a means of keeping children's homes together for them now so they will grow up normally into productive adult citizens. . . . No community can afford *not* to invest in its own future by providing for its dependent children.[94]

Of course, this broad expression of support for the program avoided altogether the details of determining the sort of mothers who were worthy of public aid and those who were not. Local case workers spent a great deal of energy fretting about the wrong type of people drawing assistance, and state policy makers obliged them with restrictive policies that local workers could enforce.

The general public also settled into a broad consensus on welfare provision. As one observer commented in a 1960 essay in *Harper's* magazine, "the Eisenhower Administration . . . leaves with the New Deal Policies enshrined in comfortable respectability and anchored in the consensus of a broad moderate majority."[95] To the extent that the general public depended on elite media sources to raise issues and frame a debate on the state of welfare, they were not encouraged to think much about it. On the political left and right, respectively, the pages of *The New Republic* and *The Public Interest* virtually ignored poverty throughout the boom decade of the 1950s. To scan these media, one would not suspect the deep discrimination that was occurring as applicants were discouraged from applying for welfare or that successful applicants' lives were scrutinized so invasively. Further, there was almost no acknowledgement that the country still faced a 20 percent poverty rate or that fighting poverty would play a key role in the next decade's national political agenda. As the 1950s closed, fundamental arguments about welfare provision had been overshadowed by talk of an affluent society. All that would change in the first few years of the next decade.

## NOTES

1. Devine 1914, pp. 73–75.
2. *Public Papers of the Presidents of the United States, 1935*, p. 19. Franklin Roosevelt's State of the Union address. January 4, 1935, pp. 15-25. Washington, DC: General Services Administration.
3. Hunter 1904, p. v.
4. Himmelfarb 1983, chap. 14; Riis 1971 [1890].
5. Hunter 1904, pp. 22–25.
6. Fisher 1997.
7. Hunter 1904, p. 63.
8. Ibid., p. 82.
9. Devine 1914, p. 75.
10. Heisterman and Keener 1934.

11. Klein 1968, chap. 10.
12. Grace Abbott 1966 [1941], p. 267.
13. *Proceedings of the National Conference of Social Work, 1912 (Cleveland)*, p. 268.
14. Axinn and Stern 2005, p. 154.
15. Grace Abbott 1966 [1941], pp. 269–70.
16. Ibid., pp. 3–5, citing 1939 speech.
17. Ibid., pp. 11–12.
18. Teles 1998, p. 27; Roosevelt 1908.
19. Teles 1998, p. 28.
20. Leff 1973, p. 407.
21. Sidel 1986, p. 52.
22. Leff 1973.
23. Mink 1995, chap. 3.
24. Teles 1998, pp. 29–30.
25. Leff 1973, p. 403.
26. Ibid., p. 404.
27. Ibid., p. 397.
28. Lens 1969, p. 212.
29. Leff 1973, p. 411.
30. Axinn and Stern 2005, p. 144.
31. Leff 1973, p. 399.
32. Ibid., p. 399.
33. Grace Abbott 1966 [1941], p. 262.
34. Ibid., p. 231–32.
35. Ibid., p. 265.
36. Ibid. pp. 266–67; Zimmerman 1930.
37. Leff 1973.
38. Ibid., pp. 401–2.
39. Skocpol 1992.
40. Breckinridge 1927.
41. Linda Gordon 1994.
42. Amenta 1998, p. 65.
43. Leff 1973, pp. 413–14.
44. Axinn and Stern 2005, p. 187.
45. Teles 1998, p. 26.
46. Amenta 1998, pp. 112–113.
47. Ibid., p. 111.
48. Ibid., pp. 110–112.
49. Grace Abbott 1966 [1941], p. 23.
50. Ibid., p. 313.
51. Edith Abbott 1936, pp. 400–401.
52. Axinn and Stern 2005, p. 194.
53. Amenta 1998, p. 70.
54. Axinn and Stern 2005, p. 189.
55. Jacobs 1968, p. 45.

56. Ibid.
57. Linda Gordon 1994, p. 258; Hamilton and Hamilton 1997; Steiner 1966, chap. 2.
58. Linda Gordon 1994, p. 270.
59. Amenta 1998, p. 120.
60. Lieberman 1998, p. 51.
61. Ibid, p. 51.
62. Ibid.
63. Teles 1998, p. 32.
64. *Alabama Social Welfare* 18, no. 2 (February 1953).
65. Burke and Burke 1974, p. 8.
66. Lieberman 1998.
67. Ibid., p. 54.
68. Ibid., p. 54.
69. Ibid., p. 120.
70. 74th Congress, 1st sess., *Congressional Record* 79 (1935): 14,761.
71. Amenta 1998, p. 157; *Social Security Bulletin* 2 (July 1939): 55
72. Howard 1943, p. 766.
73. Bell 1965.
74. Steiner 1974, pp. 49–51.
75. Teles 1998, p. 38.
76. Axinn and Stern 2005, p. 201.
77. *Report of the Department of Welfare of the Commonwealth of Kentucky*, June 30, 1945, p. 7.
78. Ibid., pp. 7, 9.
79. Lieberman 1998, p. 48.
80. Amenta 1998, p. 145.
81. Ibid., p. 205.
82. Steiner 1974, p. 52.
83. Rein 1982, p. 8; Amenta 1998, p. 157.
84. Brenner 1950.
85. Bell 1965, chap. 6.
86. Ibid.
87. Trattner 1999, p. 310.
88. Melnick 1994, p. 72.
89. Brenner 1950.
90. Ibid.
91. Orchard 1960.
92. Steiner 1974, p. 49.
93. Block et al. 1987, p. 86.
94. Saunders 1950, p. 109 (emphasis in original).
95. Drucker 1960, p. 46.

# 4

# The Rise and Fall of the War on Poverty

When viewing the government interventions of the 1960s, it is entirely possible to be both surprised by how much was done and aggrieved by what was not done. Learning from those years requires a more complicated and sophisticated evaluation.

—Lance Liebman (1974)[1]

The broad ideological consensus that developed during the 1950s truncated the range of debate, for the vast majority of Americans, over the proper role of government in social and economic life. The political schisms of earlier years—separating those who supported government welfare provision from those unalterably opposed to it—had given way to a notion that Americans had become masters of a large portion of the globe and skillful directors of their own economy. This national self-confidence, bordering on hubris, led those in government to believe that the American version of capitalism was a machine that could resolve not only most problems here on earth but, without exaggeration, could also send men to the moon. If the market machine ran imperfectly from time to time, the occasional economic glitch was a matter for fine-tuning of technique, not indicative of any fundamental flaws. Throughout During the 1950s, most conservatives finally bought into Rooseveltian ideas, after years of resisting them. Beyond the political class, academics and others did as well.[2] Harvard professor Louis Hartz wrote in what would become an enduring classic, *The Liberal Tradition in America,* of how a Lockean liberalism guided much of the nation's thinking. Hartz, Richard Hoffstadter and other midcentury consensus historians constructed an understanding of America that drew on what they took to be broad and deep agreement on first principles: procedural due process, Keynesian economics, universal suffrage, and social and political institutions that spoke of something approaching equality of opportunity for broad swaths of the population. These points of consensus led political scientists such as David Truman to write of the robustness of groups as platforms for broad political participation in tones that strongly suggested the ability of the haves and have-nots to compete on an essentially level playing field of national politics. Not every group would win any given conflict, but they would all enjoy substantial enfranchisement in the struggle.[3]

What Truman and others dramatically underappreciated was the lingering racism that had fostered poverty rates among African Americans that hovered around twice the rate for whites. Once government began to measure poverty systematically in 1963, and the nation's attention to poverty was awakened once again largely by Michael Harrington's *The Other America,* it proved fairly noncontroversial within this broad consensus for Lyndon Johnson to declare an "unconditional war on poverty" in January 1964.[4] The metaphor of a war proved a handy rhetorical devise. It suggested a truly national effort to combat economic privation. It lent itself to a clear definition of an enemy to be defeated. It also fostered the understanding that there would be, perhaps within a decade, a victory, and that this agenda item could then be retired, another accomplishment to chalk up to the technical prowess of that optimistic age.[5]

Within a few years, however, Johnson's rhetorical formulation proved wrong in several important ways. The war was not unconditional. Instead, the effort to combat poverty was very much conditioned on not unsettling the existing distribution of wealth or opportunity. The president rarely endorsed the idea of expanding transfer payments, and when he did in 1967, Congress declined to enact a federal requirement for more uniform and generous welfare payments. Local political elites resisted the broad mobilization of people and levels of government to enact the host of programs developed by the Office of Economic Opportunity (OEO)—Community Action—at various steps of the way and for many reasons. Big city mayors resented losing control over federal grants upon which, in part, they had built their own machines. Members of Congress felt threatened by litigation brought by community activists against federal agencies. Southern politicians feared the momentum toward black empowerment that a stream of federal dollars directed to nongovernmental groups would foster. Governors thought these programs would outflank them and their role in the federalist power structure. Community Action was attacked by people who should have been its friends, notably in Daniel Moynihan's widely discussed book, *Maximum Feasible Misunderstanding.* Finally, the war was not truly a war; it appeared more like a skirmish, or as the political historian Ira Katznelson later wrote, a "timid call to arms."[6] Liberals and conservatives alike pointed out the limited and sometimes ineffective nature of federal efforts during the 1960s to address the multifaceted problems of health care, employment, education, housing, and other issues. President Johnson explicitly and appropriately portrayed poverty as a cluster of problems, not simply a lack of money; but the administration also proved its unwillingness to engage the poor on their own terms, instead wringing its hands in the wake of urban riots and noisy protests.

The optimism that marked the early 1960s, generally, and the opening volleys of the War on Poverty, specifically, would, within a few years, give way to pessimism, disillusionment, and confusion over both the ends and means of fighting poverty. The consensus that seemed so solid a few years earlier would have its many cracks revealed, troubles over race being only one of them. As the consensus historians of the midtwentieth century had underestimated subterranean conflicts over some fundamental issues, the War on Poverty did not adequately appreciate the profound misgivings on various sides that would rise to the surface once again during this period of the welfare debate.

## THE ORIGINS AND DECLARATION OF THE WAR ON POVERTY

In the early 1960s, the rediscovery of poverty, a faith in the power of the modern state to confront a wide range of problems, and a sufficiently liberal policy orientation among those in government converged to make a significant effort against poverty possible, even if short-lived. Leveraging the power of the market, it was widely thought that government could successfully tackle a set of problems as large as poverty and much of what goes with it. Complementing this, there was a pervasive belief in government that the science of policy analysis could crack the nut that was persistent poverty and bring about a Great Society.[7] In the context of this overarching national confidence, a growing awareness that one-fifth to one-quarter of Americans still lived in squalid conditions, below what would, in 1963, come to be quasiofficially labeled the federal poverty line. Michael Harrington's 1962 book, *The Other America: Poverty in the United States,* significantly advanced a national conversation about poverty. Awareness about Harrington's book was helped along by Dwight Macdonald's lengthy 1963 review essay in *The New Yorker* magazine, a review that may have been more important than the book itself in that it reached a large and politically important readership, including the most visible resident of 1600 Pennsylvania Avenue.[8] Kennedy's advisor Ted Sorenson gave the president a copy of Macdonald's article and of Harrington's book and urged him to read both.[9] This built on the powerful impressions made on Kennedy by his visits to central Appalachia during the 1960 presidential campaign.

Harrington's passionate writing highlighted the ways in which poverty had been ignored in America. The liberal economist John Kenneth Galbraith's influential book, *The Affluent Society*, which topped best-seller lists following its 1958 publication, argued that America had essentially solved the age-old problem of poverty and scarcity, and that the persistence of poor populations was a mere anomaly in a society where the gross national product had grown at an annual rate of approximately 3.5 percent following the Second World War.[10] He believed that poverty was confined to Appalachia and the Deep South, and that poverty was no longer a serious affliction but rather only a low-level problem. Serving as a corrective to Galbraith's optimism, Harrington made two important points. First, relying on Commerce Department reports, he documented that instead of isolated pockets of poverty involving only marginal portions of the population, the United States was actually home to between 40 and 50 million poor people, some 20 percent of the population, and that their problems involved not only a lack of money, but also a shortage of spirit and opportunity after being beaten down for so long. Second, Harrington dampened the widespread belief that America was making steady progress in reducing poverty, when in fact the rate of reduction of poverty had slowed throughout during the 1950s, not accelerated as Galbraith asserted. Not only did Harrington's writing stand as a corrective to Galbraith's optimism, more importantly, Harrington's book prompted those on both the political left and the right to renew a conversation about poverty, which had virtually fallen off the nation's agenda since the end of the Great Depression. Reviewing elite media outlets such as *The Nation, The National Review,* and *The New Republic* during the 1950s reveals very little attention to welfare in particular or even to the politics of poverty more generally in their pages. Instead, politicians and scholars throughout during this period were heavily focused on the Cold War and the spectacle of the nation's economic growth. Illustrating this point, Walter Heller, who chaired Kennedy's Council of Economic Advisors and would be an engineer of the early War on Poverty, addressed the National Conference on Social Welfare in 1960 and offered an optimistic assessment for the decade to come. He noted that given even a modest projected annual growth rate of the nation's productivity throughout the 1960s, America would experience a 50 percent increase in GNP by 1970. As a sidelight, Heller, presaging Harrington in this observation, pointed out that there appeared to be a persistent poverty population whose boats would not likely be buoyed by the national economy's rising tide.[11] That point, however, was submerged in a rosy overall assessment. If Heller's point was that the nation's economic glass was three-quarters full, the 1962 publication of *The Other America* dramatized how it was still one-quarter empty. Harrington prompted a national conversation that would animate the federal government for at least a decade to come.

Solidifying claims by Harrington and Macdonald was the 1963 publication by Mollie Orshansky, a statistician in the Social Security Administration, of poverty thresholds based on Department of Agriculture minimum food budgets. Orshansky, having grown up in poverty herself, based her poverty thresholds on the assumption that low-income families spend approximately one-third of their money on food. Multiplying a minimum food budget by three and adjusting for family size and urban/rural residence, she developed the first federal poverty thresholds. They would be officially adopted by the federal government in 1969.[12] Her primary interest was to create a reliable diagnostic tool, but her work was instead borrowed by the OEO in 1965, which used it as a benchmark to work against in evaluating how well the War on Poverty was working.[13] By Orshansky's measure, nearly one-third of children in America were poor. However, the Johnson administration's 1964 report, produced by the Council of Economic Advisors, indicated that only one child in six was poor, in what is likely an intentional understatement of the problem. Despite this, Orshansky's findings of widespread poverty helped raise awareness of how bad things were, even among working families. She found that in 1963 the head of household worked in 30 percent of all poor families, meaning full-time employment was no guarantee of rising above poverty.[14]

In addition to the growing realization of stubborn poverty in the early 1960s, Americans also gained an awareness during this period that the makeup of the nation's welfare caseload had evolved since ADC's enactment a generation before. Where ADC had begun as a program mostly for widows and their children, by 1960 this type of recipient made up only about 8 percent of those on welfare. Two-thirds of beneficiaries were attributable to the absence of a still-living father.[15] This transformation of the welfare clientele had caused resentment among state policy makers during the 1950s. Aside from occasional skirmishes with administration officials over patterns of (mostly racial) discrimination under ADC, relatively little of consequence had surfaced in the way of a public discourse on welfare during the 1950s. This relative silence would give way to a cacophony of critical voices by the mid-1960s, including attendance by some 200,000 people during the August 1963 March for Jobs and Freedom in Washington, D.C., capped by a historic speech by the Reverend Martin Luther King, Jr., in which he called for America to make good on its promise of economic opportunity for all.

One other factor in prompting the War on Poverty deserves mention: presidential maneuvering. John Kennedy's 1960 margin of 0.2 percent of the vote almost certainly led him to search for ways to shore up his standing with voters. It is not difficult to imagine that mobilizing urban voters would be an efficient approach. In early pursuit of this, in 1961 Kennedy successfully advocated for a $10 million appropriation to combat youth delinquency in inner-city neighborhoods. Kennedy pushed this line of thinking further with the assistance of the head of the president's Council of Economic Advisors, Walter Heller, who saw poverty as something to be reduced through more aggressive economic growth and tax reductions. Heller and Kennedy had begun their conversation about fighting poverty as early as December 1962, and it was barely interrupted by Kennedy's assassination in November 1963.[16] The day after Kennedy's death, Heller met with newly inaugurated President Johnson, who asked him to continue developing a major push in combating poverty.[17] Over the Christmas vacation, Johnson settled on the term *War on Poverty* because of the mobilizing power it promised and how it connoted strong possibilities for victory.[18] Despite fairly good evidence that economic growth alone would not eliminate poverty—recall the 20 percent poverty rate at the end of the prosperous 1950s—the Council of Economic Advisors couched the War on Poverty in those terms because it represented the dominant thinking by experts at the time, including Heller and University of Wisconsin economist Robert Lampman. There was never an agreement within the Kennedy or Johnson administrations about fundamental redistribution or upsetting the economic order in any significant way, nor was the federal government going to create large numbers of public-sector jobs. The administration would instead pursue the War on Poverty through the expansion of educational and workforce training opportunities.

Being aware of the malleable nature of public opinion, President Johnson and his allies very much adopted a moral tone to their rhetoric when discussing the need for cities, states, and the federal government to cooperate in fighting poverty. In addressing the Advertising Council in 1964, Johnson noted that "it is almost insulting to urge you to enlist in this war for just economic motivations. This is a moral challenge that goes to the very root of our civilization."[19] Many of the president's speeches through these early years verged on being utopian in nature as he spoke of the need to perfect American society by eradicating poverty and race and class discrimination. Motivated by his own humble upbringing in a poor community in central Texas, by Kennedy's death, and by his landslide reelection in 1964, Johnson very much saw himself as the heir to the Roosevelt tradition.[20] Typical of his style, Johnson used oversized language to sell Congress on his program. In February 1964, barely weeks after first announcing his War on Poverty in the State of the Union address, the president sent a memo to the speaker of the House and the president of the Senate declaring emphatically that "it is now clear that the war against poverty has touched the hearts and the sense of duty of the American people. This cause has truly become their cause."[21] Polls conducted during the summers of 1964 and 1965 suggest that the administration's rhetorical push had paid off somewhat, though the public remained deeply divided on the efficacy of confronting poverty. When asked by the Opinion Research Corporation, "Do you think Johnson's war on poverty will help to wipe out poverty in this country, or don't you think it will be much help?" 34 percent of the national adult sample in July 1964 responded that it would help, and 48 percent took this position in an August 1965 poll by the same organization.[22]

Using the platform of his January 1964 State of the Union address, President Johnson declared "unconditional war on poverty in America" and dedicated a major portion of that speech to this issue.[23] He sketched out in broad strokes some of his goals: extending employment and job training opportunities, improving schools and public libraries, and expanding housing and health care. He made no mention at the time of enhanced or expanded cash welfare. The president promised to achieve these goals through restructuring and redirection rather than through tax increases. Later that month, in his economic address to Congress, Johnson obliquely referred to expanded eligibility under "our Federal, State, and local network of programs of insurance and assistance" but did not mention welfare expansions specifically.[24] He focused on improved job opportunities and education. Further, when the president spoke to the American Society of Newspaper Editors in April 1964, he insisted the program's aim was "not a giveaway. It is not a program of doles . . . it is concerned . . . in making taxpayers out of taxeaters."[25] He repeated this same idea when signing the Economic Opportunity Act in August 1964, saying "We are not content to accept the endless growth of relief rolls or welfare rolls. We want to offer the forgotten fifth of our people opportunity and not doles. . . . The days of the dole in our country are numbered."[26] Clearly, this was not a call for welfare expansion.

Through the process of legislation, it became apparent that the administration was more enthusiastic about fighting poverty than was Congress. When Congress created the new OEO, which would administer most of the Great Society programs over the coming decade, it placed a broad mission on its shoulders. In time, however, Congress would limit the scope of many of the new initiatives. Throughout this early period, cash welfare, which Congress renamed Aid to Families with Dependent Children (AFDC) in 1962, received little discussion as a poverty fighting strategy. However, when the Johnson administration did discuss it, the focus centered on three areas: dissemination of information about how to apply for public aid; the need for litigation to challenge state and local discrimination against welfare recipients; and support for organizations that served welfare clients, mainly in the form of information and legal assistance.

An early criticism of the War on Poverty that endured for years was that President Johnson never clearly defined his goals. Others wrote that while well intentioned, the War on Poverty provisions were "doomed from the moment of their enactment."[27] A common criticism was that the varied programs that made up the Great Society initiative were too ambitious for any government to achieve. A cynic might attribute Johnson's high-flown talk about an unconditional war on poverty as being at least in part an artifact of election year politics and an attempt to establish what might pass for continuity with the Kennedy presidency. Lyndon Johnson, an aggressive voracious consumer of polling data, would likely have been aware that many voters could be convinced to base their choice in the autumn of 1964 on an idea so grand as a war on poverty.[28] As it turned out, a November 1964 poll by the Opinion Research Corporation found that 35 percent of respondents said the War on Poverty had a "great deal" to do with their recently cast vote for president, and another 35 percent said it had a "fair amount" to do with their votes.[29]

Thanks in large part to large Democratic majorities in the House and Senate, the Johnson administration achieved impressive achievements in expanding social insurance, including the creation of Medicare and Medicaid in 1965. However, the Achilles' heel of the initiative was its failure to clearly define the goals for the War on Poverty. Over time, these criticisms came from liberals and conservatives. Job training programs did not offer goals for placement, leaving the door open for arguments about what constituted success.[30] Public health indicators were poorly elaborated. The meaning of participation was not debated in Congress during the creation of the Economic Opportunity Act and its Community Action program.[31]

Some liberals accused the administration of overselling the OEO and noted that expectations were raised too high, and insufficient attention was given to the needs of African Americans. A common perspective from the political left was that the administration was excessively focused on raising incomes to some minimum standard and not sufficiently focused on changing the nation's economic system to remove the causes of radical inequality. There were never any serious attempts to guarantee jobs. The 1946 Full Employment Act was never fully funded. In fact, the Johnson administration did not pursue funding for full employment because it was doubtful such a thing could pass Congress.[32] From many places on the ideological spectrum, perhaps the most damning development was the slow realization that certain changes were arguably beyond the capacity of government to achieve.[33] Teaching young children to read may have provided one such example. This final line of argument would be pursued vigorously by neoconservatives from the late 1960s forward.

## LEGISLATING THE WAR ON POVERTY

For a piece of legislation that created such an important agenda item for the decade of the 1960s, the passage of the Economic Opportunity Act was approved by Congress with relatively little opposition. Republicans attempted to stir up concerns among southern Democrats about threats to states' rights and fears of racial mixing in housing projects funded by the bill, but these maneuvers were ultimately unsuccessful.[34] Committee consideration was simplified in part by House Education and Labor Committee chair Adam Clayton Powell's limitation of questions in mark-up sessions by Republican members and his exclusion of Republicans from the final mark-up of the bill.[35] Debate on the substantive merits of the legislation on the House floor was also more limited than a bill of this magnitude might be expected to elicit, due in part to the use of manipulative parliamentary procedures and to reputed arm twisting from the administration to push the bill through.[36] One of the most visible parts of the bill, Community Action, with its "maximum feasible participation" mandate, was greeted with virtually no discussion.[37] Senate consideration of the bill ran along similar lines to those seen in the House, with deep partisan cleavages but otherwise widespread agreement with the House provisions, ultimately approved by a voice vote.[38]

Within seven months of Johnson's call for a war on poverty, Congress passed the Economic Opportunity Act, which created the OEO, an independent agency to be headed by Kennedy brother-in-law and former Peace Corps director Sargent Shriver. The most prominent work of the OEO was the Community Action program, funded with $350 million for its first year. The philosophy of Community Action was to empower local people by allowing them autonomy on program design to meet local educational and social service needs. The OEO drew ample criticism from conservatives, particularly in the south, as they saw Community Action grants as government subsidies to outside agitators and civil rights workers. In symbolic response to these concerns, Mississippi Democratic Representative John Williams asked for and easily won a provision in the bill requiring Job Corps enrollees to swear an allegiance to the United States. The law also required other recipients of aid to promise, in writing, that they do not support the violent overthrow of the government.[39]

Other objections were more of the garden variety. Critics called the program a "poverty grab bag" or "the Santa Claus of the free lunch."[40] House and Senate Republicans called the bill an "election year gimmick" and a "hodgepodge" of only vaguely related programs, largely redundant of already existing programming.[41] Many big city mayors objected to the flow of millions of federal dollars directly to grassroots organizations because those funds allowed groups to create separate political loyalties among beneficiaries.

Before the OEO was closed by Congress in 1974 it had attempted a plethora of programs. The substantial optimism that had attended its creation had been infectious among its many beneficiaries in locales around the country, but its controversial approach to local empowerment and its frequent failure to show concrete results ultimately developed for the OEO more enemies than supporters.

## WELFARE EXPANSION AS A MINOR PART OF THE GREAT SOCIETY ERA

Several major changes in the social safety net during the Great Society era were hallmarks of the period. The expansion of the food stamp program throughout in the early 1960s; the creation of Medicare and Medicaid in 1965; the dramatic enhancement of AFDC eligibility guidelines throughout during the late 1960s and very early 1970s; the expansion of old-age and survivors' insurance payments and the linkage of them to inflation, creating annual cost-of-living adjustments in 1974; and the creation of the Supplemental Security Income program for the nonaged disabled, also in 1974, gave the Great Society era its enduring legacy of putting in place transfer programs that reduced by nearly one-half the poverty rate in the United States.[42] Of these five changes, all but the expansion of welfare were formally legislated. The expansion of welfare eligibility, in contrast, was mostly a product of a series of U.S. Supreme Court rulings that transformed what had been essentially a privilege into something akin to a property right.[43] Over the course of a decade—one that often saw intense conflict between the federal and state governments over discriminatory practices directed at people of color and women who had children outside of marriage—state governments essentially fell in line with this expanded understanding of Title IV of the Social Security Act. Following the Court's unambiguous instructions, welfare for "all eligible individuals" was to be read literally as "all eligible individuals," not as an invitation for state and local discretion about worthy versus unworthy poor applicants.[44]

The poor and their allies at the grassroots aggressively sought change in how welfare agencies handled requests for assistance. The National Welfare Rights Organization (NWRO), which by 1968 had some 300 local affiliates across the nation, as well as various older civil rights organizations, advocated for the poor from Congress to city halls, to local welfare offices and in the streets.[45] While most of this advocacy was peaceful, some of it assumed an abrasive edge. Tensions over cross-racial disparities in income and opportunity came to a head in the mid-to-late 1960s. With the Harlem riots of 1964, a wave of urban unrest began that fundamentally altered white America's attitudes toward the urban poor, renewed strained race relations, and contributed to white flight and the suburbanization of the population with the means to leave the cities.[46] Expressing some of the anger and frustration of urban blacks in the mid-1960s, Stokely Carmichael, fresh from jail in 1966, told the audience at a large rally that "the only way we gonna' stop them white men from whuppin' us is to take over. We been saying freedom for six years and we ain't got nothin.' What we gonna' start saying now is Black Power!"[47] Carmichael and others like him sought to transform the colonial analogy into a call for national action on behalf of the poor. Their use of this language was not unfounded. In 1965, 43 percent of black families lived below the federal poverty line, and the black unemployment rate was twice that of whites. Political disenfranchisement complicated economic disenfranchisement. In Mississippi only 7 percent of blacks were registered to vote in 1964, prior to the passage of the Voting Rights Act. The average percentage of African Americans registered to vote in the south in 1964 was 36 percent, compared to 73 percent among whites.[48]

As a result of this broad advocacy for political and economic rights, welfare caseworkers in many locales adopted a presumption of eligibility when people applied for AFDC, departing from the widespread earlier posture of placing the burden of proof on the applicant.[49] In two related ways these changes—at the administrative and popular levels—led to a dramatic increase in the population receiving AFDC between the mid-1960s and the mid-1970s. First, the proportion of eligible families who actually applied for welfare, the take-up rate, doubled after 1966. This rate stood near 30 percent in the early to mid-1960s but moved to 60 percent by 1972. It would drop back to 45 percent by 1988, but not before causing considerable criticism that the poor had become overly demanding of a handout. Complementing this trend of more widespread requests for aid by the poor, welfare agencies granted aid to a rising percentage of their applicants throughout this period. The percentage of welfare applications that were approved increased from one-third in the early 1960s to some 90 percent by 1971.[50]

One other very important factor that fueled the steep rise of the AFDC take-up rate after 1965 was the creation of Medicaid, which became available to most AFDC recipients in 1966. The addition of this program—funded jointly by federal and state dollars—significantly enhanced the welfare package and made signing up for assistance much more inviting.

## THE CULTURE OF POVERTY AND THE MOYNIHAN REPORT

In what would ultimately become an ironic evolution of language and social insight, a cluster of liberal-minded observers during the late 1950s and 1960s elaborated on the culture of poverty thesis. Prompted by their findings of chronic, intergenerational poverty, these thinkers attempted to explain why a portion of the nation's poor appeared persistently stuck in their economic destitution despite the broad and growing affluence of the nation around them. This new sort of poverty was markedly different from that witnessed during the Great Depression era, in that it was not as widespread as the earlier suffering and was not as readily attributable to structural problems in the economy as had been the case in the 1930s. The irony was that what began as an academic effort to describe patterns of social and economic status became a pejorative tool used by critics who adopted a certain amount of hopelessness and animosity toward the poor. In time, both liberals and conservatives, for different reasons, distanced themselves from the notion of a culture of poverty, but not before elements of this way of thinking had engrained themselves in the popular mindset, politically undermining efforts to ameliorate the conditions among inner-city and rural populations. Liberals, such as Columbia University sociologist Herbert Gans, could point to this moment as important in moving from what they initially saw as a war on poverty to what they would, 20 years later, consider a war on the poor.[51]

Building on early twentieth-century poverty studies in Britain and the United States, the anthropologist Oscar Lewis described this phenomenon in his 1959 book, *Five Families: Mexican Case Studies in the Culture of Poverty,* and in later work, notably his more widely read 1965 work, *La Vida,* on Puerto Ricans. Lewis described a pattern of myopic thinking, failure to defer gratification, sexual promiscuity, and unemployment. This learned pattern of behaviors was said to be taught to children very early in life. Lewis wrote that "by the time slum children are age six or seven they have usually absorbed the basic values and attitudes of their subculture and are not psychologically geared to take full advantage of changing conditions or increased opportunities which may occur in their lifetime."[52] Lewis distinguished between garden variety deprivation and this particular culture of poverty. He estimated that this culture applied to only about 20 percent of America's poor, making this subpopulation a relatively thin slice of the larger body of the poor. Several qualities were important in Lewis's identification of persons trapped in a culture of poverty, including poor integration into the larger society, which translates to severely depressed levels of political participation; a sense of hopelessness; often an awareness of middle-class values and at times an ability to recite them, but an absence of these values at play in their own lives; shortened childhoods, with early initiation into sexual activity; a failure to develop an ethos against family abandonment; a lack of impulse control, undermining habits of planning for the future; and a high tolerance of psychopathologies of various types.

This formulation of a culture of poverty crucially implies that its victims are largely unable to take advantage of opportunities that might come their way. In a strongly-stated version of this perspective, the implication is that because people trapped in a culture of poverty are so difficult to extract from their perverse situations, remedial efforts are a waste of time and money unless efforts are directed intensively at very young children. This implication, of course, would be hotly contested for years to come.

If Lewis, as a chronicler of self-destructive behaviors among the poor, was open to charges of being unsympathetic (he arguably was not) to slum residents, no one accused Michael Harrington, a former Catholic Worker movement veteran and a person of reasonably well-established socialist credentials, of failing to identify with the poor. But even Harrington, in his explicit effort to generate positive attention to the situation of the down and out, bought into the culture of poverty argument in that he saw the poor as living in a world apart, not quite sharing in the same rationality as mainstream society. He wrote that "there is, in short, a language of the poor, a psychology of the poor, a worldview of the poor. To be impoverished is to be an internal alien, to grow up in a culture that is radically different from the one that dominates society."[53] In his opening chapter, Harrington asserted that "the poor live in a culture of poverty."[54] In a sense, the irony of Harrington's treatment is that though his reliance on the culture of poverty argument was quite general, something Oscar Lewis would later point out,[55] he was employing a perspective that would later become the core rationale for his libertarian opponents, Charles Murray chief among them.[56] Edward Banfield would also pick up on this theme, writing in 1968 that "the lower-class person lives from moment to moment, he is either unable or unwilling to take into account the future or to control his impulses. . . . He is likely . . . to be a poor husband and father."[57]

For most non-libertarians, both liberals and conservatives, it came clear within a few years that the culture of poverty thesis was an invitation to stop the conversation about helping the poor. If the culture's victims were substantially unable to avail themselves of opportunities, why bother extending them? This understanding of the culture of poverty thesis as a conversation ender would, in time, steer nearly all writers on poverty away from it; but by the time that could happen in the early 1970s, a popularized version of it had merged with the historic dichotomy of worthy and unworthy poor making it more difficult politically to mobilize large-scale programs to assist the chronically impoverished. It mattered little that some of those who studied the culture of poverty would view myopic behaviors among the poor as rational, albeit suboptimal, adaptations to difficult circumstances, as did Lewis and Harrington.

The conversation about a distinct subculture among the chronically poor took another turn, one that explicitly injected race into the mix, in 1965. That year Labor Department analyst Daniel Patrick Moynihan wrote *The Negro Family: The Case for National Action* as a policy paper intended for internal consumption. This report was initially provided to President Johnson confidentially in March.[58] It was only made public later. In June of that year, the president relied on the report in his commencement speech at Howard University. He related his understanding that

The great majority of Negro Americans—the poor, the unemployed, and the dispossessed—are another nation. . . . For them the walls are rising and the gulf is widening. . . . The isolation of Negro and white communities is increasing, rather than decreasing, as Negroes crowd into the central cities and become a city within a city. . . . Negro poverty is not white poverty. Many of its causes and many of its cures are the same. But there are differences—deep corrosive, obstinate differences—radiating painful roots into the community, the family, and the nature of the individual.[59]

The Moynihan Report was subsequently leaked to the press. The report's strong language was probably designed to grab Lyndon Johnson's attention and to spur him to action. As it turned out, Moynihan's language also led many to label him racist. Many African Americans saw Moynihan's report as insulting rather than enlightening. For them, this constituted a case of blaming the victim. Despite the subtitle —*The Case for National Action*—the report appeared to many to depart from a liberal perspective, a view that would point out that the ghetto is in terrible condition and that the nation should do something about it. In its place, an interpretation emerged that was seen by many to foster a different argument, one informed by the culture of poverty thesis, that the ghetto is in terrible condition and government should cut its losses by not investing in it further.[60]

The Moynihan Report made several key points. First, it acknowledged that three centuries of overt racism had left African Americans in a severely disadvantaged position in a variety of social and economic spheres. Most recently, this had contributed to a rise in female-headed households. Related to this, secondly, it argued that the social pathologies that afflict black people are largely the result of dysfunctional families. Third, it argued that approximately one-half of the black population was incapable of responding to opportunities because of an unsuited psychological temperament. Fourth, regarding welfare, the historic relationship between unemployment rates and AFDC use changed after 1962, suggesting that people were relying on welfare for reasons independent of a lack of opportunities in the labor market. Prior to 1962, as the unemployment rate rose, so did welfare use. After 1962, however, that relationship was broken. Others would point out that Moynihan's analysis of aggregate statistics masked subgroup differences and that a more careful study of welfare use was in order. For instance, unemployment varied across groups dramatically. In 1967 the unemployment rate for whites age 16 to 21 was 11.8 percent, compared to 24.8 percent for blacks of the same age group.[61] Further, the unemployment rate for young black men and young white men did not move in parallel throughout the early 1960s. In the end, some other explanation is needed to explain the onset of a negative AFDC-unemployment relationship. In a more cultural vein, critics pointed out that matriarchy, often criticized by middle-class whites and by Moynihan specifically as a pathology, is a mode of living adopted by many oppressed peoples through history.[62] Social pathology, this line of argument goes, is in the eye of the beholder. As anthropologist Carol Stack reported in her 1974 book, *All Our Kin,* matriarchal arrangements are often associated with networks of support that exceed those of the traditional nuclear family.[63] On the more general point, it is important to note that Moynihan did not share Oscar Lewis's view that the culture of poverty was adaptive. Instead, this "tangle of pathologies," as Moynihan described it, borrowing a term from E. Franklin Frazer, is something to be stamped out.[64] Due in large part to its arguably ham-handed framing of this and other problems, Moynihan's report engendered far more controversy than illumination, but like the culture of poverty thesis it implicitly employed, the report provided what many considered a distinctly unconstructive frame of reference for studying poverty among African Americans.[65]

The backlash against Moynihan's report was a primary factor in leading scholars to distance themselves from the culture of poverty argument for years to come. As sociologist William Wilson would later observe, the controversy over the Moynihan Report stunted the vast majority of scholarly conversations about urban poverty, particularly among liberals.[66] The apparent connection between black family breakdown and persistent urban poverty, based in part of a misreading of the 1965 report, inhibited many scholars from pursuing serious investigations of the plight of poor urban residents out of an urge to seek out less inciting subject matter. Interest in urban poverty and discussions of this purported urban underclass would renew in the late-1970s, but until then the academic community experienced what would come to be seen as a lost opportunity.

Despite the document not making any policy recommendations that one side or another of the debate might favor, another lasting effect of the Moynihan Report was the way in which it helped cement a linkage between the culture of poverty thesis and conservative thought.[67] Edward Banfield's use of these ideas in his 1968 book, *The Unheavenly City,* recognized little family loyalty among inner-city poor populations, implying that any large-scale effort to intervene would be a waste of resources. Relying on Oscar Lewis's notion about the depressed ability of those caught in the culture of poverty to respond to positive incentives, conservatives were led to advocate a benign neglect, as Moynihan counseled President Nixon. This neglect is substantially what happened throughout during the 1980s as federal funding for large urban areas declined precipitously.[68]

In hindsight, the short-lived culture of poverty thesis left a lasting impression on poverty discourse. According to liberals, such as historian Michael Katz, this line of thinking turned social scientists into sophisticated critics of the poor.[69] Conservatives of an economic determinist stripe instead saw the culture of poverty as a dead-end alley, rendering further conversations about prompting the poor toward self-improvement as unproductive. Some researchers attempted to undermine Lewis's thesis by challenging it head-on. The studies focused on just how sticky this culture really may be and produced evidence that the chronically poor indeed still respond to training and employment incentives when those are offered.[70] To the extent that members of Congress and the general public came away from this episode with diminished hope for antipoverty programs, those efforts to create opportunity would be weakened.

## CREATING WORK INCENTIVES FOR THE POOR

As the 1960s wore on, there developed a debate in the Johnson administration and in Congress over the wisdom of steering welfare recipients into jobs or training programs. Many in the administration believed the 1964 tax cut would help stimulate jobs, and though the unemployment rate fell from just over 5 percent in 1964 to just under 4 percent in 1967, employment among the poor remained stubbornly high.[71] The president was also explicit that he did not want to get the government into the business of providing public sector work. Adam Yarmolinsky, a senior aide in the Kennedy and Johnson administrations, noted in 1973 that the decision was made, with some dissent within the Johnson administration, to focus on preparing people for existing jobs rather than creating jobs for them.[72] Not all members of Johnson administration agreed with this view. Willard Wirtz, Secretary of Labor under Kennedy and Johnson, advocated the rapid creation of employment for the poor, through public sector jobs if necessary. Johnson received this proposal coldly, making it clear that he wanted nothing to do with large-scale public sector job creation or radical income redistribution. It seems that despite Johnson's effort to shed his conservative Texan reputation, he was not willing to go as far as some in the Department of Labor had in mind.[73] A few years later, rising unemployment in the early 1970s would prompt Congress to create the Comprehensive Employment and Training Act, but that moment would have to wait for a more significant slowdown in the economy.

In the short term, Congress wanted to see more welfare recipients work, even if members of Congress were not willing to support the creation of public sector positions for them on a large scale, beyond $70 million appropriated for work experience programs in late 1967.[74] As a compromise of sorts, amendments to federal welfare law in 1967 created the Work Incentive Program (WIN). Under WIN welfare recipients with children over age six were required to register for work or training, even if neither of those activities were actually required for a given client. A study in 1970 found that of the 1.7 million recipients who had been screened for work or training, only 20 percent of them were eligible for placement, and only three-quarters of those were actually placed into positions, thus the impact of these work and training requirements was modest.[75] This legislation marked somewhat of a departure from the mind-set that had prevailed just five years earlier when the 1962 amendments emphasized instead an expansion of social services for recipients, not work. The National Advisory Council on Public Welfare, appointed by the secretary of the Department of Health, Education, and Welfare, voiced support in its 1966 report for a continuation of services to welfare clients "as a matter of right."[76] But the 1967 legislation instead focused on obligations and introduced work requirements for the first time. These work requirements, as unambitious as they were, appeared not to place downward pressure on welfare caseload levels. Instead, enrollment continued its steep climb.

The efficacy of WIN was dubious on another count as well. The program was criticized for failing to impart needed skills to a population of women who very much lacked marketable experience. Very few of the women enrolled in WIN in 1967 had any prior experience beyond service work. Only 2 percent had ever held professional, technical, or managerial positions. Only 14 percent had clerical or sales experience, and only 12 percent had craft skills.[77] WIN supporters pointed at these same figures to argue that the new interventions were indeed aimed at the most needy. Though controversial at the time, the move to push mothers of young children into the workforce was facilitated by a gradual shift in workforce participation by women. Throughout During much of the 1960s women entered the workforce at three times the rate of men. This trend continued until 1968. By that year fully one-half of women with school age children worked outside the home. With these behaviors already in place, Americans seemed primed to depart from the earlier wisdom that mothers belonged in the home to raise their children. While WIN led only a small portion of welfare mothers into jobs, in hindsight its lasting impact came in providing a wedge that would eventually clear the way for much more ambitious work requirements for welfare recipients.

## CRITICISMS OF THE WAR ON POVERTY AND A BREAKDOWN OF THE LIBERAL CONSENSUS

The year 1967 proved to be a turning point for support for the War on Poverty. Urban riots focused attention on the inner-city poor, and a more general sense that the War on Poverty had been overly ambitious began to set in. Congress expressed skepticism by creating the Workforce Investment Act, and the Johnson administration feared Congress would terminate funding for the War on Poverty altogether. Instead, Congress approved $1.8 billion appropriation for a variety of programs, though the somewhat close call signaled growing congressional unease with the overall effort.[78]

Signs of discomfort with welfare appeared elsewhere that year. As part of the 1967 amendments, a provision inserted into law by Democratic Representative Wilbur Mills mandated a freeze on federal money paying benefits to welfare cases resulting from desertion or out-of-wedlock births. The legislation allowed the executive branch to suspend this provision, and Johnson did so. Later, the Nixon administration continued the suspension, and eventually Nixon quietly orchestrated the provision's repeal. The saving grace for families threatened by this pending provision was a stream of complaints from states about the potential withholding of these federal funds.[79]

Another conflict between the Johnson administration and Congress that year involved a presidential request that all states pay AFDC benefits large enough to bring all enrolled families up to their respective state's needs standard, or the amount of income a state determines as a minimum livable income for a given family size. This would have leveled the cross-state differences somewhat, but Congress declined to adopt this provision.[80]

Several factors contributed to doubt about the War on Poverty throughout as the late 1960s wore on. First, the 1966 congressional elections saw the defeat of many incumbents who supported the War on Poverty and the election many new Republican members who had stated their opposition to any further increases in spending.[81] Second was a growing sense that the multiplicity of programs under the broad umbrella of the War on Poverty were overly ambitious and insufficiently focused. Further, welfare caseloads grew at a very steep rate starting in 1967, indeed at twice the rate they had grown throughout during the earlier 1960s.[82] The result was a billowing welfare population: 4.4 million in 1965, 8 million in 1970, and 11 million in 1973.[83] Instead of gratitude from the poor, many Americans primarily saw civil unrest. A writer for the conservative *National Review* observed with bitterness in 1968 that the irony of the War on Poverty is that government resources were being used, in the billions of dollars, to create among the poor a stronger sense of class consciousness, which in turn produced growing pressure on the government to do more. If government failed to address this newly awakened sense of entitlement, some neighborhoods' track records promised riots, a scenario that appeared as a case of government organizing the poor so the poor could in turn blackmail the government.[84] Valid or not, this interpretation contributed to a growing disillusionment among some former liberals, advancing the evolution of a nascent wave of neoconservatism.[85] This ideological shift, combined with emergent inflation and stalled growth in the gross national product and the purchasing power of wages, prompted many on the political right to ratchet up their criticisms of the War on Poverty. They had been much quieter up to that point.[86]

Beyond the efforts of advocacy organizations to foster a sense of welfare entitlement, the U.S. Supreme Court also played a very important role in this area throughout the late 1960s and early 1970s. Through a series of rulings the Court sought to enforce federal standards and to minimize state efforts to discriminate against potential aid recipients. The upshot of these rulings was that the Court converted welfare from a discretionary act on the part of states into substantially a property right. Repeatedly the Court ruled that if a person is categorically eligible—a child deprived of two-parent support or the parent of that child—and in a family with sufficiently low income and financial resources (as determined by states), states must extent aid when that aid is requested. The central issue of these cases was whether to view Title IV of the Social Security Act—AFDC's enabling legislation—as a language empowering states to exercise discretion or to carry out federal mandates. The U.S. Department of Health, Education, and Welfare favored the view that states must look for permission in the act before imposing new restrictions. The states preferred to look for restrictions on what they could do, assuming all other nonprohibited avenues would be available. From 1968 to 1975 the Supreme Court decided 18 AFDC cases, adopting pro-welfare positions in most of them.[87]

The case of *King v. Smith* (1968) illustrates the Court's thinking throughout this period. This conflict arose from an Alabama rule excluding from AFDC women who had sexual relations with men other than their husbands. Mrs. King was reported by an anonymous informant as having a boyfriend— Mr. Williams—and was consequently removed from Alabama's AFDC program. The Supreme Court ruled unanimously in Mrs. King's favor, interpreting the Social Security Act to preclude a distinction between the worthy and unworthy poor. Chief Justice Warren opined that while at an earlier time it may have been appropriate for states to enforce moral codes, it was not legitimate in 1968. The second prong of Alabama's argument, that AFDC should go to truly deprived children but not to those who have a substitute parent, did not survive the Court's scrutiny because the absence of a marriage also implies the absence of the nonparent to support the children. A visitor is not a parent. The Court pointed out that congressional amendments to welfare law throughout in the 1960s made it clear that legislative intent supported states' obligation to offer assistance to all needy children and that states may not discriminate based on lifestyle considerations. From the Court's perspective, discrimination had been sweeping in its impact. From June 1964, when Alabama's law became effective, to January 1967, the total number of recipients in the state fell by 22 percent.

Other important cases, including *Shapiro v. Thompson* (1969), which struck down state residency requirements, and *Carleson v. Remillard* (1972), which upheld a ruling of parental absence in the case of a father serving in Vietnam, enlarged further the scope of welfare as a right. The growing inclusivity of welfare throughout the late 1960s and early 1970s was not so much due to legislation or explicit executive branch action, but rather to court rulings and other nonmajoritarian factors. The expansion of welfare, something the Johnson administration explicitly disavowed in 1964, became a central feature of the history of the War on Poverty and a focal point for criticism from Congress and state governments. By 1972 one of every three black children in the nation was on AFDC, and 43 percent of welfare families contained at least one child born out of wedlock.[88] Certainly this invited some measure of resentment toward welfare recipients. The creation of welfare as a right marked a departure from a long historical understanding and was a move that helped undermine popular support for the Democratic Party, though its support for the Civil Rights Act and the Voting Rights Act had already set that in motion. Thus, to the extent Americans associated expanding welfare with Democrats, developments in anti-poverty policy contributed to the Democrats' fall from supermajority status beginning in the late 1960s.

## NIXON'S FAMILY ASSISTANCE PLAN: A LIBERAL-CONSERVATIVE CONVERGENCE?

In an unusual confluence of ideas borrowed from two very different camps, Richard Nixon proposed, in summer 1969, a Family Assistance Plan (FAP) that would guarantee poor families with children a minimum annual income. Adults who could work would be expected to do so in order to receive benefits. While the legislation ultimately foundered in the Senate in 1970 due to a substantial refusal on both sides to compromise, the episode highlighted both the promise of new thinking and the difficulty of responding to poverty in an age of growing partisan polarization.

The core of this federally financed FAP was a negative income tax. Families would be encouraged to work by being allowed to keep a portion of their welfare grant in addition to their earned income. The transfer payment would decrease by 67 cents for each dollar earned through work. The more low-income adults worked, the more money would accrue to their households, and they would be guaranteed an annual minimum income of $1,600 for a family of four. The transfer payment would continue until a family's total income reached approximately $4,000. The idea was the brainchild of the conservative economist Milton Friedman, though University of Wisconsin economist Robert Lampman is also credited with articulating the idea simultaneously. Friedman first advanced the concept in his 1962 book *Capitalism and Freedom*.[89] He reasoned that rather than spending a lot of money on conventional welfare programs that he considered of dubious effectiveness, it would be preferable to give money to poor people, who would spend it, helping themselves and in turn stimulating the economy. This was a point on which liberals and conservatives could agree. This transfer would also simplify welfare's bureaucracy. The Social Security Administration would implement the program, bypassing the complicated social work apparatus of the Department of Health, Education, and Welfare. Even the liberal economist John Kenneth Galbraith liked the idea, calling it one of the "two or three new ideas in economics in 25 years."[90]

Though often attributed to the Nixon administration, in their exhaustive book on this episode, Vincent and Vee Burke narrate how the FAP was largely a holdover plan from Democrats in the Johnson administration, principally OEO director Sargent Shriver, who had built on Friedman's and Lampman's negative income tax idea. President Johnson's Commission on Income Maintenance Programs, appointed in January 1968, had recommended this idea, but the administration lacked the time in office to carry forth with a proposed bill.[91]

When the Nixon administration inherited the plan, it advanced it with at least two goals in mind. One goal was to reduce the influence of the welfare caseworker lobby. Nixon's domestic policy advisor Moynihan expressed a clear disdain for social workers as a group. In his book, *The Politics of a Guaranteed Income,* he wrote that social workers were "only trying to keep their jobs, keep up their payments on the rather complex insurance arrangements the [National] Association [of Social Workers] sponsored, and perhaps get promoted after accumulating a few more credits at night school."[92] Nixon's distancing of himself from the social work community contrasted sharply with the approach taken by Abraham Ribicoff, President Kennedy's first secretary of Health, Education, and Welfare. When organizing a 1961 meeting of his Ad Hoc Committee on Public Welfare to discuss welfare and food stamps, Ribicoff selected 24 members, 23 of whom were affiliated with schools of social work.[93]

The second goal was to beat congressional Democrats to the punch and propose something before they devised a more liberal alternative. Nixon's suspicion that Democrats would produce a more liberal plan if given an opportunity proved correct. Senator-turned-presidential-candidate George McGovern proposed a $6,500 per year minimum income for poor families during the 1972 campaign. That year, however, Congress finally passed a bill creating Supplemental Security Income for the disabled, but the FAP was stripped from the bill.[94] In the end, conservatives thought the FAP was too generous, and liberals, who pointed out that the benefit amounted to less than one-half of the federal poverty threshold, thought it was too stingy.[95] From the perspective of the NWRO, a key player in this debate that worked aggressively to kill the bill in the Senate, the FAP was "anti-poor, and anti-black . . . a flagrant example of institutional racism."[96]

Various postmortems dissected the failure of FAP, seen by most observers across the political spectrum as a tragic lost opportunity. Objections voiced during the struggle over the legislation at the time seemed more significant than they tended to appear in hindsight. The chief point of difference was of the amount of the transfer payment. The NWRO insisted on annual payments of $4,000 (raising that figure to $6,500 by the early 1970s), while some fiscal conservatives believed Nixon's $1,600 was excessive. The NWRO encouraged people to try to live on Nixon's minimum figure for a week, and several Congress members' wives attempted just that, leading them to conclude that doing so would require not only a college degree in home economics but also a high tolerance for hunger.[97]

Another point of resistance arose over unequal distribution of these federal resources across regions of the country. Estimates revealed that cash benefits would increase in the south, which paid below-average benefits, but that federal welfare funds would remain largely unchanged elsewhere, which meant members of Congress from other regions saw little to gain in the proposal. Their states' benefits already exceeded the federal minimum.[98] Southerners feared that a guaranteed income would provide an exit option from the labor market for low-wage workers, particularly tenant farmers. Objections about workfare included complaints that forcing women with young children into the workforce would undermine quality parenting. Finally, compelling more workers into the labor market seemed a challenge with the economy slowing down and unemployment at approximately 6 percent.

In the end no one wanted to take credit for the failure of the FAP. The bill passed the House twice but foundered in the Senate. Nixon's bill went down to defeat with little protest from the president. Nixon later commented that preserving his electoral coalition trumped his support for the FAP and that he did not want to waste political capital trying to win votes from liberals.[99] White House chief of staff, H. R. Haldeman, later revealed that Nixon had instructed him to "be sure the [FAP was] . . . killed by the Democrats and that we make a big play for it."[100] There were other recriminations as well. Moynihan's came in the form of his book on the episode.[101] The National Association of Social Workers ran a bitter essay in its journal, *Social Service Review,* in the fall of 1973 that took Moynihan to task over the book and which distanced the Association from the opposition to FAP, insisting that no formal vote of its membership was ever taken on the bill.[102] It appears no side in the debate wanted to appear obstructionist.

Experiments conducted between 1967 and 1977 sought to empirically verify the effects of a guaranteed income on low-income adults. These extensively analyzed projects provided a guaranteed income to groups of low-income families in four locations: New Jersey, Gary, Seattle, and Denver. During the early years, the project went forward in New Jersey under the title "Graduated Work Incentive Program," so named to offer some political cover to this controversial idea. The project involved control groups whose members were not required to work and experimental groups whose members received varying amounts of monthly income, varied intentionally to check the effects of differing levels of income. The experiment in New Jersey ran for three years and tended to show only very small effects on work effort. Males worked approximately two hours per week less but earned more per hour. Apparently men used this grant as a stable position from which to look for and find better jobs. Women whose families received the grant worked 36 minutes less per week and earned about $1 less per week [103] Results from the other sites produced similar results, with slightly depressed work effort, and slightly increased rates of family dissolution among white women.[104] Both liberals and conservatives claimed the results supported their positions to a degree. Conservatives pointed to diminished work effort and increased rates of family dissolution. Liberals pointed out how slight the changes in work effort had been and noted that rates of marital separation varied by group. To the extent women were able to exit destructive relationships thanks to a measure of economic independence, liberals saw this demonstration project as illustrative of a need generally neglected by society.

## EVALUATING THE WAR ON POVERTY

Even in hindsight, interpretations of efforts to fight poverty during the 1960s remain deeply conflictual and very much depend on one's premises regarding the role of government. The period also stands as a high watermark for confidence in social science to show the way forward in combating what was and is, unarguably, a national problem. Historian Michael Katz writes that

Great Society poverty research proved to be the last hurrah of twentieth-century liberalism. It rested on the expectation that reason, science, and experience could inform public policy and persuade a benevolent state to engineer social progress. By placing government policy on a scientific basis, poverty researchers hoped to transcend politics and ideology. In the end, although they won several battles, they lost even the intellectual war.[105]

If this line of thinking is correct, and many believe it is, the War on Poverty stands as a testimony to the power of the adage implicitly used by the already convinced: "My mind is made up. Don't bother me with the facts." High-quality social science shed considerable light on the dynamics of poverty and programs designed to alleviate it, and to some extent this improved analytic sophistication fostered a broadened range of arguments about how to engage the poor. Academics and think tanks joined trade unions and employer groups as interlocutors in these policy discussions.[106] Unfortunately, however, much of this insight was and is lost on the general public, so these new research methods and careful tabulations of poverty dynamics likely exert only marginal influence on public debate.[107] The questions these improved studies address tend to be the same ones that have dominated public discourse on poverty since the beginning of the 1800s: Does welfare provision weaken work incentives? Does welfare undermine stable families? Does welfare receipt diminish recipients' work ethic? To the extent both the left and the right were asking these same questions, the debate remained remarkably stable throughout the 1960s. Henry Aaron of the Brookings Institution observed after the fact that "none of the ideas embodied in the Great Society or the War on Poverty was really new. All had been foreshadowed in the New Deal or Fair Deal."[108] Aaron was right regarding ideas but less so with respect to government's willingness to put some of the ideas into action. The War on Poverty represented a certain boldness in experimentation not seen since the Great Depression, and systematic thinking about policy effects on people, if imperfectly executed during the 1960s, certainly set that decade apart from the rest of the twentieth century.

Critics of the War on Poverty have tended to point to failings that run along at least four lines. Lance Liebman neatly articulated these dimensions in a 1974 essay in the conservative journal *The Public Interest*. First, social conditions improved but still fell short of rising expectations. The poverty rate fell, but society seemed simultaneously to adjust upward its expectations for livings standards among the poor. Second, poverty warriors realized there are things we do not know how to do. Reducing the rate of out-of-wedlock births may be one example. Third, public delivery of services can be inefficient. A domain other than welfare provides a powerful example here. Trash pick up in New York City during the 1970s cost much more per ton collected by the city government than by private contractor. The difference came to a factor of three-to-one. Fourth, insufficient resources were brought to bear on fighting poverty and lack of opportunity, given the diversion of funds to the Vietnam War.[109] President Johnson's initial promise to wage unconditional war on poverty while not raising taxes was proved to be completely unrealistic.

Examining the intellectual roots of the war on poverty, it becomes clear that the Kennedy and Johnson administrations attempted to merge incongruous elements from conflicting schools of thought. Participation of the poor in anti-poverty programs was attempted haltingly because of a reluctance to unsettle the status quo. Welfare was made more attractive by the improvement of social services after 1962 and the addition of Medicaid in 1965, but then policy makers were disappointed when welfare use increased. In an ironic juxtaposition, the Johnson administration endorsed the culture of poverty argument, but it also embraced maximum feasible participation, very much at odds with Oscar Lewis's theory. Johnson also made much of expanding opportunity, but he resisted any large-scale public sector jobs creation program. Fundamentally, the overall vagueness with which the Johnson administration discussed its approaches to poverty was probably intentional, as that allowed them to combine multiple tactics and to appeal to various constituencies, including the 40 percent on the Gallup Poll who believed the poor were at fault for their own poverty.

If the Great Society era had its failings, it also left some lasting marks on America's social and economic landscape. The creation of Medicare, Medicaid, Supplemental Security Income, automated cost of living adjustments for Social Security recipients, and food stamps produced a reduction of the post-transfer poverty rate from just over 22 percent in 1959 to 11 percent by 1973. It has remained between there and 14 percent since then. The elderly and racial minorities were especially helped by this decline in the poverty rate. The percentage of senior citizens below the poverty line declined from 25 percent in 1959 to only 16 percent in 1980.[110] In 1959, 55 percent of African Americans were poor compared to only 31 percent in 1973, and 24 percent in 1999. Critics have pointed out that the reduction of pre-transfer poverty rates changed much less through this period, but the dramatic drop in economic insecurity among the elderly, for example, had enjoyed strong political support across virtually every part of the political spectrum. It is also difficult to argue with a one-third decline in the nation's infant mortality rate between 1965 and 1972.

The growing disillusionment with the War on Poverty in the early 1970s—compounded with urban unrest, rising welfare use, stagnating wages among the middle-class, the Vietnam War, and a conservative shift in public opinion—saw it end with little more than a whimper. Congress closed the OEO in 1974, and Gerald Ford signaled that welfare reform would not be on his agenda. The flight of the middle class, and many industries, from the cities to the suburbs left behind concentrated pools of poverty that would, within a decade, witness declining federal urban aid.[111] That demographic shift also hastened a change in the way Americans talked and thought about inner-cities and their residents. The percentage of Americans who believed we are spending "too little" on "solving the problems of the big cities" fell from 48 percent in 1973 to only 39 percent in 1978.[112] The 1970s and 1980s would mark, depending on one's perspective, either a time of retrenchment, or a course correction.

# NOTES

1. Liebman 1974, p. 19.
2. O'Connor 2004, chap. 2; Hodgson 1976.
3. Truman 1951; Hartz 1955; Hofstadter 1948.
4. See Lyndon Johnson's January 8, 1964 State of the Union address in *Public Papers of the Presidents of the United States, 1963–64,* bk. 1 of 2, p. 91. Washington, DC: General Services Administration.
5. Zarefsky 1986, p. 21; Tobin 1967; Katznelson 1989, p. 200.
6. Katznelson 1989, p. 198; Gans 1995, p. 3.
7. Katznelson 1989, p. 188.
8. Macdonald 1963.
9. O'Connor 2004, p. 55; Zarefsky 1986, p 25; Patterson 1994, p. 99.
10. Galbraith 1958.
11. Heller 1960.
12. Fisher 1997.
13. Iceland 2003, p. 18; Fisher 1997.
14. Burke and Burke 1974, p. 12.
15. Steiner 1974, p. 55.
16. Sundquist 1969, p. 42.
17. Katz 1989, p. 80; Zarefsky 1986, p. ix.
18. Zarefsky 1986, pp. 22–24.
19. Ibid., p. 36.
20. O'Connor 2004, p. 50; Caro 1983, 1990. Johnson shared his humble background from time to time with audiences, as he did on a trip to West Virginia in April 1964. See *Public Papers of the Presidents of the United States, 1963/64,* bk. 1 of 2, p. 293. Washington, DC: General Services Administration.
21. Zarefsky 1986, p. 61.
22. "Do you think the Johnson Administration's war on poverty will help to wipe out poverty in this country, or don't you think it will be much help?" Opinion Research Corporation, 1,040 adults interviewed in late July 1964, and 1,027 interviewed in early August 1965.
23. *Public Papers of the Presidents of the United States, 1963–64,* bk. 1 of 2, p. 91. Washington, DC: General Services Administration.

24. Ibid., p. 165.

25. Ibid., p. 270.

26. Ibid., bk. 2 of 2, p. 528.

27. Ginzberg and Solow 1974b, p. 213.

28. Eisinger 2003.

29. "Here are some of the issues that were discussed in the presidential election campaign. How much did each of these have to do with your final choice of which presidential candidate to vote for? . . . The war on poverty." Opinion Research Corporation, 778 adults interviewed between November 4 and 8, 1964.

30. Miller and Roby 1968, p. 71.

31. Rubin 1969, p. 15.

32. Miller and Roby 1968.

33. Ginzberg and Solow 1974b.

34. *Congressional Quarterly Almanac,* 1964, p. 208.

35. Zarefsky 1986, pp. 53–54.

36. *Congressional Quarterly Almanac,* 1964, p. 226.

37. Rubin 1969.

38. *Congressional Quarterly Almanac,* 1964, p. 228.

39. Ibid., p. 208.

40. Trattner 1999, p. 324.

41. *Congressional Quarterly Almanac,* 1964, p. 208.

42. Katz 1989, p. 106.

43. Melnick 1994, chap. 5.

44. Melnick 1994, p. 91.

45. PBS Video 1995.

46. Pole 1993, chap. 13.

47. Katz 1989, p. 55.

48. Lawson 1976, p. 331.

49. Rein 1969.

50. Jencks and Edin 1990.

51. Gans 1995.

52. Lewis 1965, p. xlv.

53. Harrington 1962, p. 17.

54. Ibid., p. 15.

55. Lewis 1965, p. xlii.

56. Charles Murray 1984.

57. Banfield 1968b, p. 54.

58. O'Connor 2004, p. 65.

59. Rainwater and Yancey 1967, pp. 127–28.

60. Lemann 1986a, p. 58.

61. Miller and Roby 1968, p. 74; Carper 1968, p. 200.

62. Carper 1968, p. 200; O'Connor 2001, p. 255, n. 48.

63. Stack 1974.

64. Gans 1995, p. 29.

65. Rainwater and Yancy 1967, for a comprehensive treatment of this debate.

66. Wilson 1991.

67. Katz 1989, pp. 29–30; Banfield 1968a.

68. Caraley 1992.

69. Katz 1989, chap. 2.

70. Padfield 1970.

71. U.S. Department of Labor, Bureau of Labor Statistics, . "Employment status of the civilian noninstitutional population, 1940 to 2006" (table available on-line at http://www.bls.gov/cps/cpsaat1.pdf; accessed June 18, 2007).

72. Yarmolinsky 1973, pp. 286–88.

73. Katz 1989, pp. 93–94.

74. *Congressional Quarterly Almanac,* 1967, pp. 1059–60.

75. Steiner 1974, p. 60.

76. Axinn and Stern 2005, p. 256.

77. Pearce 1978.

78. *Congressional Quarterly Almanac* 1968, pp. 1058–65.

79. Steiner 1974, p. 58; Burke and Burke 1974, pp. 35–36.

80. Burke and Burke 1974, p. 23.

81. Zarefsky 1986, p. 160.

82. Teles 1998, p. 21.

83. Steiner 1974, p. 64.

84. van den Haag 1968.

85. O'Connor 2004, chap. 4.

86. Hodgson 1976, chap. 24.

87. Melnick 1994, chap. 5.

88. Burke and Burke 1974, p. 5.

89. Friedman 1962.

90. Burke and Burke 1974, p. 18.

91. Burke and Burke 1974, p. 3; Axinn and Stern 2005, pp. 293–94.

92. *The Social Service Review,* 47, no. 3 (Sept. 1973; no author given); Moynihan 1973, p. 319.

93. Steiner 1974, p. 54.

94. Katz 1989, p. 102.

95. Schorr 1969.

96. Quadagno 1994, p. 133 (quoting *The New Yorker,* December 7, 1973, p. 23).

97. PBS Video 1995.

98. Burke and Burke 1974, p. 5.

99. Quadagno 1994, p. 133.

100. Trattner 1999, p. 341.

101. Moynihan 1973.

102. National Association of Social Workers 1973.

103. Burke and Burke 1974, p. 22; Pechman and Timpane 1975.

104. Online, see http://www.econlib.org/library/enc/negativeincometax.html (accessed June 18, 2007) for description of findings.

105. Katz 1989, p. 121.
106. Block et al. 1987, pp. 49–52.
107. Katz 1993, pp. 14–15; Katznelson 1989.
108. Katznelson, 1989: 199.
109. Liebman 1974.
110. Katz 1989, p. 113.
111. Caraley 1992.
112. National Opinion Research Center (University of Chicago), General Social Survey, cumulative data file, 1972-2004.

# 5

# The 1970s and 1980s—Backlash and an Emerging Neoconservative Consensus

In a passage from *The Snows of Kilimanjaro*, one of Ernest Hemingway's characters observes that the very rich differ from the rest of us in that they have more money, not that they are somehow more exotic. Conversely, one might suppose that their lack of money is all that sets the poor apart from the rest of us.[1] Though Hemingway offered this perspective in 1961, by the early 1970s, many Americans had ceased to believe that the differences between rich and poor were so simple. The idea would come to be widespread that welfare provision had changed the poor both in spirit and habit. Richard Nixon gave voice to fears of welfare fraud and offered a moralistic critique of the poor.[2] This shift of thinking in the late 1960s and early 1970s was part of a waning of popular support for welfare spending through the coming decade, a trend that would not reverse until the 1980s. This conservative reorientation on welfare was a constituent part of a broader movement to the political Right that would effect changes in federal governance. With four new justices joining the U.S. Supreme Court between 1969 and 1971, a significant rise in the success of the conservative coalition of Republicans and southern Democrats in Congress from the mid-1960s to the mid-1970s, and Republicans in the White House, the turn away from an expanding welfare state appears to have been, in hindsight, almost inevitable.[3] Partisan forces working to curtail welfare expenditures were complimented by growing inflationary pressures and a federal budget deficit, both of which augured against continued support for welfare spending at the levels seen in the 1960s.

By the mid-1970s, the purchasing power of AFDC checks would begin to lose ground to inflation and would continue to do so through the 1990s. For states, saddled with what they saw as a load of federal mandates to expand welfare payments to a steeply increasing percentage of eligible families, curtailing welfare's generosity was one of the few legal options available to exert control over their caseloads. State governments took full advantage of this flexibility, and the real value of AFDC payments fell by 28 percent between 1967 and 1980.[4]

Of critical importance, the rise of conservatism that marked the latter half of the 1970s and the Reagan administration afterward contributed to a widespread sense that much of the previous 20 years of fighting poverty had been misspent. Critiquing the War on Poverty would become a mainstay of conservative argument on welfare, and social policy more generally, for a generation. Various lines of argument emerged, but two dominated. First, critics pointed out how billions of dollars had been spent on programs, ranging from community action to food stamps to welfare to legal aid, with only modest impacts on pretransfer poverty rates. This was to say that the money spent to deliver in-cash and in-kind assistance to the poor had done very little to help people make their way out of poverty through earned income. Whether the money spent fighting poverty constituted a lot or a little was widely debated. One way to contextualize the federal investment in the poor during this period is to note that the Johnson administration spent 25 times the amount of money on the Vietnam War than it did on antipoverty programs.[5]

In a second line of critique, others renewed the well-worn argument that generous welfare provision corrupts recipients' commitment to work. Combined, these two critiques fostered a distinctly negative public discourse of welfare queens and of women sitting home watching TV, birthing more children out of wedlock, and drawing a monthly check. Numerous stereotypes emerged: adolescent pregnancy was an epidemic, one that was spreading most rapidly among blacks; unmarried black mothers made up most of the welfare caseload; welfare availability led teenagers to become pregnant; sex education and the easy availability of contraceptives and abortion encouraged teens to have sex at an earlier age than in years past; and never-married women with children comprised the core of this persistent welfare-dependent class. As it turns out, none of the stereotypes described here squared with the facts, but that lack of veracity did little to inhibit their endorsement by commentators and a large swath of the general public.[6] Public opinion polls from the late 1970s through the 1990s consistently found that a majority of respondents believed that most of the people who receive money from welfare could get along without it if they tried.

Anecdotes, however unrepresentative of the larger trends, presented themselves as debate fodder. In the District of Columbia, Jacqueline Williams, a mother of 14 who was receiving welfare, carried on a public row with D.C. Mayor Marion Barry. The mayor publicly critiqued her fertility. She claimed a God-given right to reproduce and commented in 1987 to a *Washington Post* reporter while pregnant with her 15th child that "I don't intend to stop until God stops me. . . . I don't want to mess up my body with birth control."[7] It is perhaps difficult to imagine a better case study for antiwelfare advocates. Though liberal scholars such as William J. Wilson offered sound structural arguments for persistent poverty and the emergence of an urban underclass, the general public seemed more persuaded by conservatives' behavioral explanation.

The backlash against welfare programs gave birth to an indictment of welfare rights advocates themselves. Some observers, mostly on the political Right, argued that welfare advocates had developed a constituency among poor people, and that these political professionals cultivated the poor in a neocolonial fashion. In one of its more cynical forms, this argument suggested that liberals wanted to continually redefine poverty to ensure that their professional services would continue forever in demand. In an April 1972 essay in the *National Review,* A. Lawrence Chickering wrote that "under present circumstances, and for the foreseeable future, poverty cannot cease to be a problem in America, because [the Left] need[s] the poor too much."[8] To

**Table 5.1.**
**Can welfare recipients get by without assistance?**

"Do you think that most of the people who receive money from welfare could get along without it if they tried, or do you think they really need this help?" (Nationally representative samples by CBS/*New York Times,* except as noted; sample size > 1,100. Cell entries are percentages.)

| | October 1976* | July 1977 | November 1980 | September 1981 | December 1994 | April 1995** |
|---|---|---|---|---|---|---|
| Could get along without welfare | 51 | 54 | 51 | 55 | 57 | 53 |
| Really need help | 36 | 31 | 39 | 32 | 36 | 33 |
| Don't know | 13 | 14 | 10 | 13 | 7 | 13 |

*Survey of registered voters only.
**Survey by Hart and Teeter Research Associates.
*Source:* Survey data from the Roper Center's Public Opinion On-Line database, available via Lexis-Nexis.

the notion of redefining poverty as a percentage at the bottom of the income scale, Chickering noted that "defining poverty as a percentage, rather than in absolute terms, guarantees a supply of 'poor' people for all time"[9] A similar argument had been advanced in this publication in 1968, then noting that the "war against poverty has created agencies . . . with a vested interest in the poor—they make their living and derive their power and status from the existence of the poor. They will not let their clients disappear."[10] This type of argument carried forward to the 1990s. In criticizing low-income-housing advocates, the editorial staff of the *Pittsburgh Post-Gazette* lambasted "career bureaucrats," "sociologists," and "healthcare professionals" for their mission to ensure that "their heirs and their assignees can suck at the public welfare teat in perpetuity."[11]

Public discourse about the poor would grow more complicated through the late 1970s and into the 1980s as a newly emergent urban underclass came into sight. Those on the political Left and Right would grapple with this problem—how to define it, how to explain its origins, and how to respond to it—in a profoundly racialized fashion for a pair of decades. Proposed solutions would be scarce, given the flight of the middle-class from urban areas during these years and the federal government's concomitant neglect of the cities and their pain.[12]

## SIGNS OF AN URBAN UNDERCLASS

In the late 1970s, many Americans came to believe that a new urban underclass had emerged. As the sociologist Herbert Gans details in his history of the term, *underclass* originated with the Swedish economist Gunnar Myrdal in his 1963 book, *Challenge to Affluence*. Originally, the term referred to those disenfranchised from the mainstream labor market and was intended as a normatively neutral, not a pejorative, behavioral label. However, by the early 1970s, the term had taken on a distinct tinge of a subpopulation troubled with chronic unemployment and poverty, long-term welfare dependency, sexual promiscuity, criminal behavior, and drug use.[13] The term *underclass* also served as a euphemism for poor urban blacks and the unworthy poor more generally. Commentators disagreed on whether life in the midst of this urban dislocation and social isolation was primarily a symptom or a cause of individual behaviors associated with persistent poverty. Experts also vacillated between applying the term to people or places. For some, an operative part of the definition of the underclass involved census tracts suffering greater than 40 percent poverty. In this mode of inquiry, the focus turned to neighborhoods. For others, particularly those who focused on lingering racism as a cause, investigators examined classes of people. Rightly or wrongly, and despite its substantially undefined parameters, notions of the underclass tainted discussions of urban life, complicating efforts to address the problems, both for welfare recipients and for cities more generally.

Some objective indicators sketched the broad outlines of the underclass. In the late 1970s, the U.S. National Center for Health Statistics began reporting that more than half of black children were being born out of wedlock. The comparable 1950 figure had been 17 percent.[14] Social scientists also noticed a substantial increase in the number of places experiencing extremely high rates of poverty. Poverty in Chicago's inner-city neighborhoods rose by 12 percent between 1970 and 1980. Although this was not the trend in all large cities, Chicago was not unique. Many northern Rust Belt cities suffered similar concentrations of poverty.[15] More broadly, between 1970 and 1980, the percentage of African Americans living in areas of extreme poverty rose by 148 percent, compared to only 24 percent of whites living in such areas.[16]

Press accounts during the 1970s fostered these beliefs and helped cement this term in the American lexicon. One month after the July 1977 blackout in New York City and its accompanying looting rampage, *Time* magazine published a cover story on the American underclass. The article painted a grim picture of inner-city America, drawn largely on scenes from New York City, and left the distinct impression that problems with this subpopulation vastly outnumbered solutions. Photos accompanying the story portrayed people who were about as worn out as the dilapidated buildings they lived in. Both the photos and the text of the story emphasized how the underclass was largely African American. Of the 21 persons shown in the story's accompanying pictures, 19 of them were black. As it turns out, the skewed portrayal in that story was not an isolated one. Martin Gilens documented this pattern in the media on a widespread basis in his study spanning news coverage from 1950 through 1992.[17] This growing sense was that there were two very separate needy populations: whites, who were the victims of plant closings, and blacks, who were unwilling to work, chronically poor, and dangerous. This reinforced the old distinction between the worthy and unworthy poor.

An important salvo in the effort to establish some intellectual credentials for the concept of the underclass came in the 1982 publication of Ken Auletta's book, *The Underclass,* based on a study of New York City.[18] The major issues included a debate over personal versus structural causes of chronic poverty, the roles of culture and family structure, and antipoverty institutions and programs. Overarching these themes was the question of why so much poverty persists despite years of efforts to minimize it. Auletta developed a four-way categorization of members of the underclass, including the passive poor, the hostile street criminals, the hustlers, and the traumatized homeless. Despite their obvious differences, Auletta saw a common theme in a lack of mobility

connecting them.[19] While Auletta did not intend the book to be an ideological tract, the work in fact divided the poor into two groups, one defined by its
deviant behavior, the other as unfortunate victims. This in turn reinforced a
now centuries-old dichotomy between an implicitly worthy versus unworthy
poor. In the 1968 welfare case of *King v. Smith,* Chief Justice Warren asserted
that "the most recent congressional amendments to the Social Security Act
further corroborate that federal public welfare policy now rests on a basis
considerably more sophisticated and enlightened than the 'worthy-person'
concept of earlier times."[20] Of course, saying it did not make it so. Whether
the U.S. Supreme Court desired it or not, the bifurcation of the poor was
once again very much part of the popular and academic vocabulary.

Liberals and conservatives alike continued to disagree into the 1980s on
exactly what the term *underclass* meant, but in time, the term, despite its
lingering morally pejorative undertones, came to enjoy a certain currency,
even among scholars engaged in serious study of urban problems. The term's
acceptance was as much due to it having become a permanent part of the lexicon as that, in the eyes of many, it is functional.[21] For liberals, admitting the
functionality of the term was not the same as admitting that cultural instead
of structural economic factors were to blame for the problems of poor, urban
residents. The most visible embrace of the term on the political Left came in
the 1987 publication of University of Chicago sociologist William Wilson's
*The Truly Disadvantaged.*

Wilson distinguished himself sharply from the culture-of-poverty writers
in his attribution of deep poverty to largely structural factors, primarily a
spacial mismatch between low-skilled workers trapped in the inner-city and
good-paying jobs that had fled to the suburbs.[22] This mismatch contributed
to inflated rates of unemployment among men, especially among black men.
In Wilson's view, unemployed men are not marriageable men, and assuming that women become pregnant at a more or less constant rate whether
they are married or not, the deficit of marriageable men leads directly to
elevated rates of out-of-wedlock births. In addition to the question of out-of-
wedlock births, an emaciated pool of marriageable men stunts family forma-
tion beyond childbirth and increases the likelihood of family breakup. This
in turn leads to an increase in mother-only households, which experience dramatically lower income and roughly twice the rate of poverty of two-parent
households.

In *The Truly Disadvantaged,* Wilson considered cultural factors, such as
rates of crime commission, but they played a secondary role to structural
explanations of poverty. In time, Wilson would adopt a more blended view,
opening the door for a more prominent role for cultural factors. Most,
though not all, liberals remain loathe to rely on cultural explanations for

economic underachievement. For example, Jared Diamond's Pulitzer Prize–winning *Guns, Germs, and Steel* is one such effort to explicitly shun cultural explanations when examining economic underdevelopment across societies.[23] Christopher Jencks and Kathryn Edin articulated this point explicitly in their 1990 essay in *The American Prospect,* arguing that "single mothers do not turn to welfare because they are pathologically dependent on handouts or unusually reluctant to work. They turn to welfare because they cannot get jobs that pay any better than welfare."[24] An exception to the voluntary moratorium on cultural explanations of poverty appeared in a significant, two-installment exposé on the underclass in the *Atlantic Monthly* in 1986. Nicholas Lemann noted after spending time with poor blacks on Chicago's south side,

A fundamental reason that so many unmarried teenagers have children in the ghetto today seems to be that having them has become a custom—a way of life. The story I heard over and over from teenage mothers was that their pregnancies were not accidental. Their friends were all having babies. Their boyfriends had pressured them into it, because being a father—the fact of it, not the responsibility—is a status symbol for a boy in the ghetto.[25]

In time, Wilson and others would cautiously distance themselves from the *underclass* label. In his 1990 address to the American Sociological Association, Wilson gingerly stepped away from the underclass as an analytical concept, due to its poor ability to generate theoretical insights or even to support a clear definition, but advised a dedication on the part of poverty researchers to continue their work.[26] Outside of the academy, in the rough and tumble of partisan discourse, liberals such as Wilson were accused of attempting to enforce an "etiquette of silence" surrounding the culture of poverty and, by extension, talk of a largely black underclass, in the hope of perpetuating a welfare state.[27]

## THE ASCENDANCY OF NEOCONSERVATIVE WELFARE IDEAS

If conservatives were divided over prescriptions for welfare during the 1970s, they achieved greater unity by the early 1980s, along with Republican control of the presidency and the U.S. Senate.[28] That control translated to a shift in the war of ideas about poverty. In a tactic of fighting ideas with ideas, an approach suggested in the late 1970s by neoconservative Irving Kristol, the new administration saw to it that federal grants to centrist and left-leaning think tanks were significantly curtailed, helping to clear the field for its own supply-side economic philosophy.[29] This idea involved economic theory that in its traditional formulation, remained somewhat inscrutable to nonexperts. However, George Gilder, a Reagan speech writer, repackaged supply-side theory into an arguably simplistic, but at times eloquent, praise of capitalism in his best-selling *Wealth and Poverty*. Media commentators critiqued the almost fanciful quality of Gilder's writing. *Newsweek* noted that Gilder's arguments against various contemporary lines of sociological thinking "required the reader to take some fairly dizzying leaps of faith."[30] Fanciful or not, Gilder's book reputedly became the bible of the new administration.[31] With talk of a "Reagan revolution" in Washington, national politics was ripe for a renewed conversation about how to confront welfare. The first two years of the Reagan administration would see dramatic reductions in aid programs for the working poor and a refocusing of federal employment policy away from public-sector employment to more of an emphasis on private-sector work. This period also saw the beginning of earnest efforts to condition welfare eligibility on job training and job-placement programs designed substantially by state governments, in keeping with a so-called new federalism, a shift to more state control over social programming.

As controversial as it was, *Wealth and Poverty* helped popularize the idea that "the only dependable route from poverty is always work, family, and faith. The first principle is that in order to move up, the poor must not only work, they must work harder than the classes above them."[32] Gilder was criticized for his overt sexism as regards his ideas about the harm done, at the micro and macro levels, by women in the workforce, and his rather uncomplicated layman's sociology; but he should be credited for helping turn poverty discourse away from the culture-of-poverty thesis that had been so pervasive just a few years before. While praising Edward Banfield's insights on the urban underclass, Gilder substantially qualified their applicability to the poor more generally.

In Gilder's view, men are ruled by disruptive sexual aggression unless yoked by family life and the expectations of supporting a wife and children. In this sense, Gilder is something of a biological determinist, hanging much of his explanation for poverty on the sexual aggressiveness of unattached men. Gilder argued that if a culture of poverty exists, it is limited to unmarried men, and that stable marriage and a job can powerfully convert them. For their part, mother-only families are a recipe for social and economic disasters. In Gilder's words,

once a family is headed by a woman, it is almost impossible for it to greatly raise its income even if the woman is highly educated and trained and she hired day-care or domestic help. . . . A married man, on the other hand, is spurred by the claims of family to channel his otherwise disruptive male aggressions into his performance as a provider for a wife and children. These sexual differences alone, which manifest themselves in all societies known to anthropology, dictate that the first priority of any serious program against poverty is to strengthen the male role in poor families.[33]

To appreciate Gilder's contribution to a changed poverty conversation, one might consider how, in Oscar Lewis' formulation, the culture of poverty is, in a sense, sticky. It was said to dramatically reduce its victims' ability to respond to positive incentives, such as a job opportunity. A logical implication of this view of poverty is that certain people are essentially beyond economic remediation or moral redemption. Policy remedies simply do not work with this crowd. In contrast, Gilder, with his heavy emphasis on the power of capital markets, instead saw work, even low-end jobs, as empowering, despite not being as financially rewarding as poor people would like or expect. In this view, the vast majority of poor people will indeed respond to market incentives if not dissuaded by the temptation of public assistance. Distancing himself from the sociopathology perspective of earlier writers and instead adopting a homo economicus paradigm, Gilder wrote that "the poor choose leisure not because of moral weakness, but because they are paid to do so."[34]

In keeping with this vision of work as the solution for the able-bodied, the Reagan administration won a one-quarter reduction in low-income assistance programs, particularly those aimed at the working poor, during its first two years in office. Changes in federal legislation lowered the income ceilings for AFDC eligibility, and over 400,000 families were removed from the program. Some of these cuts were restored in 1984, but the downward trend in AFDC enrollment continued until 1987.

Although this mixed record of achievement on welfare policy caused some commentators to declare the failure of the Reagan revolution, a more subtle reading of these conflicts suggests that the administration may have lost some legislative battles—in the form of reversed budget cuts and the like—but that it won the ideological war.[35] This victory accelerated federal and state welfare reforms during the late 1980s and early 1990s, a movement that would culminate in 1996 with the most sweeping federal social-policy legislation in a generation.

If Gilder's moralizing about welfare's disruptive role struck a sympathetic chord among libertarian-leaning conservatives, it also left somewhat abstract the point of just how policy should respond to poverty. Filling this void in 1984 was Charles Murray's highly influential book, *Losing Ground*. This more closely argued and more methodically presented work highlighted how the expansion of welfare through the latter half of the twentieth century had detracted from the pain of being poor, and thus had made welfare use a more appealing option than it had been prior to the 1960s. Murray largely avoided the sexism that marred Gilder's work (that would change in his early 1990s writings), focusing instead on what he saw as the perverse economic incentives imbedded in AFDC. In keeping with growing expectations that poor mothers would work, he explicitly noted that the harmful impacts of women's entry into the workforce had been exaggerated. In taking this position, it should be noted that Murray still found himself at odds with some social conservatives who continued to point to the negative social impacts of working mothers on their children.[36] Murray, like Gilder, sidestepped the culture-of-poverty argument, seeing it as a conversation ender for those interested in pursuing policy solutions instead of hand-wringing or a posture of detached cultural relativism. He illustrated his points about the incentives of changing welfare eligibility rules through the literary devise of a hypothetical young couple facing decisions about work, marriage, and childbearing.

Murray enjoyed substantial support in promoting his ideas. The publication of *Losing Ground* was sponsored by the Manhattan Institute, whose president, William Hammett, raised funds to support Murray for two years during the writing of the book. The foundation also helped promote the book upon its publication by spending some $15,000 to mail free copies to 500 politicians, academics, and journalists. Hammett also hired a public relations agent to oversee the campaign promoting Murray's book. Further, to drive home the point, the institute organized a two-day seminar on *Losing Ground* and invited a group of influential people to attend, paying them between $500 and $1,500 in addition to housing them in New York City hotels. The book contained what many considered powerful arguments, but its successful launch was not solely due to the force of Murray's intellect.[37]

The core of Murray's argument was illustrated by a fictitious young couple—Harold and Phyllis—who faced the option of getting married (or not), and of having a child (or not) in the early 1960s and again in the 1980s. The argument was that the growth of welfare programs through the 1960s made working less appealing to Harold and made having a child under these less-than-ideal circumstances less of a negative prospect than it had previously been. In 1960 it would have made economic sense for Harold to take and keep whatever low-paying job he could find, regardless of how distasteful the work was. By 1970, owing to changes in family composition rules under AFDC, the couple's options had changed and made it possible, indeed likely, that the couple would live together without getting married, and that they could have survived without any earned income from Harold.

Murray decried several specific policy changes, including the elimination of the man-in-the-house rule in 1968 as a result of the U.S. Supreme Court's ruling in *King v. Smith*. Under this new regime, states were not allowed to disqualify women due to the presence of their live-in male friends. Further, the 1961 creation of AFDC for unemployed parents (AFDC-UP) made many two-parent families eligible, so long as the primary breadwinner was out of work. (As it turns out, recipients under the AFDC-UP program never made up more than 8 percent of the national caseload.) Lastly, the 1967 creation of the rule that required states to disregard the first $30 and the remaining one-third of earned income meant Harold could work part time and still not render the couple ineligible based on his income. Murray argued that the $30 and one-third rule reduced work effort.

Murray summed up *Losing Ground* with a list of grievances specific to AFDC as well as what he took to be a series of troubling assumptions behind economic redistribution generally, along with several patterns he asserted to be so-called laws of social policy—including critiques that the involuntary redistribution of money, in the form of taxes to support public assistance programs, was tantamount to robbery, and that the perverse incentives embodied by welfare mean that nonmarket efforts to help the poor inevitably do more harm than good. In the final analysis, Murray offered an argument, presented as a thought experiment, for the complete elimination of welfare programs, sparing unemployment insurance due to its contributory nature. This would force working-age people to either work or rely on local charities, which presumably would make normative decisions about deservingness on a case-by-case basis. The previously welfare-dependent would regain their social status as independent persons.

Despite the social-science trappings of much of Murray's work, many of his arguments proved factually flawed. Some critics insisted they were mostly wrong.[38] Perhaps most glaring was Murray's assertion that allowing working parents to disregard a portion of their earned income in determining eligibility—under the $30 and one-third rule—would depress work effort. Nearly all the states recognized the positive incentive of this rule, and most adopted expanded versions of it in the 1990s, discounting an even greater portion of earned income in an effort to smooth welfare recipients' transition into full-time work.[39] Further, numerous studies found increases in work effort once this rule went into effect. Also, according to Murray, because welfare caseloads move in parallel with benefit levels, enrollment should have fallen dramatically through the late 1970s as benefits lost purchasing power. However, they did not. Many other examples of contrary evidence exist. Most social scientists have come to judge Murray's work as much more of a political broadside than as a piece of serious scholarship.

In a very real sense, however, Murray's analytical mistakes are beside the point. *Losing Ground* resonated powerfully with conservatives of a libertarian bent and provided a rationale for welfare retrenchment at a time when the Reagan administration and many states were highly sympathetic to such a move. By the late 1980s, a near consensus on work requirements and child support enforcement would emerge, substantially bridging the gap between liberals and conservatives—at least in Congress—on those specific issues.

The power of *Losing Ground* lay in its use of the conventions of liberal policy analysis—objective statistics and the like—to undermine liberal goals. As the intellectual historian Alice O'Connor put it, "behind Murray's tables of aggregate statistics was a highly charged political tale of social policy gone wrong."[40] Appearing dispassionate, Murray advanced an ideological crusade that was anything but. Adding to its influence, *Losing Ground* appeared at a time when states were beginning to explore both additional services for welfare recipients, such as Massachusetts' Education and Training program, and to condition welfare on work, as illustrated by California's Greater Avenues to Independence program. While few politicians endorsed Murray's suggestion for a complete abolition of welfare, his writing made other less dramatic proposals, such as mandated work in exchange for welfare, or workfare, seem more reasonable than they otherwise might have.

If Murray's libertarianism was too strong for some, a more neoconservative argument from Lawrence Mead in *Beyond Entitlement,* laying out a case for stiffer obligations to be imposed on welfare recipients, found a receptive audience among both federal and state lawmakers before the 1980s came to a close.[41] An important part of Mead's objections to the American welfare state was how permissive it was, not how large it was. Neoconservatives, born of disillusionment with the perceived excesses of liberalism during the era of the Great Society, were, after all, attempting to "repeal the 1960s, not the New Deal."[42]

Neoconservatives, or liberals who had been "mugged by reality" in Irving Kristol's formulation, were frequently former liberals who had become disaffected with what they saw as the excesses of liberalism during the 1960s, splitting away from the Left, and who generally supported a welfare state but one that insisted on minimizing what they saw as destructive incentives of excessive social provision.[43] These thinkers, including some prominent experts on welfare policy such as Daniel Patrick Moynihan, believed their former colleagues held significantly exaggerated impressions of what government could achieve.[44] Mead fit squarely within this camp and made a compelling case for imposing obligations on welfare recipients, arguing that benefiting from welfare should trigger a responsibility on the part of the recipient to accept available employment and, more generally, to play by the rules. If society is to support poor people through welfare, those people should give back through hard work, law abidingness, and responsible personal behavior. In this work and his follow-up book in 1992, *The New Politics of Poverty,* Mead carefully avoided engaging in a culture-of-poverty argument and instead emphasized the relationship between regular employment and economic stability.

Advancing a parallel line of thinking was Harvard professor Nathan Glazer. A partner in the neoconservative journal *The Public Interest* with

Daniel Bell and Irving Kristol, Glazer envisioned what he and others took to be a more rational approach to welfare provision, one that self-consciously acknowledged the limits of government intervention in the market and that envisioned poor people as quite capable of responding to positive economic incentives. In his 1988 book *The Limits of Social Policy,* Glazier argued that when government-funded welfare programs displace more traditional, community-based institutions, they make matters worse, not better.[45] Ironically, in our attempts to ameliorate poverty, welfare teaches people to rely on it instead of strengthening their own self-reliance, goes this argument.

Echoing a sentiment was a post-mortem on the War on Poverty by Lance Liebman in *The Public Interest.* Liebman argued that social provision generally—cash assistance, health provision, and the like—artificially raised popular expectations about how much comfort people ought to enjoy, compliments of the government.[46] Thus, regardless of how much poverty actually exists, rising expectations continually expand the degree of perceived disadvantage and under-privilege. The revolution of equality that began in the 1960s ensures that our sense of inequality will only grow more severe. Pursuing a solution only makes the problem look worse. None of this is to say that Glazer and those like him were completely opposed to welfare. He had supported a modified version of President Nixon's Family Assistance Plan—one including stricter work requirements—when it was pending before Congress. This was more than many other conservatives at the time could bring themselves to tolerate. The emphasis on reciprocal obligations, however, made all the difference for neoconservatives like Glazer.

If Glazer exhibited a big faith in the rationality of the poor to respond appropriately to constructive incentives, social scientist Neil Gilbert challenged that assertion. He called not for the abolition of welfare as had some other conservatives of a more libertarian persuasion, but rather for stiffer requirements to accompany welfare receipt in what eventually came to be viewed as a new paternalism. Gilbert challenged the assumption that the vast majority of parents—rich and poor—were competent to raise their children without outside supervision. This assumption of competence had, combined with burgeoning caseloads, dissuaded welfare agencies since the early 1970s from conducting regular home visits. Gilbert argued that young mothers required structured guidance in child rearing and that institutional living might be appropriate. He denied that his argument was one for a return to the poorhouse, but the thrust of his essay certainly leaned toward a modern version of that type of group home.[47]

The weight of these conservative but strong-government arguments resulted from their ability to tap into a powerful but largely underappreciated point, at least among liberals. There was a desire to save money by cutting social spending, but there was a stronger urge to do no harm with dollars spent on social policy. In his February 1981 address to a joint session of Congress, Reagan touted the estimated $520 million that would be saved in fiscal year 1982 by tightening welfare eligibility and the estimated $1.6 billion that would be saved by curtailing the federally subsidized school lunch program.[48] However, the overriding concern among the public and ultimately among conservative politicians had more to do with the social, rather than the fiscal, implications of welfare reforms. This point, however, was difficult to recognize at the time.

The decade of the 1980s witnessed growing income and wealth disparities between rich and poor. A survey of households in Los Angeles, for instance, showed that over that decade, the number of households earning $50,000 or more annually nearly tripled from 9 percent to 26 percent, and that the number of households earning less than $15,000 annually also increased, from 30 percent to 40 percent.[49] Nationwide, between 1980 and 1990, the income of the poorest one-fifth declined by 5.2 percent (adjusted for inflation), and that of the richest one-fifth rose by 32.5 percent.[50] In this context, cuts in welfare at the national level combined with a sense in the popular culture—perhaps best evidenced by the 1987 movie *Wall Street* ("greed is good," opined Michael Douglas's character)—that Republicans were out to stiff the poor, left many if not most liberals viewing new restrictions on welfare as an effort to do away with the federal program. This impression was almost certainly fostered by Reagan's proposal in the early 1980s to cede federal control over the program in exchange for the federal government assuming full responsibility for the Medicaid program—the so-called great swap, an effort that ultimately failed. In time, however, strongly stated free-market capitalist arguments rallied a scant following outside of the circles of ideologically charged policy advocates. Instead, what the public took away from the 1980s debate over welfare was strong support for obligations of citizenship to be tied to welfare receipt. Work and law-abiding behavior should accompany welfare receipt. Poor women should clearly see incentives to limit their fertility while dependent on public aid. Policy should foster an expectation that welfare will be a helping hand in time of need, not a way of life. Objections over how welfare dollars were spent, not that they were spent at all, came to comprise a core element of congressional action on the Family Support Act of 1988 and public sentiment on welfare by about the same time.[51]

## POLICY CHANGES IN WELFARE

Ronald Reagan entered office in 1981 with several key goals, among them to curtail social welfare spending and to shift greater responsibility for welfare to the states. Reagan argued extensively for a new federalist relationship in which select powers would devolve to state governments. The impetus for this was at least two-fold. First, Republicans were coming to hold more governorships by that time, so the devolution would put power in the hands of the president's ideological kin. Second, as a former governor, Reagan saw advantage in moving social policy closer to the front lines. The pro-devolution argument that close government is good government and that policy makers closest to the problems should be allowed to create solutions to those problems was, at that time, mainstream Republican doctrine. The administration clearly did not believe in a one-size-fits-all model of welfare administration. Robert Charleson, a welfare advisor to Reagan, commented in 1986 that "I don't believe it's possible for the federal government to run a workfare program. . . . The country is too big, with too many variations in the labor market. Detailed federal regulations won't work for New York City and rural Idaho and Puerto Rico at the same time."[52] The argument for devolution was, in part, a softened version of earlier states' rights doctrine coming out of the Civil Rights era. This line of reasoning would not continue to square with (pro–federal government) Republican legislation beyond the late-1990s.

A second rationale for devolution to state governments was that it would curtail direct federal aid to cities, most of which were still controlled by Democratic leadership and their labor union allies. Not all of the administration's policies would cut strings that had bound the state governments, and the frequency of federal laws preempting certain state actions would increase through the 1980s. But with regard to welfare, states were granted greater authority to craft programs more to their liking than had been allowed in the past.[53] If this new federalism was embraced by Congress and the administration, it was not always fully integrated in the thinking of the general public. Polls during this period often revealed an apparent public desire to have it both ways: greater state discretion but continued federal financial backing.[54]

Two important pieces of federal legislation during the 1980s set states on what would prove to be a bumpy and indirect course toward greater state control over welfare programs. The first was the 1981 Omnibus Budget Reconciliation Act. The second was the Family Support Act of 1988.

With Reagan's first budget, AFDC eligibility was limited by lowering income standards and allowing states to begin mandatory work programs for certain adult recipients. An immediately significant change was the reduction of the income ceiling for AFDC eligibility. Prior to this act, states were prohibited from using federal dollars to pay cash benefits to families with incomes above 185 percent of a state's need standard. (The need standard was the minimum amount of income a state determined that a family of a given size needed to get by.) In 1981 the ceiling was lowered to 150 percent.

Furthermore, the rule allowing a portion of a family's earned income to be disregarded for eligibility computation purposes, an incentive to enter the workforce, even if only gradually, was limited to the first four months of employment. Under this new regime, aid recipients were expected to make their transitions to full-time employment in short order. The net effect of these changes was an elimination of assistance to many working poor families. AFDC usage during the first quarter of 1982 was 3 percent lower than the previous quarter and over 8 percent lower than the first quarter of 1981. The reductions saved the federal and state governments some $1.1 billion but came at a high price for thousands of families (estimated as a loss of $1,555 in benefits per AFDC family during 1983). As a result, some 408,000 families lost eligibility, and another 299,000 families saw their benefits reduced.[55] Congress restored some of these cuts in 1984.

The 1981 legislation also provided states greater opportunity to innovate with their welfare programs. Amendments to AFDC law in 1962 had created a mechanism by which states could seek permission to innovate outside the conventional parameters of federal law.[56] The 1981 amendments eased the way for states to use this provision. Waivers granted under section 1115 of the Social Security Act allowed states, within bounds, to innovate with their welfare-to-work programs and in other areas. A state's innovations were not permitted to increase the federal cost for that state's AFDC program above what it would have been in the absence of the pilot project. This posed an obvious limitation on the level of up-front investment states could afford to make in welfare-to-work efforts. Within these boundaries, states adopted a number of strategies, including job searches, job training, employability training, and paid and unpaid community-service work.[57]

By 1985 California became the first to mandate workfare. Designated aid recipients were required to look for and accept work as a condition of their continued AFDC eligibility. Other states followed. Taking a different tack, Massachusetts used the opportunity to create an elaborate, voluntary education and training program. The innovation opportunities worked politically for the Reagan administration, bolstering its devolution credentials, and also for governors, who could tout their welfare reforms. Many other innovations were undertaken, involving everything from minor administrative reforms— simplifying reporting requirements and the like—to relaxing family composition requirements in efforts to remove incentives for family dissolution.

Lessons learned through these pilot programs helped create a new set of expectations about welfare recipients seeking and finding work. By 1988, 45 states were either operating or developing pilot projects to enhance their welfare-to-work programs.[58] The result, after nearly two years of negotiations in Congress, was the Family Support Act of 1988. This law accelerated innovation in the states because, for the first time, states faced hard targets for placing aid recipients in work.

## LINGERING ISSUES OF DEBATE THROUGH THE LATE 1980s

Although some pointed to this moment of agreement in Congress on work and child support enforcement as one of consensus between liberals and conservatives, the furor over both issues continued in other quarters. Liberals argued that extracting child support from low-income fathers, under threat of jail sentences, was unlikely to be successful and was indeed counterproductive. Forcing poor fathers to pay child support was, from this perspective, akin to efforts to squeeze blood from a turnip. Instead, employment assistance programs would help those fathers become more economically stable, rendering them more likely to support their children. In cases where absent fathers—dubbed deadbeat dads—were located and pressed for support, their poverty would make them unlikely to be able to pay and would often contribute stress to any existing relationship between the father and caretaker mother. Jailing noncompliant fathers, a tactic used around the nation, including a sweep of 549 fathers in the predawn hours of December 11, 1990, in New Jersey, marked the aggressive end of the scale of states' responses.[59] Other states garnished wages, publicized most-wanted lists, and suspended hunting and fishing licenses of delinquent fathers.

Another point of contention focused on the declining value of welfare benefits. As the 1980s progressed, the purchasing power of AFDC checks lost ground against inflation in most states, squeezing single parents. This led many if not most welfare parents to augment their household budgets with unreported income earned through off-the-books employment. Interviewing 50 female welfare recipients in Chicago during 1988, urban affairs specialist Kathryn Edin found that not one of the women she interviewed was able to live on her welfare check, and that most of them supplemented their budgets with undeclared earned income. This work ranged from babysitting to employment under assumed names to drug sales to prostitution. This evidence of cheating poses a conundrum for both liberals and conservatives. Liberals can point to the inadequacy of welfare payments and insist that they be increased, but in doing so, they have to confront the morally compromised nature of women on welfare. Conservatives can point to the cheating as evidence of the corrupted ways of poor welfare-dependent mothers, but they also have to admit that welfare payments are so stingy that they apparently force women into selling drugs on the side, work that Edin found earns the women only about $4 per hour. In addition to being illegal, the work is dangerous. One of Edin's subjects was murdered shortly after she was interviewed, apparently by her drug supplier over a money dispute.[60]

**Table 5.2.**
**Estimates of minimum necessary income compared with actual welfare grants.**

"What is the smallest amount of money a family of four (husband, wife, and two children) needs each week to get along in this community?"

| Date of survey | Median estimate of minimum income needed by a family per month* | Actual monthly income of average family of four on welfare (welfare grant plus value of food stamp benefit) | Welfare grant for a family of four (national average) | Food stamp benefit per month for a family of four (national average) |
|---|---|---|---|---|
| October 1969 | $516 | $186 | $159* | $26.52 |
| December 1970 | $542 | $220.20 | $178 | $42.20 |
| January 1975 | $692 | $295.60 | $210 | $85.60 |
| January 1980 | $1,075 | $411.88 | $274 | $137.88 |
| January 1984 | $1,290 | $492.96 | $322 | $170.96 |
| January 1985 | $1,299 | $518.96 | $339 | $179.96 |

*Source:* Average monthly AFDC benefit for family of four, from *1990 Green Book: Overview of Entitlement Programs,* U.S. House Ways and Means Committee, p. 4563, table 13. Food stamp figures from U.S. Department of Agriculture (http://www.fns.usda.gov/pd/fssummar.htm).
Note: Monthly welfare figure equals weekly estimate multiplied by 4.3.
* Average AFDC grant for 1969 estimated by multiplying the average cash grant per recipient by 4 (from *Advance Release of Statistics on Public Assistance,* table 6, January 1968, U.S. Department of Health, Education, and Welfare).

Paralleling Edin's evidence of insufficient welfare benefits is a finding from the Gallup Poll. Since the early 1960s, the Gallup Organization has asked Americans to estimate the minimum amount of money a family of four would need to get by in the community where poll respondents live. The median estimates appear in Table 5.2. Figures also show the actual average monthly welfare payment. After accounting for the value of food stamps, estimates of minimum expenses remained more than two times the amount of average public aid benefits between 1961 and 1985. These data suggest that if the public knew how frugal welfare checks were, it would support increases in aid.

Complementing this finding, another survey, this one asking respondents whether most welfare families receive about the right amount of aid versus too much help, the plurality of respondents (after the mid-1980s, the majority of them) said most welfare families receive "more than they need." This question was asked four times between 1984 and 1994. Clearly, most people are unaware of the amount that welfare checks actually provide, but they still resent what they perceive as a large amount of money being spent on welfare. Interpreting such polling data requires caution. Asking about spending on "welfare" versus spending on "assistance to the poor" renders very different responses. The difference across these two versions of the question is typically in the 40 percentage point range.[61] Similarly, Figure 5.1 shows the distinction Americans draw between "people on welfare" and "poor people," as measured by the American National Election Studies. People on welfare elicit significantly less sympathy, with respondents reporting, on average, a so-called thermometer rating that is about 20 points lower on a 0 to 100 scale (with 100 being the warmest). Clearly, over this period, Americans drew a distinction between those who may need assistance and those who actually avail themselves of it. That public support varies so dramatically based on question wording implies a broad rhetorical battleground for advocates of various ideological stripes on this issue. Rhetoric and question framing are not completely controlling, but they play a major role in determining winners and losers.[62]

## CHANGED THINKING ON WOMEN IN THE WORKFORCE

In addition to the racially charged discourse about inner-city poverty and state-level innovations to address welfare dependence, one of the most important developments that affected the welfare debate during the 1970s

**Table 5.3.**
**Public opinion: Too much welfare, or not enough?**

"What do you consider a more serious problem in America today—families not getting enough welfare to get by, or families getting more welfare benefits than they need?"
(Nationally representative surveys by CBS/*New York Times.* Cell entries are percentages.)

|  | September 1984 | August 1988 | May 1992 | January 1994 |
|---|---|---|---|---|
| Not enough | 29 | 25 | 31 | 21 |
| More than they need | 49 | 55 | 51 | 58 |
| Both (volunteered response) | 10 | 9 | 7 | 10 |
| Neither (volunteered response) | 3 | 3 | 2 | 2 |
| Don't know/ no answer | 10 | 9 | 9 | 8 |

*Source:* Survey data from the Roper Center's Public Opinion On-Line database, available via Lexis-Nexis.

**Figure 5.1**
**Thermometer ratings for "poor people" and "people on welfare."**

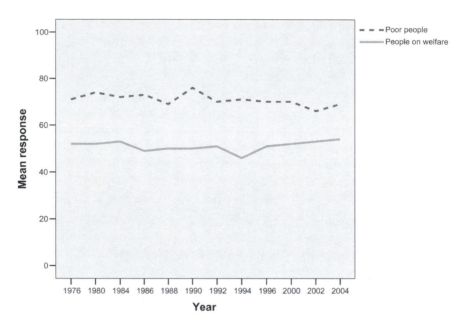

*Source:* American National Election Studies.

and 1980s was the movement of women into the paid workforce, a trend that had begun in the early twentieth century but which accelerated in the 1950s. The percentage of women working outside the home rose from 43 percent in 1970 to 59 percent in 2005.[63] While women still earn less than men, even for comparable work, their widespread entry into the labor market has reached into every corner of American life. Almost certainly as a consequence of this shift, the percentage of Americans who say they approve of married women working outside the home rose from 60 percent in a 1970 Gallup poll to 81 percent of respondents to the 1998 General Social Survey.[64] That support is stronger among the college educated than among those without college degrees, but it is high among both groups.

With the entry of women into the labor market has come strong support for work mandates for welfare mothers, including those with young children. Registration for training and employment programs has been mandatory under federal law for welfare parents with children over six years of age since 1967, through recipients were not actually required to work on a widespread basis until the 1980s. Public opinion polls have not followed this issue systematically through time, but by the early 1990s, a majority of Americans believed welfare mothers should be required to work instead of staying home to care for their children. A December 1995 CBS/*New York Times* poll found that 67 percent of respondents favored this. Of course, this is a far cry from the rationale for mothers' pensions in the early twentieth century, which were based on the idea that single mothers' time was best spent at home nurturing their children. At that early time, relatively few women, married or single, worked outside the home. An estimated 5 percent of married women were employed in 1890, and by 1920, that figure was still below 20 percent.[65] The reluctance in recent years to shelter single parents from the labor market, and instead to require them to work, facilitated a dramatic welfare policy shift through the 1980s and 1990s toward mandated work, even for women with very young children.

Through the same period that increasing numbers of welfare mothers were required to work, poverty in America was taking on an increasingly female face. Several factors were responsible for this feminization of poverty. Growing rates of family dissolution meant women, who earn less than men, were increasingly saddled with the burden of both raising children and financially supporting their households. A second factor in play through the mid-1970s was that women were systematically underrepresented on the rolls of unemployment insurance. In many states, eligibility for unemployment insurance was contingent on an applicant's willingness to work full-time, so pregnancy put this program out of reach. Also, because many women worked in marginal industries—piecework at home, bartenders, day-care providers, and the like—they were not as eligible as men for unemployment insurance. One outcome was that many women turned to welfare in lieu of more mainstream social insurance. However, relying on AFDC and food stamps has historically left most aid recipients deep in poverty. Since the early 1970s, the value of AFDC and food stamps combined has declined as a percentage of the federal poverty level, from 93 percent in 1972 to only 65 percent in 1994.[66]

Even among those women who do work full time and year-round, their earnings are significantly lower than those of men, even in comparable professions. This is due to a series of factors. Interruptions in one's career to birth children, the pejorative mommy track, is said to dampen employers' willingness to invest in high-quality training for female relative to male employees. Gender discrimination surely plays a role as well, though statistical models typically do not include this variable, as it is difficult to measure, leaving instead a portion of the gender gap in earnings unexplained.[67] All this combines to create systematically lower wages for women, which makes them less able to save for a rainy day, which, in turn, makes them more vulnerable to have to rely on welfare in lean times.

## LESSONS LEARNED

For those on the political Left, there was a bitterness about the collapse of the liberal consensus and the War on Poverty. While some of them became neoconservatives in the late 1960s and adopted a limited view of government intervention in the economy, others remained unreconstructed liberals and insisted that the answer to the question of whether the War on Poverty worked was unknown because a serious war was never waged.[68] This sentiment was shared by some neoconservatives in recognizing how irrational it was to hope for sweeping change through limited budgets.[69] The failure of the Model Cities program illustrates this point. However the political class shifted and morphed through the 1970s and 1980s, certainly a broad swath of Americans came to see excess in wide-ranging government efforts to eliminate poverty. Resentful in the sense that money may have been wasted through community action programs, urban renewal, and enhanced welfare eligibility, a growing percentage of the public opposed increased welfare spending and supported efforts to compel welfare recipients to work in exchange for their dwindling cash benefits.

The shift in federalism through the 1980s in particular was modest at the time but foreshadowed greater changes to come. By the late 1980s, a fairly clear sense prevailed that states could craft welfare programs to meet local particularities better than the federal government could design a one-size-fits-all policy. Liberals recognized that this new federalism would allow states to undermine some of the guarantees those on the Left had successfully fought for during the 1960s and early 1970s, but conservatives knew equally well that state designs would likely result in less emphasis on redistribution and more on work, imposition of local mores, and the political ability to claim partisan victories. The late 1980s would see the passage of the Family Support Act, with an emphasis on mandatory work as a condition of welfare receipt. Efforts to implement this federal law would drive a wave of state-level welfare innovations, which in turn brought about even more dramatic federal legislation in the mid-1990s.

## NOTES

1. See Harrington 1962, p. 16, for brief elaboration of the thrust of the point, though Harrington describes the Hemingway passage incorrectly.
2. Trattner 1999, chap. 15.
3. Ornstein et al. 2002, p. 174, for voting coalition data.
4. U.S. House of Representatives Committee on Ways and Means 1992.
5. O'Connor 2004, p. 80; Ginzberg and Solow 1974a, p. 10.
6. Katz 1989, p. 216.

7. Judy Mann, "Paying for Ignorance and Too Many Children," *Washington Post,* April 22, 1987, p. B-3.

8. Chickering 1972, p. 392.

9. Chickering 1972, pp. 392.

10. van den Haag 1968, p. 1261.

11. Al Donalson, "Pay the Poor," *Pittsburgh Post-Gazette,* October 25, 1998, p. B-4; see also O'Connor 2004, chap. 4.

12. Caraley 1992.

13. Gans 1995, chap. 2; Sawhill 1989.

14. Lemann 1986b, pp. 32–33.

15. Wilson 1991.

16. Wilson 1987, pp. 46, 55.

17. Gilens 1999.

18. Auletta 1982.

19. Katz 1989, p. 201.

20. *King v. Smith* (1968).

21. Nathan 1987.

22. Wilson 1987, especially chap. 2; see Kain 1968 for early research on this idea.

23. Diamond 1997.

24. Jencks and Edin 1990, p. 31.

25. Lemann 1986b, p. 67.

26. Wilson 1991.

27. Kaus 1986, p. 22.

28. O'Connor 2004, p. 119.

29. O'Connor 2001, pp. 244–47; Lane 1985.

30. Sheils 1981, p. 64.

31. Ibid.; August Heckscher, "The Unexpected Return," *Christian Science Monitor,* March 13, 1981, home forum sec., p. 20; A. O. Sulzberger Jr., "Dole Might Just Prefer His Own Ideas on Tax Cut," *New York Times,* May 10, 1981, sec. 4, p. 4.

32. Gilder 1981, p. 68.

33. Ibid., p. 69.

34. Ibid., p. 68.

35. O'Connor 2004, p. 112.

36. Gelernter 1996.

37. Lane 1985.

38. Jencks 1992; Lieberman 1998, chap. 6; O'Connor 2001, chap. 10.

39. Lieberman and Shaw 2000.

40. O'Connor 2001, p. 247.

41. Murray 1997.

42. Dorrien 1993, p. 16.

43. Podhoretz 1996, p. 20, quoting Kristol's self-description.

44. O'Connor 2004, pp. 98, 102.

45. Glazer 1988.

46. Liebman 1974.

47. Gilbert 1987.

48. *Public Papers of the Presidents of the United States, 1981,* February 18, p. 111. Ronald Reagan's address to joint session of Congress, pp. 108-115. Washington, DC: General Services Administration.

49. Davis 1990, p. 7.

50. Rose 1995, p. 127 (citing data from the Congressional Budget Office).

51. Public Agenda Foundation 1996.

52. Lemann 1986b, pp. 65–66.

53. Zimmerman 1991.

54. Shaw and Reinhart 2001.

55. U.S. House of Representatives, Committee on Ways and Means, 1987; Heclo 2001, p. 182.

56. Gallup-Black 1997.

57. Gueron and Pauly 1991.

58. Congressional Budget Office 1987.

59. Paul Taylor, "Delinquent Dads: When Child Support Lags, 'Deadbeats' May Go to Jail," *Washington Post,* December 16, 1990, p. A-1.

60. Edin 1991; Jencks and Edin 1990.

61. Smith 1987; Shaw and Shapiro 2002, 2005.

62. Lakoff 2002.

63. U.S. Department of Labor, Bureau of Labor Statistics. "Employment status of the civilian noninstitutionalized population 16 years and over by sex, 1970-2005 annual averages," data available on-line at http://www.bls.gov/cps/wlf-table2-2006.pdf (accessed June 22, 2007).

64. Identical wording of questions in both surveys. The General Social Survey is conducted by the National Opinion Research Center at the University of Chicago. See Teles 1998, p. 56, for data by education.

65. Okin 1989, p. 140; Pearce 1978.

66. U.S. House of Representatives Committee on Ways and Means 2000; U.S. Department of Agriculture, Food and Nutrition Services data available online at www.fns.usda.gov/pd/fssummarhtm; accessed July 2, 2007; Pearce 1978.

67. General Accounting Office, "Work Patterns Partially Explain Difference between Men's and Women's Earnings" (report no. GAO-04-35) October 2003.

68. Hodgson 1976, p. 476.

69. Ginzberg and Solow 1974b, p. 216.

# 6

# The End of Welfare Entitlement

In 1964 the famous war on poverty was declared and a funny thing happened. Poverty, as measured by dependency, stopped shrinking and then actually began to grow worse. I guess you could say poverty won the war. . . . The welfare tragedy has gone on too long. It is time to reshape our welfare system so that it can be judged by how many Americans it makes independent of welfare.

—Ronald Reagan (1986)[1]

The mid-to-late 1980s witnessed a substantial convergence of thinking on welfare. Neoconservatives and neoliberals, the latter typically involving centrist Democrats, came together to form a broad middle ground that supported aggressive action to move welfare recipients into training and employment programs.[2] The legislation that coalition produced in 1988 certainly drew criticism from those farther out on the left and right, but it represented thinking that was broadly embraced by the general public, a large majority of members of Congress, the Reagan administration, and many policy experts. The product was the Family Support Act of 1988, which in turn set up a chain of state-level reforms that ultimately opened the way for legislation in 1996 that in Bill Clinton's formulation, "ended welfare as we knew it."[3]

Aside from growing public frustration with welfare, stoked by journalistic accounts of fraud and abuse, many scholars also changed the way they thought and talked about people on public assistance during the 1980s. A series of quantitative studies linked single-motherhood with heightened rates of poverty, teen pregnancy, low academic achievement, and other problems. By the late 1980s, welfare use was, by and large, no longer discussed as an outcome of structural problems in the economy, but rather as a form of dependency that called out for aggressive policy interventions. Liberals contributed to this changed discourse about as much as did conservatives. For example, a 1983 research paper by Harvard University welfare analysts Mary Jo Bane and David Ellwood, one that was widely read in the analyst community, measured the length of welfare spells by recipients and concluded that the conventional wisdom of welfare use as a mostly transitory experience needed revision. They found that over long spans of time, most people who used welfare did so for short periods, less than two years. However, at any given moment, most of the people on welfare were long-term users who had drawn assistance for more than two years. Together with persons returning to welfare after a period of self sufficiency, long-term users accounted for nearly two-thirds of the overall costs of welfare.[4] One might think of this phenomenon using a hospital bed analogy. If a 100-bed hospital sees two-thirds of its beds occupied on any given day by long-term patients and the other one-third by short-term patients who rotate through every few days, over the course of a year, short-term patients will dramatically outnumber long-term patients, but that core of long-term patients will still make up most of the people in the hospital on any given day. The implication was that many welfare recipients were not simply ordinary people who had temporarily fallen on hard times, but rather chronic users. Largely a result of these findings and others like them, the language of *welfare dependency* gained substantial currency in the mass media and among analysts and politicians. Once this vocabulary took hold, the idea of aggressive interventions to break cycles of poverty no longer seemed so controversial to most policy makers. Ronald Reagan's choice to speak of welfare's existence as a "tragedy," instead of a legitimate part of the social safety net, was indicative of the dearth of public support for the program. Forces gathered for something to be done.

Within the terms of this new consensus, liberals and conservatives found substantial agreement regarding changes to welfare policy. Once defined chiefly as a problem of dependency, designing incentives to steer poor people off welfare became the chief goal. This served as the story line in wide-ranging conversations involving state governors, members of Congress, the Reagan administration, policy analysts, and the public. The earlier concern about single mothers as caretakers of children, challenged only marginally in the 1967 amendments to AFDC law and put increasingly to test through the mid-1980s under state demonstration projects, ceased to be a stumbling block for most policy makers. As Pat Moynihan, the prime Senate sponsor of welfare reform, remarked at the beginning of the process, it is "now the normal experience of mothers to work, at least part time."[5] Of course, employers who rely on low-skilled workers also favored the prospect of millions of people willing to work for low wages.

That many states had already charted some of the terrain of welfare-to-work programs simplified Congress's work when it considered reforms in early 1986. Congress could benefit from lessons learned in the states. California, with its Greater Avenues to Independence program, and Massachusetts, through its Employment and Training Choices program, had tested mandatory and voluntary work and education provisions, respectively. The former had shown significant results in terms of participants' earned income.[6] These demonstration projects convinced governors that moving forward with new congressional legislation to open the way for state innovation was preferable to piecemeal reform under waivers that had to be laboriously solicited from the federal government.

The idea of tearing down the safety net, as proposed by Charles Murray, had found friends within the Reagan administration, but not many among policy experts or the general public. A May 1992 poll by Yankelovich, Clancy, and Shulman registered 93 percent opposition to efforts to "eliminate all welfare programs entirely."[7] By contrast, the neoconservative ground occupied by those advocating mandatory work in exchange for assistance found favor in many quarters. This line of argument—that the poor should meet certain responsibilities of citizenship in exchange for the assistance they receive—appeared relatively reasonable compared to the more stridently conservative alternatives. Those who still wanted to eliminate welfare ran into the reality that Democrats controlled Congress (after 1986) and that they would have to settle for workfare rather than an abolition of welfare altogether.

The consensus on welfare did not prevent Congress from debating the matter for nearly two years before producing a bill for the president to sign. Disagreements over work incentives versus requirements lay at the center of the debate. Most congressional Democrats supported voluntary incentives to steer welfare recipients into jobs. The administration insisted on mandatory work requirements. The president ultimately got his way. Time-limited welfare eligibility, a secondary discussion that had been raised in several states, would have to wait until state demonstration projects in the early 1990s.

Supporters of voluntary incentives for welfare recipients took the position that the skills imparted through such programs should be directly relevant to the labor market. From this perspective, forcing adults into fast-food jobs does them little good in either the short or the long term. The minimum wage they are likely to earn there is not enough to lift the average family out of poverty, and the experience of flipping burgers hardly enhances one's resume. In the blunt words of Massachusetts Welfare Commissioner Charles Atkins, "sweeping streets or cleaning buildings doesn't do shit for preparing someone to go and get in a job in the private sector."[8]

On the other side, supporters of hard-work requirements viewed them as opportunities to teach important life skills. As commentator Mickey Kaus wrote in 1986,

Workfare should not be a short-term program to existing welfare clients, but a long-term program to destroy the culture of poverty. In this 'hard' view, what's most important is not whether sweeping streets or cleaning buildings helps Betsy Smith, single teenage parent and high school dropout, learn skills that will help her find a private sector job. It is whether the prospect of sweeping streets and cleaning buildings for a welfare grant will deter Betsy Smith from having the illegitimate child that drops her out of school and onto welfare in the fist place—or, failing that, whether the *sight* of Betsy Smith sweeping streets after having her illegitimate child will discourage her younger sisters and neighbors from doing as she did.[9]

Another point of disagreement arose over the extent of transitional supports for those attempting to leave welfare. Liberals wanted to ensure these bridges, such as public-sector jobs, for those pushed off welfare. Fiscal conservatives separated from their erstwhile ideological kin at this point. Most Americans supported the idea of spending more money in order to help welfare recipients move to independence. Public opinion polls through this time found strong support for increased spending in order to move poor people off welfare and into jobs. Even after public frustration with welfare had reached its peak in 1994, a *USA Today* survey found that 68 percent of respondents expressed their willingness to "pay more taxes for a system that would get people off welfare," compared to only 27 percent who would not.[10] Neoconservative columnist Mickey Kaus, who admitted not having the stomach for eliminating welfare outright, wrote in 1986 that these short-term interventions to implement workfare would likely cost more. But he asked rhetorically, "Who cares? The point isn't to save money."[11] Many fiscal conservatives disagreed, but they tended to downplay that part of their agenda.

## THE FAMILY SUPPORT ACT OF 1988

Following up on conversations with members of the Senate Finance Committee, who had begun considering welfare reform in the spring of 1986, the National Governors' Association, then chaired by Arkansas Governor Bill Clinton, transmitted a set of recommendations to Congress after its summer 1986 meeting.[12] These suggestions, endorsed by 49 of the 50 governors, formed the basis of much discussion on Capitol Hill over the next year and a half. The state executives were particularly interested in a jobs program that would divert would-be welfare recipients from enrolling on public assistance in the first place. Clinton said of the plan that "this is an old-fashioned conservative idea that advances investment rather than maintenance."[13] Conservative or not, the governors' bipartisan plan would have been expensive, an estimated one to two billion dollars per year. Delaware Republican Governor Michael Castle, chair of the governors' task force on welfare prevention, enthusiastically endorsed what he called a shift from "primarily an income-support system to a job program with an income component."[14] The governors envisioned a series of transitional supports, including extended Medicaid, help with day care and transportation expenses, and enforced child support orders in place to encourage poor people to avail themselves of the education and training programs as a path away from welfare. The governors found an ally in Senator Moynihan. In keeping with his long-held attitudes toward what he saw as traditional welfare's permissiveness, he believed that welfare in its current state placed too much emphasis on income maintenance and too little on job preparation.[15] Moynihan's expertise on social policy and his moderate ideology gave him the credibility to lead in bipartisan fashion.

After some 20 months of negotiation, Congress produced a bill that required states, over the next three years, to place 20 percent of their AFDC recipients into training positions or jobs. The White House prevailed in its quest to make job preparation mandatory, not voluntary. Though opposed by a majority of congressional Democrats, the president's insistence and the seeming imperative to pass bill opened the way for sticks in addition to carrots to be made part of the new law.[16]

Most observers commended the Family Support Act. The *New York Times* celebrated the law's passage in an editorial, approvingly commenting on how this legislation altered the social contract between the government and the poor, and that injecting an element of training, work requirements (16 hours a week), extended Medicaid, and child-care subsidies would bring about a long overdue reform of a broken system.[17] In retrospect, some of the governors remained dissatisfied with the new law owing to the constraints it placed on state governments. Delaware's Castle stated that "the proposed rules will actually force significant changes in current programs, often the very programs that served as the models for the law itself."[18] Despite this, states enthusiastically set to work crafting welfare-to-work plans under the new Job Opportunities and Basic Skills program with the help of just over three billion new dollars from Congress. Critics raised concerns over what they saw as the detrimental effects of forcing mothers of young children into the labor market during "the most precious years of childhood," but in hindsight these work requirements, imposed on parents of children over age three, came to seem like a modest step.[19]

To the extent that history credits the passage of the Family Support Act with redirecting the nation's efforts on moving welfare recipients into jobs, most of that credit should go to state governments for their initiatives under the law. Despite growing caseloads due to the economic recession of 1990–1991, the Bush administration exerted very little effort to advance welfare reform initiatives during that period. Following rather unproductive discussions with poverty workers in the spring of 1992, one White House official characterized the president's effort as, "keep playing with the same toys, but let's paint them a little shinier."[20]

## STATES INNOVATE UNDER WAIVERS

In response to the Family Support Act, states became the primary drivers of welfare reform. Innovations grew both in number and scope and were driven by the economic recession that began shortly after the passage of the law.[21] Three types of innovations stand out in this respect. Work requirements became more sweeping. Wisconsin emerged as a leader. That state's 1993 Work-Not-Welfare demonstration required recipients in two counties to participate in work, education, or training activities in exchange for their cash benefits. Wisconsin's initiative garnered significant national attention and was followed by 37 state demonstrations involving similar requirements over the next two years. Incentives to preserve intact families also grew in popularity. In 1992, New Jersey's Democratic governor, Jim Florio, signed into law a family cap. This meant additional children born on AFDC in that state would not draw additional cash benefits. The difference would have amounted to $64 per month. Other states followed with variations on this theme. By October 1995, 14 states had obtained waivers allowing them to copy New Jersey's experiment. Also under the family composition rubric were requirements that minor mothers must live either with their parents or with some other responsible adult. California led in July 1992 with this rule, and by July 1995, nine other states had implemented similar policies.[22]

Growing state experience with welfare-reform demonstrations combined with the recession of 1990 and 1991 to lend urgency to the movement. From 1990 to 1994, the population receiving AFDC grew from 11.4 million to just under 14 million, a 19 percent increase.[23] As the fiscal burden grew, many states' budgets were overwhelmed.[24] During fiscal year 1991, 40 states reduced or froze their AFDC benefit levels, 10 cut emergency assistance funding, and 14 reduced general assistance programs for childless adults.[25] Liberals rebelled at the cuts, especially when accompanied by rhetoric from governors such as California's Pete Wilson, who voiced confidence that the 9 percent reduction in AFDC benefits he proposed in 1991 would leave welfare recipients "able to pay the rent but . . . [with] less for a six-pack of beer."[26] Widespread mandatory work programs also became quite common as states either replaced or expanded earlier workfare experiments, in many cases implementing them

statewide as opposed to running them in only a handful of counties or municipalities. By the time Bill Clinton assumed the presidency in 1993, welfare
receipt without reciprocal obligations was becoming a thing of the past.

Clinton had campaigned on overhauling welfare and once in office threw
open the doors on federal waivers, granting 29 in his first two and a half years
in office, more than presidents Reagan and Bush combined. By mid-1996,
Clinton had granted over 200 waivers, at least one to every state. States in
turn applied for more waivers, and the calls for reform at the national level
grew. Of particular importance was the urging from Republican governors
to Republican leaders in Congress to switch to a block grant in exchange for
more state autonomy over the program. The shift to a block grant meant that
states would face the prospect of running out of money once a year's grant was
exhausted, but they valued flexibility enough to make this worth the risk.

The Clinton administration's use of waivers to allow states to experiment
at the margins with their poverty programs was calculated to produce less
fundamental change than was contemplated by congressional Republicans.
Clinton noted in a 1995 speech to the National Governors' Association that
"if you just look at these . . . waivers, I have pretty much gone along with
anything the states wanted to do to move people from welfare to work."[27]
However well calculated the president's strategy might have been, the Republican victories in 1994 and the imminent 1996 presidential balloting proved
too compelling for Clinton, who had pledged a welfare overhaul.

In addition to the substantive debate over how strict work requirements should
be or how short to make time limits, there was a parallel argument about federalism. States' rights proponents argued that in order to tailor welfare-to-work programs to state preferences and needs, states should be given extensive latitude in
crafting their own programs. Governors were tired of going to Washington, hat
in hand, or, as Wisconsin's Tommy Thompson said in 1994, "on bended knee
to kiss the ring" of some federal bureaucrat for permission to innovate.[28] As it
turns out, analysis of the actions taken by states under federal waivers from 1982
through 1996 revealed that national factors such as caseload size and growth,
not state measures of welfare demand, offer the better explanation for why states
undertook welfare reform under federal waivers. This suggests that states tended
to look outward, toward national factors, when considering waiver requests,
rather than looking inward when contemplating reforms. This supports a view
that sees states as part of a herd rather than idiosyncratic entities with each moving according to its own circumstances. These findings imply that loosening
federal controls on policy was not likely to produce state-tailored reforms, but
rather behavior that involved state governments following the crowd.[29]

Empirical explanations aside, the wave of state welfare innovation took
on a life of its own. It was accelerated by rising unemployment through the

recession of the early 1990s that pushed millions more people onto welfare. Social welfare agencies were aware of this, and the American Public Welfare Association published in its winter 1991 edition of *Public Welfare* an article, entitled "The Gathering Storm," about how local administrators were dealing with sharply increased demands on their services.[30]

Members of Congress noticed as well. Senator Moynihan characterized the changes contemplated by his Finance Committee in the spring of 1992 as attempts at "behavior modification,"[31] that is, efforts to reduce school truancy, to lead parents to work more, and to discourage women on welfare from giving birth to more children. The welfare debate had taken on a tone characterized by the American Public Welfare Association as "the New Paternalism."[32] Members of Congress and policy experts disagreed on the relative effectiveness of sanctions versus incentives, much as they had during the passage of the Family Support Act in 1988, though this time around there would be more of a foundation to build on, given the extensive experiences of states and their demonstration projects. The competing schools of thought were training up front versus work first. Work first won.

Welfare reform would likely have been considered by Congress during 1993 had it not been for the White House's intense focus on health care. That bill moved first because the administration believed welfare reform would be simpler once the related health care issues were settled. When, in the summer of 1994, it became evident that health-care legislation would not pass that year, the president sent a welfare proposal to Congress. However, by then it was too late to act, and by the time Congress could return to the issue, new Republican majorities controlled both chambers. Strident conservatives, especially in the House, did not share Clinton's vision regarding transitional supports, and the welfare reform conversation became highly contentious.

## CLINTON'S WELFARE REFORM PROPOSAL

Bill Clinton's penchant for governing from the center led him to propose a two-pronged approach to moving welfare recipients to work. First were the sticks. The president's mantra of "two years and you're off"[33] combined with support for time limited assistance meant the contract between poor people and the government would be contingent on recipients making discernable progress toward economic independence over a relatively short period of time. Second, Clinton emphasized transitional supports: extended Medicaid benefits for those departing the welfare rolls, child-care and transportation subsidies for those who needed them to hold a job, training programs, and increased efforts to collect child support. For political centrists, each part of the plan required the other in order to make sense. To strip away one side or the other would undermine the vision that Clinton touted regularly, that those who work hard and play by the rules should not be poor. Candidate Clinton believed in 1992 that this could be accomplished with some $1.7 billion of extra spending over the following three years.[34] As it turned out, the estimated price tag grew considerably over the next couple of years. In 1994 the administration said its job-training program would cost some $9.3 billion per year more than the $20 billion annually that welfare cost at the time. The price seemed worth it, however. For the administration, moving welfare recipients into jobs should be "the cornerstone, not the afterthought" of welfare reform, insisted his lead public assistance architect, David Ellwood.[35] This was the plan, anyway. Clinton, like many modern presidents, however, seemed to forget that Congress would have quite a bit to say on the matter before new law could be made.

Clinton met David Ellwood at a conference of the National Governors' Association in the late 1980s. Ellwood's 1988 book *Poor Support* intrigued the Arkansas governor.[36] Ellwood's plan involved several points that Clinton adopted once in the White House as part of his own reform plan.[37] Ellwood, a liberal by most estimations, recognized that although Charles Murray had been wrong about many things in *Losing Ground,* he was probably right when it came to values. As Ellwood wrote, "no amount of tinkering with benefit levels or work rules will change" how Americans feel about the need for welfare recipients to take responsibility for their own success.[38] In this way of thinking, any tenable welfare program must honor the autonomy of the individual, the virtue of work, the primacy of the family, and the desire for and a sense of community.[39] These values resonated powerfully with Clinton, who incorporated much of this thinking into his 1994 welfare overhaul proposal to Congress.

By the summer of 1994, when Clinton's plan was delivered to Capitol Hill, not only members of Congress but also the public had become wary of the administration's talk of government's ability to solve problems. Clinton would ultimately have to admit that the era of big government was over, and Congress acted accordingly, depriving the president of formal votes on his welfare proposal—neither chamber even scheduled committee hearings on the bill.[40] When the fall elections gave control of Congress to the Republicans, the balance of power tipped to favor conservatives who differed from the president in at least two respects. First, they were more focused on the issue of family breakup than on income maintenance. Second, they were less impressed with the need to provide transitional supports for those attempting to work their way off welfare. If Clinton's proposal embodied tough love, congressional conservatives wanted a cold-turkey approach to getting people off public assistance.

One of the significant tensions, indeed the ultimately unsolved problem with Clinton's proposal, was how to help former welfare recipients. Ellwood and his former Harvard University colleague Mary Jo Bane recognized this problem years earlier. Their liberal peers noted it as well. Mark Greenberg at the Center for Law and Social Policy commented on this point, noting in 1993 that his primary worry was that welfare reform was being undertaken in a "harsh political context with very limited resources."[41] Liberals were clearly worried about the fates of those leaving welfare. The lack of assurance of smooth transitions arguably lay at the center of their preoccupation with the long-term outcomes of welfare reform. For them, the bumper-sticker rhetoric of ending welfare as we know it fell flat. Patricia Ireland, president of the National Organization for Women, complained in 1993 that the president should drop the "politically popular catchphrases" and start talking about "ending poverty as we know it."[42]

While the president certainly found little comfort on his left, the harshest criticism came from Republicans who belittled the president's bill as doing nothing to discourage out-of-wedlock births, providing too much flexibility about time limits, and continuing some social services to immigrants. House Republican whip Newt Gingrich chortled that the "president is brilliant at describing a Ferrari, but his staff continues to deliver a Yugo," referring to the budget subcompact car from Eastern Europe.[43]

## AMONG CONSERVATIVES, MORE COMMON GROUND THAN DISAGREEMENT

With Republicans in ascendance, insisting on the Ferrari version of a welfare overhaul became increasingly implausible from a strategic perspective. Bill Clinton's middle way now clashed with increasingly strident proposals from the Right, forces that could no longer be dismissed out of hand. In a 1993 essay in the *Wall Street Journal,* Charles Murray had sounded an alarm about rising rates of out-of-wedlock births, warning of an emerging white underclass.[44] Identifying mother-only households as the nation's gravest problem, Murray suggested strong medicine to stem this tide. He argued that immature and unprepared single mothers fail when it comes to socializing their sons, meaning the nation is facing the prospect of "*The Lord of the Flies* writ large" as these young men grow up badly without father figures. Murray recommended that unmarried women be forced to take care of their children without welfare. He proposed helping the children but not the mothers. This would, he acknowledged, likely force up the rate of adoption, foster care, the use of orphanages, and the frequency of marriages prompted by unplanned pregnancies, developments he did not lament: "Stigma and shotgun marriages may or may not be good for those on the receiving end, but their deterrent effect on others is wonderful—and indispensable."[45] A year later, in the fall of 1994, Speaker-elect Newt Gingrich picked up on Murray's idea and suggested that welfare reform ought to involve denying welfare money to any woman unable to establish the paternity of her children or who bears children as a minor, and that children of unfit mothers ought to be sent to orphanages. The comments drew criticism from many quarters: adults who had grown up in orphanages, Catholic bishops, charity organizations, and the White House. First Lady Hillary Clinton lambasted Gingrich, calling his idea "unbelievable and absurd" and warning that welfare reform must be done right unless the nation wants to see a dramatic rise in the ranks of the homeless.[46] Initially, Gingrich stuck to his argument and suggested that the first lady should view the Mickey Rooney's nostalgic 1938 film *Boys Town* about life in an orphanage. The president publicly opposed Gingrich's idea and insisted that government ought to interfere in family life less, not more.[47] After nearly two months of acrimony, Gingrich retreated, acknowledging that rhetoric that sounds "clever" in Republican circles perhaps is not so prudent with the general public and that such comments "are just wrong when you're the speaker of the whole house." The Speaker-elect stopped short of apologizing.[48]

Conservative circles also saw some minor disagreements on the role of women vis-à-vis their children. Reverend Jerry Fallwell grieved the decline of traditional, stay-at-home motherhood: "In a dramatic departure from the home, more than half of the women in our country are currently employed. Our nation is in serious danger when motherhood is considered a task that is 'unrewarding, unfulfilling, and boring.'"[49] Most conservatives, however, strongly supported the idea of pushing welfare mothers into the workforce, even those with young children.

Not withstanding Fallwell's concerns or these other disagreements among players on the political Right, by the mid-1990s, many conservatives had merged in much of their thinking and had given up on entitlement-based welfare altogether. Social commentator and pillar of the neoconservative movement, Norman Podhoretz, observed that conservative victories over the 1970s and 1980s had gone a long way toward eliminating the need for distinctions among conservatives of various stripes.[50] Conservatives had become completely convinced that the liberal provision of cash assistance to the able-bodied poor was a disaster in terms of family decomposition, work effort, and good citizenship more generally. Neoconservatives and more strident old school conservatives still disagreed on the finer points of women's involvement in the labor market, the meaning of motherhood, and what to do with children in severely broken households; but their concurrence on the general need for work requirements, strict law abidingness, and limited welfare provision created ample common ground for legislation that would, in 1996, overturn 60 years of poor provision. From the early 1990s onward, conservatives argued effectively for welfare reform based less on fiscal concerns than from a position of compassion for those stuck on public assistance rolls.[51]

The task of uprooting what they saw as a corrupt AFDC program was arguably made easer by Clinton's rhetoric over years, which had contributed to welfare appearing unredeemable in the eyes of many, effectively burning a bridge across which liberals and moderates might have dragged welfare-reform legislation to make it a vehicle for, as those on the left saw it, support and dignity for recipients attempting to work their way off assistance. By the time negotiations over the new law came down to their details—and the details mattered a great deal—Clinton and congressional Democrats had worked themselves into a corner, effectively unable to renege on their promise to overhaul the nation's chief public assistance program. Through the spring of 1996, senior White House staff, including Rahm Emanuel and Bruce Reed, privately told congressional Republicans almost daily that if they would sever the Medicaid provisions from the welfare bill, the president would probably sign the AFDC overhaul.[52] After two presidential vetoes, Republicans peeled off those divisive issues and sent the president a bill he thought he had to sign if he was to remain true to his campaign pledge.

Conservatives also had the backing of the general public on some of the broad themes of welfare reform. In a spring 1996 study by the Public Agenda Foundation, 93 percent of survey respondents, including 88 percent of those living in welfare households, wanted the current public assistance system changed. Sixty-five percent of respondents voiced that their primary complaint was not about the money welfare programs cost, but rather the ways in which welfare was out of step with the values of work and personal responsibility. Where the general public disagreed with congressional Republicans was on the need for transitional help for those whom states hoped to move off the welfare rolls. Fully 77 percent of respondents said that mandatory job training was essential.[53] These findings were in substantial agreement with a 1995 study by the Kaiser Family Foundation.[54]

## THE PASSAGE OF TEMPORARY ASSISTANCE TO NEEDY FAMILIES

When it came down to turning broad ideas into specific legislation, the partisan cleavages were somewhat more complicated than the ideological divisions discussed above. Both parties in Congress found themselves splintered on exactly how to proceed. Republicans disagreed among themselves on how radical the reform should be. Moderate Republicans wanted to turn federal funding into a block grant for the states to do with largely as they liked. More conservative Republicans wanted to severely restrict welfare before handing it to the states, imposing limits on welfare for immigrants, children born out of wedlock, and minor mothers, as well as a restriction on additional monthly payments for children born on welfare, or the family cap.[55] Speaker Gingrich fell into this latter camp, though he protested publicly that he did not want to "replace the social engineering of the left with the social engineering of the right" by imposing strict national standards on the states.[56] Senator Nancy Kassebaum, Republican of Kansas, suggested handing welfare and its funding entirely to the states in exchange for a federal takeover of Medicaid, an idea proposed by Ronald Reagan in the early 1980s. That idea achieved no traction.

For their part, Democrats realized the need to talk about the values of personal responsibility, work, and family. Representative Mike McCurdy, a moderate Democrat from Oklahoma, ran television campaign ads back home in which he talked about how work is an important value and said in interviews that he fully appreciated how welfare crystallizes the values of work and broken government in one issue.[57] More liberal Democrats took a defensive posture, focusing their efforts to try to ensure a safety net for welfare recipients who move off assistance into low-paying jobs or those who are unable to find work. Liberals got substantial mileage from forecasts developed by the Urban Institute, indicating that just over one million additional children and another million adults would be thrown into poverty under the Republican bill. Simultaneously, many Democrats privately expressed discomfort at appearing to the president's left on this issue, given the public's strong support for reform.[58]

Following two earlier vetoes of Republican welfare bills, in July Congress removed the Medicaid provisions that had been most objectionable and sent the president what remained. In this moment, with the president teetering on the edge of a decision, the Children's Defense Fund organized a mass march in the nation's capital to persuade Clinton to stand by his convictions, to hold out for guarantees for the poor. They reiterated the Urban Institute's estimate of millions thrown into poverty under the Republican bill.[59] On the other side, polls that summer revealed that most Americans considered moral decline—often associated in the popular mind with welfare use—more important than economic problems.[60] House Ways and Means Committee chair Bill Archer announced, "Mr. President, we are calling your bluff. It's time to either put up or stop the rhetoric."[61] Despite misgivings about the sparse provisions for transitional support and the absence of public-sector jobs as a last resort, the president indicated he would sign the bill.

Liberals were devastated. Democratic Senator Christopher Dodd complained that the bill was "an unconscionable retreat from a 60-year commitment that Republicans and Democrats, 10 American presidents, and congresses have made on behalf of American's children."[62] Patricia Ireland, president of the National Organization for Women, said she would hold her nose and continue to support Clinton during that election season.[63] Even Senator Moynihan, who by then had denied his neoconservative label, decried the new policy bitterly, saying "this bill is not welfare reform, but welfare repeal. It is the first step in dismantling the social contract that has been in place in the United States since at least the 1930s. Do not doubt that Social Security itself . . . will be next."[64] Despite the anger, however, Congress passed the bill with margins of approximately three-to-one in both chambers. Democrats were nearly evenly split.[65] The bill lacked provisions for public-sector jobs for those departing welfare, something Clinton had called for in 1994. He also agreed to time limits, work requirements, and to a family cap provision, ostensibly to attempt to discourage women on welfare from having more children. The bill he signed in the summer of 1996 was indeed a far cry from what he had proposed two years before.

Surrounding himself with welfare recipients, Bill Clinton signed into law the Personal Responsibility and Work Opportunity Reconciliation Act on August 22, 1996, ending 61 years of entitlement-based welfare and creating Temporary Assistance for Needy Families (TANF). States began submitting their TANF plans to the federal government later that day. Wisconsin was first. Under this new order, families would be eligible for federal cash assistance for no more than 60 months, recipients would have to work within two years of going on welfare, minor mothers would not be permitted to establish their own welfare cases, and states could implement a family cap at their discretion. Significant cuts were also called for in food stamps for immigrants and Supplemental Security Income (SSI). The savings under the 1996 law were projected to amount to $54 billion over five years.[66]

Just over half of the fiscal savings of the bill came in provisions regarding food stamps and assistance for immigrants. Most legal immigrants already in the country and most future legal immigrants would be denied SSI and food stamps. States would have the option of denying them Medicaid as well. New immigrants would be excluded from most means-tested programs during their first five years of U.S. residency. At the time, some 880,000 legal immigrants received SSI. Most were cut off. Curtailing aid to these new arrivals was expected to save $22 billion over six years, constituting approximately 40 percent of the bill's savings. The food stamp savings were estimated at $24 billion. Half of those savings would result from across-the-board cuts in enrollment due to a change in eligibility rules. For unemployed adults under age 50 without children in their homes, food stamps would be withheld for three months out of every three years. The liberal Center for Budget and Policy Priorities called this last change "probably the single harshest provision written into a major safety net program in at least 30 years."[67] Between 100,000 and 200,000 children were to be removed from SSI. Another three billion dollars was cut from day-care and low-income food programs.[68] As it turned out, most of the savings promised by the legislation were erased with the 1997 substantial reestablishment of the previous year's food stamp and SSI reductions.

The elimination of the entitlement basis of welfare worked on two levels. In addition to the individual entitlement for welfare coming to an end, states would no longer receive a stream of federal welfare funds based on the investments they made into the program. Instead, the states would share a $16.4 billion annual block grant. Although by the time the 1996 legislation was signed, caseloads had begun their decline and were expected to shrink more, accepting a block grant in place of open-ended federal funding represented something of a gamble for states. If welfare expenses rose much beyond their projected levels (there was a small emergency fund established), states would bear this burden entirely out of their own treasuries.

The bill contained no requirement that states provide any cash assistance at all. They became free to spend their entire welfare budget on in-kind assistance or even administration. In 1996, 73 percent of AFDC dollars were distributed as cash benefits. That figure would decline to approximately one-third by 2004.[69] Under a maintenance of effort provision, states were required to continue spending at least 75 percent per year of what they had spent prior to the new law's passage. This averted the widely feared race to the bottom, as states vied to be less generous than their neighbors. The time limits were perhaps the most anxiety-producing part of the new law from states' perspectives. To alleviate some of this concern, the law permitted states to exempt up to 20 percent of their caseload from this requirement.[70]

The public supported the new law. In opinion polls fielded in the months following passage, solid majorities supported it. A January 1997 survey found that 53 percent approved of the bill, and 16 percent disapproved, though 31 percent did not know enough to answer. The next month, another poll found that 75 percent of respondents favored the law, 22 percent opposed it, and only 3 percent volunteered that they did not have an opinion.[71]

For Republicans, this legislation represented the fulfillment of one of the points on their 1994 Contract with America, a campaign document enumerating legislative priorities. Perhaps more important, this welfare legislation represented for them a significant step toward building family stability through provisions they hoped would reduce out-of-wedlock births and voluntary nonwork. Though Clinton's decision to sign the bill deprived them of what would surely been a powerful campaign issue that summer, for Republicans, the victory was worth the price.

## POLITICAL FALLOUT ON THE LEFT

President Clinton's insistence that Congress needed to revisit the new welfare law to correct shortcomings did little to assuage the anger liberals felt as their hopes for what they took to be a humane bill were dashed. Democratic partisans distraught over the matter found themselves in a curious position that August. At that month's Democratic Convention, they bravely rallied behind their president and advanced the argument that Clinton must be reelected, along with a Democratic Congress, in order to ensure that the law would indeed be fixed. To the logic of renominating the president who had just signed a bill many Democrats hated, *Washington Post* columnist David Broder wrote, "If you think Clinton should be rewarded with a second term for that, you have to believe that Jack the Ripper should have been given a scholarship to medical school."[72]

Liberals were angry that Clinton did not insist on a bill that would provide supports for poor people about to be pushed off welfare or who had already been removed from the rolls. Three senior officials in Clinton's Department of Human Services resigned over the president's decision to sign the bill, including Wendell Primus, Mary Jo Bane, and Peter Edelman.[73] David Ellwood had resigned the year before when it became apparent that Clinton was unwilling to fight hard for the kinds of transitional supports that were so central to Ellwood's thinking.[74] Indeed, the president secured three billion dollars for work-preparedness programs as part of the 1997 budget agreement, but to many on the left, that seemed like too little too late.[75]

One particularly sharp critique of Clinton's handling of the episode came from Peter Edelman. In a 1997 essay in the *Atlantic Monthly* titled "The Worst Thing Bill Clinton Has Done," Edelman—the husband of Marion Wright Edelman, the president of the Children's Defense Fund—laid blame squarely on the president. He argued that Clinton should not have promised a welfare overhaul in the first place. He complained that the administration had been too sluggish, failing to pass welfare reform prior to the 1994 Republican takeover of Congress. He bitterly lamented the fate of an estimated 2.6 million people, according to the Urban Institute, who would be thrown into poverty. In an attempt to engage in "bumper sticker politics [and] oversimplification to win votes," Clinton had sacrificed an opportunity to constructively remake welfare into a system both its beneficiaries and the general public could respect.[76]

Mary Jo Bane lamented the weakening of federal guarantees under the new law in an *American Prospect* article in early 1997.[77] Her fears centered on the lack of guaranteed due process in the states for individuals denied aid, for neglect of the poor at the hands of for-profit companies hired to implement the program, and what to do with children in families that exhaust their 60 months of aid. While profoundly sorry to see the new law, she recognized that fixing the worst errors in the law—regarding guarantees for those who need the program, not necessarily the food stamp and immigrant provisions (those would be easy to fix if the money were reinstated)—would not be politically feasible until Americans were emotionally ready to consider a guaranteed safety net once again, something that could be years away given the rabid dissatisfaction with what welfare had been.

For his part, Bill Clinton appeared to talk out of both sides of his mouth about the new law during the remainder of the 1996 presidential campaign. In an effort to please moderates, he proudly spoke about having fulfilled his promise to end welfare as we know it.[78] To liberals he promised to fight hard to fix the flawed provisions of the law. While perhaps awkward from a rhetorical standpoint, Clinton had managed to defuse a campaign liability, at least among many moderate swing voters.

Commenting on this process after the fact, Douglas Besharov of the American Enterprise Institute critiqued the children's lobby—the Children's Defense Fund, among others—for not taking Clinton to task earlier in the process: "The liberal establishment let Bill Clinton bad-mouth welfare for four years, and this is the result. What you're supposed to do is stand up and say, 'Dumb idea.'"[79] Of course, in hindsight, to second guess strategy is easy, especially when, at the beginning of the campaign, few Democrats believed they would have to work under a Republican controlled Congress to enact welfare reform.

In the Senate debate leading up to passage, Republican Senator Slade Gordon of Washington celebrated the bill as "a magnificent new experiment."[80] Those on Bill Clinton's left were in no mood to celebrate experiments, something they saw as gambling with poor people's lives. However, from then on, the race was on to track the experiences of those on welfare and those many who would soon leave. That is the story of the next chapter.

## NOTES

1. Radio address, February 15, 1986 (available online at http://www.american presidency.org

2. Whitman 1992.

3. Weaver 2000, p. 2.

4. O'Connor 2001, pp. 252–53.

5. Rose 1995, p. 140.

6. Gueron 1995.

7. Whitman 1992, pp. 38, 40.

8. Kaus 1986, p. 27; Weaver 2000, p. 186.

9. Kaus 1986, p. 27 (emphasis in original).

10. William Welch, "Two-Thirds Back a Costly Welfare Overhaul," *USA Today*, April 22, 1994, p. 7A.

11. Kaus 1986, p. 33.

12. National Governors' Association 1987.

13. John Herbers, "Governors Seek Work Plan Linked to Welfare Benefits," *New York Times,* February 22, 1987, p. A30.

14. Spencer Rich, "Governors Would Alter Welfare to Emphasize Jobs," *Washington Post,* February 22, 1987, p. A7.

15. King 1991, p. 19.

16. Ibid., pp. 22–23.

17. *New York Times,* "Real Welfare Reform, at Last," October 1, 1988, p. A26.

18. Statement by the National Governors' Association, "Job oriented welfare reform," February 1987, quoted in King 1991, p. 20.

19. John Robinson, "Reagan Signs Bill Overhauling Welfare," *Boston Globe,* October 14, 1988, national sec., p. 1.

20. Robert Pear, "White House Spurns Expansion of Nation's Anti-Poverty Efforts," *New York Times,* July 6, 1990, p. A1.

21. Heclo 2001, pp. 184–85.

22. Listing of approved state welfare reform provisions, Administration for Children and Families, U.S. Department of Health and Human Services (unpublished document, July 3, 1996).

23. Data from Administration for Children and Families available online at http://www.bls.gov/cps/wlf-table2-2006.pdf (accessed June 22, 2007).

24. Gold 1995, chap. 2.

25. Shapiro et al. 1991.

26. Elaine Herscher, "Outrage over Wilson's 9% Welfare Cut," *San Francisco Chronicle,* January 12, 1991, p. A3.

27. Bill Clinton speech to National Governors' Association, Burlington, Vermont, July 31, 1995, transcript, White House Press Office, Washington, D.C.

28. Dan Balz, "GOP Governors Seek Shift in Power," *Washington Post,* November 21, 1994, p. A1.

29. Lieberman and Shaw 2000.

30. Connors 1991.

31. Moynihan 1992, p. 6.

32. Moynihan 1992.

33. Edelman 1997, p. 44.

34. Bill Clinton, "Welfare Reform as an Investment," December 10, 1987, *Washington Post,* p. A27.

35. Ed Anderson, "Clinton: Welfare Must Lead to Job," July 26, 1994, *Times-Picayune,* p. B4.

36. O'Connor 2004, p. 193; Anthony Flint, "Welfare Reformers Pursue Game Plan against Steep Odds," *Boston Globe,* December 28, 1993, national sec., p. 1.

37. O'Connor 2004, p. 195.

38. Ellwood 1988, p. 6.

39. Ibid., p. 16.

40. *Congressional Quarterly Weekly Report,* October 15, 1994, pp. 2956–58. Washington, DC: Congressional Quarterly Press, Inc.

41. Anthony Flint, "Welfare Reformers Pursue Game Plan against Steep Odds," *Boston Globe,* December 28, 1993, national sec., p. 1.

42. Charles Nicodemus, *Chicago Sun-Times,* August 11, 1993, news sec., p. 20.

43. *Congressional Quarterly Weekly Report,* June 18, 1994, p. 1622. Washington, DC: Congressional Quarterly Press, Inc.

44. Murray, "The Coming White Underclass," *Wall Street Journal,* October 29, 1993, p. A14.

45. Ibid.

46. *St. Louis Post-Dispatch,* "First Lady Ridicules GOP Plan," December 1, 1994, p. 18A.

47. Greg McDonald, "Clinton Denounces Orphanage Proposal as Bad for Families," *Houston Chronicle,* December 11, 1994, p. A-2.

48. Kathey Alexander, "Gingrich Retreats on Rhetoric," *Atlanta Journal and Constitution,* December 21, 1994, p. C-1.

49. Ellwood 1988, p. 50.

50. Podhoretz 1996.

51. Heclo 2001, pp. 181–186.

52. Edelman 1997, p. 46.

53. Public Agenda Foundation, press release, April 24, 1996 (available online at http://www.publicagenda.org/press/press_release_detail.cfm?list=4; accessed June 25, 2007).

54. Kaiser Family Foundation, press release, 1995 (available online at http://www.kkf.org; accessed August 10, 2006).

55. *Congressional Quarterly Weekly Report,* January 6, 1996, pp. 37–38. Washington, DC: Congressional Quarterly Press, Inc.

56. Charles Krauthammer, "House Waffling on Welfare Revolution," *Houston Chronicle,* January 23, 1995, p. A-14.

57. *Congressional Quarterly Weekly Report,* October 15, 1994, p. 2957. Washington, DC: Congressional Quarterly Press, Inc.

58. Weaver 2000, p. 327.

59. Serafini 1996.

60. Heclo 2001, p. 193.

61. Weaver 2000, p. 326.

62. Robert Pear, "The Welfare Bill: The Overview," *New York Times,* August 2, 1996, p. A1.

63. Greg McDonald, "President Signs 'Historic' Welfare Reform Measure," *Houston Chronicle,* August 23, 1996, p. A1.

64. Robert Pear, "The Welfare Bill: The Overview," *New York Times,* August 2, 1996, p. A1.

65. Weaver 2000, p. 328.

66. Jeffrey Katz. "After 60 Years, Most Control Is Passing to States," *Congressional Quarterly Weekly Report,* pp. 2190-2196. August 3, 1996 (quote at p. 2190). Washington, DC: Congressional Quarterly Press, Inc.

67. Edelman 1997, p. 48.

68. Edelman 1997, p. 48.

69. National Conference of State Legislatures, November 2002, "State of State TANF Spending, 2001" (available online at http://www.ncsl.org); Center on Budget and Policy Priorities "An Introduction to TANF," November 2005 (available online at http://www.cbpp.org/1-22-02tanf2.htm; accessed June 22, 2007.

70. *Congressional Quarterly Almanac 1996,* section 6, pp. 3–24.

71. Weaver 2000, p. 338 (the 1/97 poll explicitly offered a "don't know" opinion; the 2/97 poll did not).

72. David Broder, "The Convention vs. the Reality," *Washington Post,* August 29, 1996, p. A23.

73. *Washington Post,* "Mr. Clinton's Welfare Harvest," September 12, 1996, p. A-26.

74. Ann Scales, "After Welfare Exodus, New Criticism," *Boston Globe,* December 13, 1996, p. A20.

75. Weaver 2000, pp. 336–37.

76. Edelman 1997, p. 44.

77. Bane 1997.

78. Bill signing statement by President Clinton, August 22, 1996 (available online at http://www.presidency.ucsb.edu/ws/index.php?pid=53218; accessed June 22, 2007).

79. Serafini 1996.

80. Robert Pear, "The Welfare Bill: The Overview," *New York Times,* August 2, 1996, p. A1.

# 7

# A New World of Welfare

The abolition of AFDC and its replacement with TANF in 1996 meant that states had the opportunity to radically redesign their public assistance programs, ending cash assistance altogether if they chose. This moment also confronted states with the challenge of putting to work large numbers of welfare recipients, many of whom had few job skills, multiple obstacles to work, and thin employment records. Lastly, states experienced an imperative to move families off welfare within five years, due to the new federal limit on assistance beyond that point. States responded in a variety of ways. Many continued the programming they had launched in the early to mid-1990s under federal waivers. A few took this opportunity to fundamentally redesign their efforts. Over the first five years, a combination of more directive welfare-to-work policies and a booming economy cut the national caseload in half, though there was some debate over whether the former or the latter led to more dramatic caseload reductions. The fate of former aid recipients would also become the subject of much debate in the years that followed.

With the launch of the new TANF program, liberals had feared a race to the bottom, as they expected states to outdo each other in minimizing benefits. This did not occur, however, due to a pair of forces. First, the federal legislation included a maintenance of effort requirement, meaning that states had to continue spending at least 75 percent of the amount they had spent on welfare in 1994. Further, caseloads had already begun declining by late 1995, meaning that the block grant states received was based on larger caseloads than they actually experienced in the more recent period, creating a cash surplus. This caseload reduction allowed states to spend a much larger portion of their welfare funds on in-kind help for recipients. In 1995 nearly three-quarters of AFDC funds were spent on cash payments. By 1999 that figure dropped to 55 percent, and by 2004, to 36 percent.[1]

A chief complaint by liberals at the time of passage was that the new law lacked many of the transitional supports welfare recipients would need to facilitate their successful entry into the labor market: child care, health care, and education and training. To some extent, anger over the absence of these provisions was assuaged by state decisions to fund some of these bridges to employment out of the surplus funds resulting from caseload declines. However, education and training were deemphasized under the law so as to play very much a secondary role to an approach that stressed immediate job placement over preparatory training. For example, attending college was not considered work for the purposes of meeting federal targets. Instead, states began pushing recipients to quickly enter the labor market with whatever skills they possessed. The adage attached to this approach and one that appeared on the walls of many welfare offices around the nation ran along the lines of, get a job, get a better job, get a career. As it turned out, the assumption that people could climb the ladder to success regardless of how low they started likely underappreciated how slippery and far apart the rungs were for many welfare recipients.

For their part, conservatives—and many moderates—pointed to the decline in caseloads as clear prima facie evidence of the overwhelming success of the TANF program. Because a chief objection to welfare historically had been its purported tendency to depress recipients' self-help impulse, virtually any policy changes that were associated with steep caseload declines and more workforce participation had to be good.[2] Further, supporters of welfare reform were able to point to increased earnings and decreased poverty levels among former recipients. While just how dramatic these improvements in income were was debated, these developments certainly marked a reversal of some earlier trends.

Behind the rhetoric, this new world of welfare involved significant changes for poor people who might wish to apply for aid and for those already on assistance. Public assistance applications came to involve personal responsibility agreements, mandatory job searches, and one-time payments—such as grants to head off an eviction or utility severance—to divert would-be applicants from landing on welfare. For those on the rolls, recipients in some states encountered limitations that were stricter than those in the federal law, such as time limitations of less than five years. Idaho adopted a two-year lifetime limit and a three-strikes policy that rendered the entire family ineligible for life for those guilty of three infractions of the state's welfare rules.[3] On the other hand, states also tried to clear the way for recipients to find work. Resource limits were increased in many states. These provisions historically had excluded certain applicants and thwarted the upward mobility of others by making it difficult, for example, to own reliable transportation or to save for college without exceeding resource limits. In attempting to remove these impediments to work and schooling, many states relaxed resource restrictions. By the end of 1997, most states had increased their cash reserve limits and vehicle value limits.[4]

Through the early 1990s, a few states had been willing to pay for welfare-to-work programs involving large start-up costs, but they were a distinct minority. Washington State's experience with its Family Independence Project (FIP) provided a vivid example of a state quitting the sometimes costly positive-incentives approach in favor of cheaper methods. FIP was based on the idea of catching more flies with honey than with vinegar. From 1988 to 1993, the program offered comprehensive education and training opportunities to welfare recipients in five sites around the state, but when people began flocking to those places to enroll and program costs rose dramatically, the state aborted its planned expansion to state-wide status. At the end of the five-year waiver, the program was ended altogether. Dave Anderson, FIP's administrator, lamented the collapse of political support for the program but noted that anyone proposing an FIP-like program after Washington State's misadventure "would be laughed out of the room."[5] In the end, Washington experienced a $29 million cost overrun.[6] Other states learned from Washington's lesson.

Building on these findings and others, many states formalized their job-search processes. In Wisconsin, participants came to use county-level job centers and their professional staffs for guidance, fax machines, and phones to call prospective employers. Participants even punched time clocks to track the hours they spent looking for employment. The facilities included on-site day care for their children. Wisconsin's willingness to provide such comprehensive job-search services meant that welfare was effectively replaced by a work program for poor parents in that state.[7] Other states moved in similar directions, even if not providing support as broad as that seen in Wisconsin.

Building on these experiences, perhaps of greatest significance during the early years of TANF was a conscious decision by states to pursue a work-first strategy. This involved welfare recipients being steered into whatever jobs were available with no prior attempt to train them for more high-powered employment. While this approach was launched based on little more than a hunch and an ideological predisposition involving the presumed moral strengthening brought about by hard work, some systematic evidence appeared by the late 1990s to support the contention that steering poor people into largely entry-level jobs paid more handsome dividends than did preparatory education and training programs. One highly influential 1997 study by the Manpower Demonstration Research Corporation reported the effects of work first versus education in Atlanta, Georgia; Grand Rapids, Michigan; and Riverside County, California.[8] The study compared the income of welfare recipients who were steered into jobs versus those who were directed into education programs, such as GED courses. The study found modest returns on investments in education and training two years later. Among those participants beginning with less than a high school education, the work-first group increased their earnings consistently, but the education group experienced increases in only two of the three sites. Among the work-first group, earnings rose by approximately 20 percent. Among the education group, there were small improvements in earnings during the first year and much smaller improvements (and an actual decline in one site) in the second year. Across the three sites, education led to $882 in increased earnings on average during the first year and $172 in the second year. Across the three sites, work-first approaches led to $1,269 in increased earnings on average during the first year and $912 during the second year. A follow-up study by the same organization in 2001 examined five-year impacts across 11 sites using mandatory programs and concluded much the same: education and training programs performed no better than work-first programs in boosting income; education and training efforts cost more and were slower to connect participants with jobs than work-first programs, an important feature in a context of limited federal dollars for assistance.[9] These studies and others went a long way toward settling the debate over the best way to move welfare recipients into jobs, though they did not silence those discussions altogether.

If states became more practical in assisting poor people to move from welfare to work by redirecting surplus money to job-search strategies and by relaxing previously restrictive resource guidelines, they did less well at providing health-care coverage to low-income families struggling to leave welfare. President Clinton twice vetoed welfare legislation, in 1995 and early 1996, due to what he believed were inadequate Medicaid protections for those leaving welfare. Despite addressing this concern to some extent in the legislation that Clinton finally signed, studies of these welfare leavers routinely found that over 20 percent of children in former welfare families were left uninsured.[10] Through 1997 and 1998, Colorado, Florida, Indiana, Mississippi, New Jersey, and New Mexico all left more than one-quarter of child welfare leavers uninsured, even though the vast majority of these children would have been Medicaid eligible. Single mothers experienced similar gaps in health-care coverage. In 1997, 41 percent of single mothers who had left welfare within the previous two years were uninsured. The transition from welfare as an entitlement program to an explicitly short-term bridge exceeded expectations on both sides of the ideological debate, but it did not end arguments about how to address the most vulnerable poor, children, and the role of states versus the federal government in defining the exact nature of the obligations to be imposed on those who rely on public aid.

## THE FATE OF THE POOR AND THE RHETORIC OF POLICY EVALUATION

Because many liberals still focused on structural explanations for poverty, they remained skeptical of conservative welfare reform. They saw modern poverty as largely the result of a shift to an information and service economy through the 1970s and 1980s, a trend that left behind many low-skilled workers. Beyond this, a rising cost of living, especially in steeply increased housing costs, made getting by on stagnant wages that much more difficult. In 1973 the median wage in the United States was $12.06 per hour (in 2001 dollars). By 2001 it stood largely unchanged at $12.87. Further, between 1979 and 1997, the average income of the bottom 20 percent of Americans declined by $100, from $10,900 to $10,800 (in 1997 dollars).[11] Making welfare more punitive, as liberals saw it, was a step in the wrong direction, given persistent and fundamental problems with the labor market.

But as conservatives saw things, it was hard to argue with a better than 50 percent reduction in the welfare caseload. Given the powerful resentment toward welfare's purported dependency-building qualities, moving people off the rolls was a great policy victory. The TANF program required states to place 35 percent of recipients in work or training programs by 1999, and half by 2002—well above the levels states had achieved prior to 1996. All states met the 1999 goal in time.[12] Further, earned income rose among TANF families between 1996 and 2000, from a median of $472 per month to $738.[13] Some liberals admitted that welfare reform had succeeded to a surprising degree and focused their attention on the work ahead to help those still remaining on assistance. Others pointed to the reductions as a product of a booming economy during the mid-to-late 1990s.[14] After all, AFDC rolls had begun to shrink during 1995, a full year before the earliest states began to implement TANF. For them, the triumphant talk about strong policy interventions was only one part of a more complex explanation for the fall off in welfare use.

Welfare reform proponents, for their part, observed that single mothers increased their labor force participation at a higher rate than even childless single women. The proportion of single mothers who worked at least partial years rose from 73 percent in 1995 to 84 percent in 2000, and the proportion of single mothers who worked year-round rose from 48 percent to 60 percent during that period.[15] Single mothers still suffered an unemployment rate twice that of the overall labor force, but the increased work levels were impressive nonetheless.[16]

The increase in employment among single mothers was not enough to offset the declines in welfare use, so there remained many former recipients who did not find work after leaving assistance, or who initially found work but subsequently lost it. Studies of welfare leavers in the first few years of TANF showed that nearly two-thirds of those who left welfare did so due to finding work, and that most of those people were still employed at the time of those studies.[17] Even if the welfare reform glass was not overflowing, it seemed to conservatives, by many indicators, to be considerably more full than empty. The debate between supporters and critics of welfare reform substantially narrowed, focusing on relatively limited issues of program performance rather than continuing to be marked by broad and deep ideological conflict. No longer was the idea of putting welfare recipients to work generally a point of contention. Liberals and conservatives tended instead to argue over the detailed terms of just how that should be accomplished and how to measure success. A brief look at some specific indicators is useful in this regard.

As TANF matured in the states through the late 1990s and into the new century, various research organizations tracked the fates of those still on assistance and those millions who had recently left. The nonpartisan Urban Institute led the investigative efforts. Its study conducted during 1997 involved a nationally representative sample of 44,000 households, including an oversampling of households with incomes below 200 percent of the poverty level.[18] The project focused on people who had left welfare between 1995 and 1997. Of those individuals, 29 percent had returned to welfare by the time of the interview in late 1997. In comparing former welfare recipients to other low-income people, it was found that former recipients were almost twice as likely to be unmarried as other low-income individuals, bolstering conservative claims that stabilizing marriage is key to reducing welfare use. Once off welfare, 61 percent of former recipients who were interviewed were found to be employed. Of those with jobs, one-third of them worked less than 35 hours per week. Jobs held by former welfare recipients were comparable to those of other low-income people, concentrated in service and retail sales positions. As of 1997, 46 percent labored in service jobs, especially food service and cleaning, and another 24 percent were employed in sales. Only 14 percent of these recent welfare leavers in the late 1990s who had found work did so in the generally higher-wage manufacturing sector. Just over one-quarter of these former recipients worked mostly at night, a situation that almost certainly complicated child-care arrangements. Only one-quarter of them were covered by employer-provided health-care insurance.

When it came to earnings, successes were modest. One-half of leavers earned between $5.30 and $8 per hour. The other half was evenly distributed above and below this range, leading to a median wage of $6.61 per hour. Among those families with at least one working adult, the median annual household income amounted to $13,788, roughly equivalent to the 1997 poverty level for a family of three.[19]

If conservatives tended to view these figures in terms of success, many liberals still lamented the limited nature of welfare-to-work transitional help. Peter Edelman, one of the disillusioned former Clinton administration officials who resigned in protest over the 1996 law, noted in a 2003 article that nearly one million former welfare recipients and their more than two million children enjoyed neither a job nor public assistance on a regular basis. These people had been involuntarily removed from the welfare rolls or had been diverted from applying. For the poorest, life had become even more challenging. The average income of persons living below 50 percent of the poverty level decreased during the latter half of the 1990s.[20] Despite the rising tide generally, their boats sunk a bit more. They, Edelman maintained, lost ground.

Beyond modest incomes for most former recipients, other government services were spotty. As of 1997, not quite one-third of former recipients received food stamps, even though many more were eligible. Through fiscal year 2003, only 56 percent of eligible families—including both welfare related families and others—received this food assistance. That rate rose to 60 percent in fiscal year 2004.[21] Nearly half of former welfare families lacked health-care coverage, compared to approximately 15 percent of the population at large. Nearly 40 percent reported sometimes running out of food and lacking the means to buy more, and approximately that same number said they sometimes fell behind on their rent, mortgage, or utility bills due to lack of money.[22] A few million had left welfare, but they were not uniformly on their way to prosperity.

The financial challenges perhaps hit children the hardest, as child poverty rates remained persistently high. In 1993 nearly 23 percent of children lived in poverty. Just before the recession of 2001, the child poverty rate sunk to its lowest point in two decades when it reached 16 percent. However, by 2005 children as a group had again lost ground, with nearly 18 percent living in poverty.[23] The persistence of poverty among children remained of particular concern, as their overall well-being appeared to be more dependent on family income than on patterns of parental involvement in the labor market. Conservatives have long argued that seeing parents go off to work each day instills in children a healthier work ethic than witnessing parents stay home. While the long-term effects of this lifestyle remain an open question, in the short-term, increased household income matters more in improving children's indicators of well-being than do demonstrations of effort to find and keep a low-wage job, according to a 2002 study by Columbia University's National Center for Children in Poverty.[24]

Beyond the objective outcomes for former welfare recipients, the process of implementing these reforms drew criticism. If the rise of scientific social work in the late 1800s marked a turn away from treating poor people as members of an amorphous class toward a more individualized approach, some liberal critics argued that this new state of welfare eligibility determination represented a reversal on this point. During its first decade, TANF strongly focused on moving welfare recipients into jobs rather than on developing personalized plans for career development or tracking the substantive outcomes experienced by recipients and former recipients. Handler and Babcock, two liberal commentators, argued that little attention was given through this period to long-term viability for people who find themselves on the receiving end of work-first policies. They argued that "the common assumption is that if the family is not on welfare, everything is all right."[25] Because the goal for state welfare agencies was to move people off assistance, the latitude that case workers enjoyed in steering aid applicants toward a particular job or away from applying in the first place allowed "caseworkers to meet performance goals without ever addressing the needs of the client."[26]

Despite these critiques and signs of trouble for millions of former recipients, the broad public discourse on welfare reform through the first decade of TANF emphasized successes over failures.[27] In line with these upbeat assessments, some optimistic observers, even those cautiously so on the left, wondered why the aftermath of welfare reform had unfolded better than expected. Explaining this requires reference to multiple developments. The whole story involved more than simply pointing to large numbers of former recipients now in low-wage and intermittent jobs. In addition to this, the dramatic expansion of the Earned Income Tax Credit in the 1990s led that program to spend more annually on the working poor than the old AFDC program ever had. For a minimum-wage worker with two children, receiving the tax credit versus not receiving it, meant a 40 percent increase in income. More aggressive child-support enforcement also helped. Lastly, expanding Medicaid to the working poor, despite the gaps still persistent there, also helped reduce out-of-pocket medical expenses.[28]

One other aspect of the transition away from welfare use that probably went under-appreciated by both liberals and conservatives involved the supplemental, rather than central, role played by assistance payments in most poor people's lives. Since the mid-1980s, welfare checks have provided only about 40 percent, on average, of the income of families enrolled. The rest came from work, family and friends, and food stamps. As Edin and Lein report in *Making Ends Meet,* based on research in the early 1990s, welfare was only one part of the financial picture for poor single mothers. Portraying welfare instead as central to poor people's finances likely leads the nonpoor to see welfare as more prominent, and thus potentially more corrupting, than it really is.[29]

## WHAT'S NEXT FOR WELFARE?

Regardless of the details of how former recipients fared in this new world of welfare or of the experiences of poor people more generally, it seems unlikely that the American public will take as much interest in welfare in the near future as it did in the early 1990s. Both liberal and conservative commentators observed after 1996 that in order to win political support at all, welfare must demand work from its recipients. Americans are willing to spend significant tax money—more than the nation currently spends, according to opinion polls—to fund programs to aid people who appear to be doing all they can to help themselves, but they deeply resent spending money on those who do not. Of course, observers on the political left contest just what constitutes self-help, as they point out the difficulty of getting by in poverty.[30] However, for most middle-class Americans, the fundamental problem with AFDC was that it asked too little of its recipients. For recipients themselves, it provided little in return. The program was easy to hate.

That frustration with welfare led President George W. Bush to appoint Governor Tommy Thompson of Wisconsin as his secretary of Health and Human Services in 2001. The choice of Thompson, an aggressive welfare reformer since the late 1980s, might have seemed like a poke in the eye to liberals, but it is important to note that Thompson's efforts in Wisconsin involved much more generous transitional supports than other states, or the federal government, had offered. The Wisconsin Works program was created in the spring of 1996 and included a ladder with education and training for the least job-ready participants at the bottom and unsubsidized jobs at the top for the most prepared. The program also included subsidized jobs for those who were work-ready but otherwise unable to find conventional employment. While this formula had provided Thompson considerable political mileage in Wisconsin, the Bush administration opposed subsidized jobs and certainly public-sector work for welfare recipients. However, Thompson, even after joining the administration, continued to talk about training programs, an effort that received no backing from the White House. In a summer 2001 essay in the *Brookings Review,* Thompson looked forward to what he hoped would be the next steps of welfare reform and called for all recipients, not only the portion of them then under federal mandates, to be asked to work or combine work and training.[31] He called for more ambitious government-funded supports for those working their way off welfare, including food stamp and Medicaid coverage. Thompson also supported programming to strengthen marriage.[32]

The White House's Healthy Marriage Initiative, launched in 2002, picked up on Thompson's last point. Funded by a $200 million annual appropriation from Congress, grants to state and local governments and to nongovernmental organizations would target family breakup, a very common avenue to child poverty. Efforts to strengthen marriage merged with more strict work requirements to form the core of the administration's agenda when the time came to reauthorize TANF beginning in 2002. Conservatives had taken the administration to task for neglecting the importance of marriage and the rise in out-of-wedlock births over the past generation. To the extent this critique rang true, President Bush's initial emphasis on jobs may have been due to his awareness of greater public concern about work than about family in recent years.[33] However, in time, marriage assumed a central role in the administration's efforts. How well programs promoting marriage may work in a society where young people today wait almost four years longer to marry than young people did 30 years ago remains unknown.[34] However, for its part, the Bush administration placed great faith in this plan, while many liberals scoffed both at the idea that government can effect change of this type and that encouraging women to remain in abusive or otherwise troubled marriages is worth the trouble. Skeptics of government efforts to promote marriage point to evidence that merely growing up in a two-parent family is not necessarily a good thing. Two-parent families that experience significant conflict tend to produce children with lower academic achievement, higher rates of depression and suicidal thoughts, higher rates of behavioral problems, and higher rates of drug use than do less-conflict-ridden families.[35] That a marriage remains nominally intact provides no systematic advantage to its children if strife is a routine part of family life.

Questions of marriage and social engineering aside, the discussions surrounding reauthorization of TANF—a process that dragged out until 2006—substantially involved issues of federalism. State officials engaged this reauthorization process early and asked for an extension of this new status quo, specifically to preserve rules that allowed them to count their early welfare leavers against their job-placement targets. In 2001 state welfare commissioners communicated to Congress their desire to see the law reauthorized for six more years without major changes or stiffening of requirements on states.[36] However, when President Bush finally signed the TANF reauthorization into law in February 2006, states found themselves facing more stringent work-placement requirements than before. No longer could they use the high watermark of 1995 as their base year when calculating the percentage of recipients who met work requirements, a procedure that had allowed all states to meet their 50 percent work-placement goals with relative ease. Rather, states would be required to use 2005 as the new base year, meaning that reaching the 50 percent work-placement target would require significantly more aggressive placement of recipients into jobs.[37] Further, in light of what it saw as a need for stricter definitions of work, the Bush administration advanced a new set of rules during the summer of 2006 to require states to steer welfare recipients into conventional jobs instead of performing other activities, such as motivational reading or even studying English language skills, as some states had included under their list of approved work activities. With a nod to some flexibility on this point, federal rules were modified in 2006 to allow on-the-job training, unpaid work experience, job searching for up to six weeks per year, community service, 12 months of vocational training during a lifetime, or, of course, unsubsidized employment to count toward the work requirement.[38] Some state policy makers balked at the stricter definitions, and other critics challenged what they considered the president's narrow focus on work and marriage despite growing child poverty rates in a context of still falling welfare caseloads, findings that clearly indicated that more needy people are going without the assistance they need.[39]

When looking back over a decade of this new world of welfare, several criteria of judgment emerge. The devolution of welfare policy has indeed encouraged policy diversity among the states. To the extent that diversity fosters improved policy solutions, that is a positive development, though diversity for its own sake holds more symbolic than actual value. On the point of moving welfare recipients into jobs, certainly the policy has been a success. However, if part of the bargain is that poor people will strive to gain employment provided that government will fund the supports they need, welfare reform has been a mixed success. Recipients in many states experienced waiting lists for child-care benefits.[40] More basic problems plagued welfare in other areas. If part of the public assistance bargain is to ensure that poor people receive the basic services they need, such as Medicaid and food stamps, clearly welfare reform has fallen short. Also, if a major thrust of the law was to promote marriage and stable families, despite efforts in this direction, many observers—liberal and conservative alike—remain deeply skeptical that government can accomplish much in this arena.[41]

Even if the apparatus of government cannot fix the institution of marriage, it certainly can and has prioritized employment as a strategy for departing welfare. From all appearances across the states, processing applications for welfare has become much less about determining a family's eligibility based on income, resources, and family composition—the approach that character-ized welfare application screening through most of the twentieth century. Instead, welfare application came to more closely resemble entering a job-placement agency. Typical of this was Georgia's rule that TANF applicants must first search for work before cash benefits can be authorized. In Bibb County (Macon), Georgia, applicants were required to go through a five-week job search, contacting at least four employers per day, before they could receive public assistance. To back up this type of requirement, most states adopted full family sanctions for families where the adult refused work or to cooperate with other program requirements. This meant a loss of all cash assistance for the whole family.[42] Despite the economic hardship experienced by sanctioned families, this tool came to be widely used. Other, more mun-dane offenses, such as missing meetings with one's case worker, also led to involuntary case closures. More than half of Indiana's 14,428 case closures during one three-month period in 1997 were due to sanctions, not to recipi-ents finding jobs. In Florida during the last six months of 1997, 27 percent of the nearly 150,000 cases closed were due to sanctions.[43] New jobs were behind part of welfare exodus in the late 1990s, but so were strict administra-tive procedures.

As in the past, the future of efforts to modify welfare programming is likely to be marked not only by objective successes, and perhaps some fail-ures, but also by symbolically appealing but rather ineffective provisions. The family cap provides one vivid example of symbolic policy making. First adopted by New Jersey in 1992 as a demonstration project, the family cap, which withholds increased benefits for additional children born on welfare, spread to nearly half the states by 1996. It was written into federal law that year. The policy rested on the premise that increased cash grants for addi-tional children provided an incentive for women on welfare to have more children. Beyond being of limited plausibility—$50 or $60 additional per month for each additional child arguably cannot seem like a bargain for a poor woman who might be considering pregnancy—the evidence does not support its effectiveness. The difference in fertility rates comparing women on welfare to those not on assistance is slight. During the 1990s, women on welfare had some 2.5 children during their lifetimes, compared to approxi-mately 2.1 among non-welfare users.[44] Further, a decline in fertility among women on welfare had been underway for some 30 years prior to the advent of the family cap. The number of children living in welfare families stood at three in 1962, at 2.5 in 1973, and at 1.9 in 2000.[45] Lastly, analysis of national fertility data under the family cap shows no discernable impact on births to women on welfare. This finding holds across both white and black women.[46] However, none of those facts dampened enthusiasm for this policy. That the rate of out-of-wedlock births rose to over one-quarter alarmed many, and women on welfare provided a politically viable target for this frustration.

## WHAT HAS BECOME OF THE WELFARE DEBATE?

In keeping with the pattern seen during earlier eras, public discourse about welfare faded to a shadow of its former self shortly after the passage of TANF in 1996. While a sampling of major newspapers collectively printed well over 200 articles annually on welfare and poverty through the early and mid-1990s, that number shrank dramatically within two years of Congress' completion of welfare reform. Figure 7.1 shows the rise and fall of welfare as a public issue from 1990 through 2006, as measured by the annual count of newspaper stories in the Lexis-Nexis news archive of major U.S. papers mentioning *welfare* and *poverty*. At decade's beginning, this sample of newspapers ran between 200 and 300 stories annually, including editorials, that mentioned these terms. That number jumped to 319 in 1995, only to fall back again from 1998 thereafter. Similarly, welfare declined significantly in importance for public opinion polling organizations. Where the number of polls mentioning welfare during the mid-1990s had numbered as high as 620 in 1995, the comparable number fell to less than 150 annually beginning in 1998. Figure 7.1 shows the annual counts for both news sources and public opinion polls.[47]

Further evidence of the steep decline in attention given to welfare comes from political scientists Saundra Schneider and William Jacoby.[48] Their analysis of major television networks' coverage from 1990 to 2000 reveals a peak of coverage during 1995 and 1996, and then a dramatic fall off beginning in 1997. Nearly 100 television news stories appeared during 1995, compared to fewer than 20 per year prior to 1994 and from 1997 onward. Negativity toward welfare increased along with the volume of coverage. In both TV news and an accompanying analysis of *New York Times* reporting, the voices in these media became distinctly more critical of public assistance. On television in 1995, negative treatment of welfare overshadowed positive treatment by nearly six-to-one. In print that year, the *New York Times* ran five times as much negative treatment as positive treatment of welfare.[49] This 1995 peak of reporting volume and negativity toward public assistance stands in contrast to the years early and late in that decade, periods that witnessed substantially more balanced treatment of welfare as an issue. Schneider and Jacoby concluded that the shift in publicized elite

**Figure 7.1**
**Annual count of news and poll mentions of welfare.**

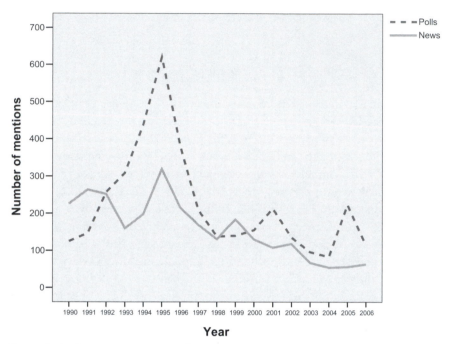

*Source:* Author's computations. See endnote 47.

discourse explained most of the shift in an antiwelfare direction during the mid-1990s.

Not only do counts of newspaper stories and questions in public opinion polls reveal a steep decline in attention paid to welfare since 1996, but evidence from elected officials in state governments shows a similar trend. Based on surveys of governors' aides and state legislators in 1996 and 2001, welfare as an issue moved down the list of issues about which constituents contact them.[50] Figures in the upper portion of Table 7.1 show that among both governors' aides and legislators, the percentage placing welfare "at or near the top" of the list of issues on which they were contacted by constituents fell between 1996 and 2001. Also, the percentage of these respondents placing welfare "at or near the bottom" of the list rose dramatically, 21 percentage points among governors' aides (from 37 percent to 58 percent), and 33 percentage points (from 28 percent to 61 percent) among legislators. Less dramatic but still significant changes appear in the lower portion of Table 7.1. Here, noticeably smaller percentages of governors' aides and state legislators reported their sense that their constituents watch the positions these elected officials take on social policy questions. Among both governors' aides and legislators, the percentage who reported being watched "very closely" declined by some 10 percentage points from 1996 to 2001.

Both of these sets of figures fit with the trends shown above regarding newspaper stories and public opinion poll questions. Together they illustrate that once welfare reform was put in place, the general public substantially lost interest and left the matter of implementation up to state officials. One explanation for why the welfare debate has largely fallen out of the public view is a sense that the earlier problems of welfare have been fixed. Recipients must work, and assistance is now time-limited. Conservative welfare scholar Lawrence Mead captured this explanation in his observation that Americans are more frustrated with welfare programs than with the poor themselves.[51] This explanation squares readily with polling evidence showing reasonably strong support for helping poor people and for welfare-to-work transitions. This help, however, only extends so far. A decade after sweeping welfare reform, the public remained largely unwilling to pay for the large-scale creation of public-sector jobs to ensure long-term, stable employment for those in need, preferring instead to rely on the existing private-sector labor market.

As this new version of welfare took hold in the states, the debate over it split and moved in two distinct directions. For the largely inattentive general public, the problem of welfare was effectively addressed through a set of policy interventions targeted at chronic welfare use, intergenerational dependency, and nonwork. To the extent that ordinary citizens paid attention to the results of TANF, what they tended to see was a program that rapidly reduced welfare use and that required recipients to actively work their way off public assistance. As far as this view goes, welfare reform was a success, and any needed changes easily fall into the category of fine tuning. For this group, the great welfare debate is over, at least for the moment.

In the other branch of the discussion, carried on around conference tables and in policy journals, welfare-reform supporters continued to focus intently on reducing welfare dependency and to celebrate the policy interventions that have led millions of individuals to no longer rely on public assistance. For critics of conservative welfare reform, however, this exactly misses the point. For them, what matters most is the well-being of poor families. Further, to characterize welfare use categorically as dependency misses the point that in a competitive labor market where less-skilled workers and single parents often end up on the short end of things, welfare provision is a crucial buffer between those families and destitution. For those adopting this perspective, welfare use is a right of citizenship, not a policy problem. This debate, however, is largely lost on a great swath of the

**Table 7.1.**
**Constituent pressure on welfare policy making.**

---

Would you say the volume of constituent contact you receive about welfare places this issue at or near the top of the list of issues about which constituents contact you, near the middle of the list, or near the bottom of the list? (Cell entries are percentages.)

|  | Governors' aides | | Legislators | |
|---|---|---|---|---|
|  | 1996 | 2001 | 1996 | 2001 |
| At or near the top | 20 | 12 | 19 | 8 |
| Near the middle | 37 | 30 | 52 | 31 |
| At or near the bottom | 37 | 58 | 28 | 61 |
| Don't know | 7 | 0 | 1 | 1 |
| *Based on sample of . . .* | *41* | *33* | *79* | *104* |

To what extent do you think your (governor's) constituents watch how (you vote/the positions he or she takes) on social policy questions? (Cell entries are percentages.)

|  | Governors' aides | | Legislators | |
|---|---|---|---|---|
|  | 1996 | 2001 | 1996 | 2001 |
| Very closely | 37 | 27 | 22 | 13 |
| Somewhat closely | 44 | 56 | 51 | 48 |
| Not too closely | 15 | 15 | 25 | 35 |
| Not at all closely | 2 | 0 | 0 | 4 |
| Don't know | 2 | 3 | 3 | 0 |
| *Based on a sample of . . .* | *41* | *34* | *79* | *100* |

*Source:* Survey of state legislators and governors' senior aides. See Shaw 2000 for details.

American people. Not until the nation's awareness of poverty as a persistent phenomenon in the midst of an otherwise affluent society rises again will the broader debate likely be vigorously engaged across the breadth of the population.

# NOTES

1. Nathan and Gais 2001; Center on Budget and Policy Priorities "An Introduction to TANF," November 2005 (available online at http://www.cbpp.org/1–22–02tanf2.htm; accessed September 11, 2006).

2. Ron Haskins, "Welfare Revisited: Young Men Need Incentives," August 22, 2006, available at http://www.npr.org.

3. Edelman 2003, p. 99.

4. Gallagher et al. 1998.

5. Author interview with Dave Anderson, Washington State Department of Social and Health Services, March 5, 1996.

6. Gordon 1994.

7. Nathan and Gais (n.d.), chap. 4.

8. Manpower Demonstration Research Corporation 1997 (available online at http://www.mdrc.org/Reports/JOBS2Approaches/JOBS2ApproachesExSum.html).

9. See 2001 report, "How Effective Are Different Welfare-to-Work Approaches?" by the Manpower Demonstration Research Corporation (available online at http://www.mdrc.org/publications/64/execsum.html; accessed June 22, 2007).

10. Center for Budget and Policy Priorities, "TANF at 10," August 17, 2006 (available online at http://www.cbpp.org).

11. Edelman 2003.

12. Blank and Schmidt 2001, pp. 80–81.

13. U.S. Census Bureau, press release, June 2, 2002 (available online at http://www.census.gov/press-release/www/releases/archives/fertility/000317.html).

14. Blank and Schmidt 2001, pp. 90–91.

15. Jencks 2002.

16. Ibid.

17. Acs and Loprest 2004.

18. Gallager et al. 1998.

19. Acs and Loprest 2004; Blank and Schmidt 2001, p. 90.

20. Edelman 2003, pp. 98–99.

21. U.S. Department of Agriculture, "Food Stamp Participation Rate Increases for Third Consecutive Year," press release, 2006 (available online at http://www.fns.usda.gov/cga/pressreleases/2006/pr_0234.htm).

22. Gallagher et al. 1998.

23. U.S. Census Bureau data from the Current Population Survey.

24. National Center for Children in Poverty 2002.

25. Handler and Babcock 2006, p. 3.

26. Ibid., p. 10.

27. Samuelson 2006.

28. Jencks 2002.

29. Edin and Lein 1997; Jencks 2002; see also Edin 1991.

30. Edin and Lein 1997.

31. Thompson 2001.

32. Ibid.

33. Mead 2001, p. 216.

34. U.S. Census Bureau data from "Estimated Median Age at First Marriage, by Sex: 1890 to Present," September 15, 2004.

35. Family Violence Prevention Fund, "Bush Marriage Promotion Plan Could Endanger Victims of Abuse, Advocates Say" (available online at http://endabuse.org/programs/printable/display.php3?NewsFlashID=495); accessed June 22, 2007).

36. Nathan and Gais 2001.

37. Fact sheets from the Administration for Children and Families, US Department of Health and Human Services, available online at http://www.acf.hhs.gov/programs/

ofa/drafact.htm    and    http://www.acf.hhs.gov/opa/spotlight/welfareauthorized.htm
(both accessed June 24, 2007).

38.  Richard Wolf, "New Welfare Rules Designed to Reduce Rolls," *USA Today,*
June 29, 2006, p. 5A.

39.  *New York Times,* "Mission Unaccomplished," August 24, 2006, p. A1.

40.  Handler and Babcock 2006.

41.  Nathan and Gais 2001.

42.  Gais et al. 2001, p. 40.

43.  Katz 2001, p. 331.

44.  U.S. Census Bureau data from "Fertility and Program Participation in the
United States: 1996" Jane Lawler Dye, May 2002 (report no. P70-82).

45.  U.S. Census Bureau data from "Participation of Mothers in Government
Assistance Programs: 2001," Terry Lugaila, September 2005 (report no. P70-102).

46.  Kearney 2004.

47.  The count of public opinion poll items asking about welfare were drawn from
the Roper Center's Public Opinion On-Line database (available through Lexis-Nexis),
and the count of news mentions of welfare and poverty come from the Lexis-Nexis
news archive (http://www.lexisnexis.com) of major U.S. news sources. The sample of
news sources were those included for every year from 1990 through 2006, inclusive,
in the "major papers" section of the Lexis-Nexis news archive. This list included the
*Boston Globe,* the *Christian Science Monitor,* the *New York Times,* the *San Francisco
Chronicle,* the *Seattle Times,* the *St. Louis Post-Dispatch,* the *St. Petersburg Times, USA
Today,* and the *Washington Post.* News stories were those mentioning *welfare* and *poverty,* while selected polls were those mentioning *welfare.* The poll and news archives
were accessed and counts were tabulated during January 2007.

48.  Schneider and Jacoby 2005.

49.  Ibid., p. 371.

50.  See Shaw 2000 for explanation of 1996 survey. The same method was used for
the 2001 survey.

51.  Mead 2005.

# 8

# Conclusions

Pervading all nature we may see at work a stern discipline which is a little cruel that it may be very kind. . . . The poverty of the incapable, the distresses that come upon the imprudent, the starvation of the idle, and those shoulderings aside of the weak by the strong . . .are the decrees of a large, far-seeing benevolence. . . . Similarly, we must call those spurious philanthropists, who, to prevent present misery, would entail greater misery on future generations. All defenders of a poor-law must, however, be classed amongst such.

—Herbert Spencer (1872)[1]

Indigence is produced not by the social or economic system, but by the deviance of the poor. The necessary punishment for deviance is poverty.

—Larry Backer (1993)[2]

You are going to have some who are just not going to be able to make it. Welfare reform didn't just present an opportunity. It also presented a certain amount of pain for not being able to take control of your life.

—U.S. Representative Clay Shaw (1997)[3]

Surveying four centuries of American poor-relief practices and rhetoric might lead one to wonder how much things ever change. The continuities of the debate are striking and include a sense of societal obligation to provide for poor people, but also in many quarters a vision of poverty as moral failure and relief as dependency builder; a need to supervise the poor; and the distinction between more-deserving versus less-deserving petitioners. Despite the underlying support for assisting those in need, the view of penury as moral failure poses a conflict for most Americans in their thinking about how to extend help to the impoverished while not simultaneously doing them harm. The centrality of this conflict hindered innovative thinking at least up until the early twentieth century. Many liberals argue that it still does. This conflict in beliefs about the poor led town councils in colonial times typically to offer help only in kind rather than in cash. Firewood, clothes, and food seemed unlikely to be abused by their recipients, while cash grants might be frittered away on drink. Outdoor relief through the nineteenth century might, it was thought, have tempted poor people to live debauched, unsupervised lives, as it left them to their own devices in their own homes. Institutionalization was intended to address both maladies, though in practice it likely undermined well-being at least as much as it helped. Poorhouse life was often grim by design, as deterrent, though not until the late 1800s did Americans' disquietude over those conditions eventually led to the widespread closure of poorhouses, first in the case of children, and later more broadly. Its difficulties not withstanding, the poorhouse represented, in its peculiar ways, the dual urges to help the poor with their material needs while steering them away from loose living. Later, from friendly visitors up through supervision by professional social workers during the middle of the twentieth century, charity and welfare beneficiaries still found themselves on the receiving end of this dual approach: aid combined with surveillance. Today's job search programs combined with personal responsibility contracts and elaborate sanctions for aid applicants echo this long-standing dualism of American welfare provision. Overseers of the poor—currently and historically—communicate to aid applicants something akin to, "We will help you, but this will not be pleasant."

For what it is worth, modern social science has not left these assumptions unexamined. The criticism that welfare provision depresses recipients' work effort, as much of a mainstay as this view has been among conservatives, finds little empirical support in studies of welfare recipients and their employment patterns. Summing up over 100 such studies, policy analysts Danziger, Haveman, and Plotnick found that transfer programs reduce the total number of hours worked annually by just under 5 percent, on average.[4] Robert Lampman, one of the nation's foremost authorities on the negative income tax, estimated the effect of transfer programs to be somewhat higher, approximately 7 percent.[5] As trifling, in liberals' view, as such figures are, they are largely beside the point for many conservatives, who instead often insist, in everyone-just-knows fashion, that welfare undermines both the work ethic and the morality of its recipients. Upon touting the accomplishments of his state's welfare-to-work programs in 1997, Wisconsin Governor Tommy Thompson was asked about the well-being of former recipients and how he knew that, in his words, "the vast majority of them have jobs and are working" and that "they're doing better, and they like it."[6] Thompson admitted the evidence to be unscientific and "anecdotal."[7] Similarly, in 1996 former Wisconsin State Senate majority leader Joseph Strohl defended his support of his state's "Learnfare" program, which sanctioned the families of chronically truant children in what turned out to be an ineffective effort to improve their school attendance. The state spent some $10 million on the program, yet the vast majority of those sanctioned did not return to school. Strohl insisted that those program expenses were "irrelevant" and that efforts to keep children in school were worth whatever they might cost, even if they were largely ineffective.[8] This seat-of-the-pants approach to welfare policy implementation is common, even if criticized from time to time by both liberals and conservatives. Conservative-minded UCLA management professor James Q. Wilson, commenting on calls to abolish welfare as a means of reducing the number of out-of-wedlock births, said the idea was dubious and "in large measure based on untested assumptions, ideological posturing and perverse priorities . . . It is, at best, an informed guess."[9] In keeping with the tradition of resisting good-quality studies of the effects of recent welfare reforms, in May 1999, the U.S. Senate rejected Sen. Paul Wellstone's, Democrat of Minnesota, bill that would have created a national study of the well-being of former recipients.[10] Conservative welfare scholar Lawrence Mead critiqued the modest impact of social scientists' input on welfare reform in a 2005 essay, writing that policy makers routinely act in ways that fit with their moral beliefs regardless of the consequences, and that "in implementing TANF, most states consulted their experience rather than systematic inquiry."[11]

Another long-standing criticism of poor relief has been its presumed connection with increased fertility. Studies of an early guaranteed-income program used in Speenhamland, England, in the 1790s show that providing a minimum subsidy to families was not associated with significantly greater fertility rates.[12] In more recent times, the income maintenance experiments of the 1970s in the United States found only modest effects on fertility rates among women designated to receive a guaranteed monthly income in Seattle and Denver.[13] Following the 1996 reforms, studies of the impact of the family cap have revealed no systematic differences in the fertility rate in states with the family cap versus those without.[14] However, such studies have done little to diminish the popular belief in welfare's destructive effects on families.

Social science has attempted to speak to the efficacy of numerous aspects of welfare provision, but the public and policy makers appear very selective in their embrace of those empirical findings. A 1997 study from the Manpower Demonstration Research Corporation, supporting a work-first approach to welfare-to-work transitions (as opposed to initial investments in education and training), had a great deal of influence over state policy makers, but that piece of careful research was the exception rather than the rule. Part of the social science–policy-making disconnect in the contemporary period is at least as attributable to academy-based poverty scholars wearing their predominant liberalism on their sleeves as it is due to policy makers who neglect empirical evidence when crafting new programming.[15] This substantial failure of social science and policy making to meet stands as a lost opportunity to shed truly informed perspectives on welfare provision.

## TRANSFORMATIONS OF THE WELFARE DEBATE

Beyond the continuities in the debate over provision for the poor, several important changes have marked the American conversation about welfare. In particular, altered thinking on motherhood, race, and appropriate sources of relief deserve a brief discussion. Since the very early years of European settlement in America, a large portion of those in need have been women and children. At the beginning of the twenty-first century, women and children still comprised 74 percent of America's 38 million poor people.[16] Once the distinction between the so-called worthy and unworthy poor was clearly drawn in the early 1800s, women and children were considered part of the former category. Poor widows and their offspring were seen as the quintessential needy cases, as they had fallen on hard times not through any fault of their own, but rather due to the untimely deaths of their male heads of household. New England town records are replete with cases of widows cared for in various ways through the colonial period. In early Philadelphia, women were housed in the city's poorhouse more regularly than men, who were instead often put to labor or hospitalized until they could return to work. Explicitly, the expectation was that men were more important workers than were women.[17] Through the late 1800s and early 1900s, women still found themselves not particularly welcome in the labor market. Labor organizer Samuel Gompers, founder of the American Federation of Labor (AFL) and its president nearly continuously from 1886 to 1924, articulated the AFL's position in 1906 by proclaiming that women's greatest contribution to society came in "attending to the duties of the home," and that they need not participate in the wage labor economy, where, after all, they might displace men and drive down male wages.[18] The U.S. Supreme Court echoed this sentiment in a 1908 decision, opining that a "woman's physical structure and the performance of maternal functions place her at a disadvantage in the struggle for subsistence . . . [since] healthy mothers are essential to vigorous offspring, the physical well-being of woman becomes an object of public interest and care in order to preserve the strength and vigor of the race."[19] This maternalistic but restrictive line of thinking was central to the rationale behind state mothers' pensions created during the second decade of the twentieth century. Women were valued as mothers but were appreciated as laborers in only limited sectors of the economy. By 1914, 27 states had passed "protective legislation" that banned women from working in establishments that sold alcohol, in mines, as taxi drivers, as elevator operators, and the like.[20] This resistance to women in the workforce persisted in the minds of some observers into the middle of the twentieth century. The journalist Norman Cousins expressed the sentiment clearly in 1939: "There are approximately 10 million people out of work in the United States today. There are also 10 million or more women, married and single, who are job holders. Simply fire the women, who shouldn't be working anyway, and hire the men. Presto! No unemployment. No relief rolls. No depression."[21]

Poor women's privileged position, if it can be called that, faded through the early part of the second half of the twentieth century for at least two reasons. As women entered the workforce in larger numbers through the Second World War and thereafter, Americans slowly became more accepting of women as wage laborers, and the restrictive pedestal women had perched aloft began to erode. Second, during the 1940s and 1950s, poor mothers were increasingly never-married women rather than widows. This demographic shift rapidly stripped away the sympathy they had received prior to this time, and Americans increasingly blamed welfare-dependent women for their self-inflicted troubles. That women continued to face discrimination in the labor market—and as of 2005, only earned 79 cents for every dollar earned by men—did little to defuse increasing calls from the mid-1960s onward to steer welfare mothers into jobs.[22] Motherhood, prized and protected in its own way through mothers' pension programs of the early twentieth century, had lost its glow 50 years later. The landmark federal welfare legislation of 1996 included a motherhood work exemption only for women with children less than three years of age, or under one year at state option.[23] After that, in the view of national policy makers, poor mothers should be led into the workforce like everyone else.

A second shift in the debate over welfare regards race. Of course, race has always played a prominent part in determining who would receive assistance and who would not. Early American communities expended many fewer resources in relieving poverty among people of color than among European Americans. Records from eighteenth-century New England reveal that black and Native American women rarely received public aid, and African

Americans were disproportionately warned out from early American cities and towns.[24] In the South, free blacks were routinely excluded from what assistance programs existed, and when Charleston, South Carolina, sponsored the first municipally funded orphanage in 1790, black children were not welcome.[25] County-level data from the South through the mid-twentieth century illustrate that African American families were less likely to receive welfare, and when they did, it tended to be less than comparable white families received.[26]

Racial discrimination certainly created a second-class citizenship with regard to relief up through the middle of the twentieth century, but after that time, discrimination spilled over to taint welfare as a whole. As the face of the national welfare caseload became more black after 1950, the tone of the welfare debate shifted to a more pejorative one than had been heard during the second quarter of the century. By the 1960s, the race-based animosity toward AFDC was unmistakable, and by the 1970s, the specter of a persistently poor, racial minority urban underclass served as a dominant trope for discussions of welfare. Mass-media coverage through the 1980s and 1990s lent its part to this highly color-conscious depiction of the poor by portraying them as overwhelmingly of black or brown skin, even though most poor Americans were then, and still are, white.[27] European Americans also made up the majority of those on AFDC until welfare use began its steep decline, due to policy changes and a strong economy, in the mid-1990s.[28] As racial minority recipients in fact finally came to account for the majority of all those on welfare, the convergence between America's lingering racism merged with the long-simmering resentment of the poor generally and discomfort with welfare in particular, and poor provision came to be seen more as a black and Latino problem and less as one to solve on behalf of particularly deserving Americans.[29]

A third significant shift in the welfare debate has turned on questions of the proper sources of poor relief. From the early decades of European settlement, towns and churches extended aid to needy residents. In time, organized philanthropies joined the effort. Publicly funded assistance was common by the middle of the seventeenth century and was the dominant model of providing assistance by the early 1800s. The construction of municipally funded poorhouses in eastern cities, particularly from the 1730s onward, was driven in part by an effort to care for the poor more efficiently than was being accomplished through outdoor relief, but it also represented a long-term public commitment, in infrastructure costs, to the poor. Not until the third quarter of the nineteenth century did calls for the abolition of public relief approach a critical tipping point. Several eastern cities abandoned their assistance programs throughout the 1860s and 1870s, but most continued poorhouse or outdoor relief. The beginning of the social- work-movement in the late 1800s crystallized the argument that public relief was destructive of private charity and of the newly emergent notion of treating poor people as individuals with unique circumstances amenable to social-workers' interventions. Complaints that making relief public would subject it to political corruption held some sway throughout this period, but by the second decade of the twentieth century, this fear too had fallen in the face of rapidly spreading publicly funded mothers' pensions. Despite the power of the argument for private relief bound together with individual mentoring, private charity simply could not meet the demand of widespread urban poverty. Only governments could muster the needed resources.

At the beginning of the twenty-first century, the George W. Bush administration advanced the idea of harnessing the charitable impulses of faith-based organizations to administer selected welfare-to-work programs, but that effort has been limited by very modest budget allocations and by a resistance on the part of some religious groups to compartmentalize their primary mission: saving souls.[30] For them, maintaining a separation of church and state undermines their interest in partnering with governments.

In light of lessons learned historically about the fiscal need for government involvement in poor relief, and considering the deep ideological stakes both conservatives and liberals hold in this policy area, it seems extremely unlikely that either side would seriously entertain ceding responsibility for welfare to private sources to any significant degree. This particular part of the welfare debate appears to have been settled for the foreseeable future.

## WHITHER THE WELFARE DEBATE: LOOKING FORWARD BY LOOKING BACK

The history of the discourse surrounding poverty in America has been one of several long periods of muddling through various depths of complacency, punctuated periodically by concerted efforts to think anew about who should receive assistance, how much, and under what conditions. Thinking about where the welfare debate may go from here is probably most effectively grounded in a view of where it has been. In this sense, the pattern of historic punctuations or upheavals in poverty thinking suggests not only that Americans will indeed revisit this issue—by no means did the landmark 1996 legislation settle the matter—but also that the next visitation will likely be prompted by a rediscovery of significant poverty in the midst of our erstwhile affluence, something many Americans appear to strive to ignore despite its substantial constancy. As Americans have rediscovered poverty from time to time, they have reacted alternatively with hopefulness, discouragement, modernized versions of old measures, and occasionally with new approaches. The

Earned Income Tax Credit is one example of this last case. The initial rise of urban poverty in the 1730s and a second wave of the same in the mid-1800s led to institutionalization of the poor, more dramatically the second time than the first, but on both occasions reflecting an urge to control the perceived threats of vagrants and mendicants. The rise of social work in the late 1800s saw poverty workers approach poor people less as a class and more as individuals with, to some extent, idiosyncratic needs and situations. Toward the end of the first decade of the twentieth century, policy makers once again rediscovered poverty and responded with a far-reaching wave of state-level mothers' pensions, which in turn laid the groundwork for the creation of ADC under the Social Security Act. But no sooner had the seemingly affluent 1950s ended than it was once again discovered that some one out of five Americans remained stuck in poverty. In 1964 the Johnson administration declared "unconditional war on poverty," but again the enthusiasm faded, and by 1974, Congress dismantled the Office of Economic Opportunity, the administrative soul of the Great Society programs.[31] Poverty discourse drifted through the next decade amid a vague but growing awareness of an emerging urban underclass before middle-class white Americans once again awoke to the difficulties of caring for the poor, this time to the conservative assertion that welfare was doing at least as much harm as good. The resulting federal legislation of 1996 would rely on labor market mechanisms to move the welfare recipients into jobs, but once the initial celebration (or lament, depending on one's perspective) of that political process was done, the poverty conversation contracted back to one largely limited to experts and social workers.

These periodic bouts with poverty—whether wars, merely skirmishes, or simply periods of policy reform—leave one interesting fact largely unchanged: the percentage of those living in poverty, measured before accounting for transfer programs. From the earliest enumerations of poverty in the 1870s to the present, some one out of five Americans have found themselves in households with less earned income each year than is deemed necessary to meet basic needs. Robert Hunter found this in New York and Boston in the 1890s.[32] The Commerce Department documented it in the late 1950s. In the early 1960s, Michael Harrington brought it to America's attention, and Molly Orshansky formalized the measure on which this conclusion was based.[33] The conservative Charles Murray decried it in the 1980s, and the liberal Center for Budget and Policy Priorities published this finding again in the 1990s (though for very different reasons than Murray).[34] Despite this measure of neediness remaining persistently high, the public's interest in discussing it instead runs in cycles, as the political salience of welfare use, inequality, and urban problems wax and wane. If liberals point to this troubled one-fifth of the nation's population as a case of lingering economic injustice and as an argument for protecting the safety net, conservatives see it instead as evidence of failed governmental attempts to engineer the market, efforts that counter-productively defer the pain of personal irresponsibility.

Various observers have pointed to rising economic inequality as a trigger for a renewed public discourse about poverty in America. A compelling case can be made in these terms regarding the nineteenth century, but perhaps less so for the twentieth century.[35] If dramatic inequality were such a catalyst, one might suppose the nation to be poised for a great conversation at the opening of the twenty-first century. However, this does not seem to be the case. Over the last 50 years, high-income households have gained considerable ground, while low-income households have moved ahead only very modestly. The standard measure of income inequality, the Gini index, which indicates the skew to the distribution of income across the population, stood at 0.399 in 1959. By 2001 it reached 0.466, indicating that even more of the nation's income is accruing to those on the high end of the income scale than was the case some five decades ago.[36] Put differently, near the height of the war on poverty, in 1967, the lowest quintile of Americans received 4 percent of the nation's income, compared to 44 percent of the income going to the top quintile. By 2001 those figures had shifted to 3.5 percent for the poorest one-fifth and fully 50 percent to the top one-fifth.[37] Focusing on the 1990s, income changes hit the poor very hard. Between 1995 and 1997, the poorest 20 percent of female-headed households with children—including both those on welfare and those not—experienced an average decline of $580 in annual income, including housing assistance, the Earned Income Tax Credit, and food stamps. The bottom 10 percent of female-headed households with children fared even worse, with a loss of an average of one-seventh of their incomes during that period.[38] Measures of accumulated wealth inequality also indicate a vast chasm between the haves and the have-nots, particularly along racial lines. In 2000 non-Hispanic white households had a median net worth of $79,400, compared to only $7,500 for the median black household. Even among the poorest households, there exist dramatic cross-racial differences. The lowest quintile of non-Hispanic white households in 2000 had a median worth of $24,000, compared to a mere $57 for blacks.[39] Inequality stands at an all-time high, yet the welfare debate, for the moment, has gone substantially quiet. It would seem that Americans pre-occupy themselves less with the gaps between rich and poor than they do with perceptions of how many of the poor ask for help. This conclusion certainly fits with rising welfare use in the early 1990s and falling reliance on it through the latter half of that decade.

In the end, welfare reform is a recurring process. Early twentieth-century mothers' pensions later facilitated the creation of ADC, which in time ran afoul of middle-class sensibilities and prompted changes through the 1980s that set up another revisiting of policy in the 1990s. In this sense, each phase of welfare reform can be seen as a step toward the next, inevitable round of reform. Because poverty relief involves truly difficult trade-offs of collective provision and widely perceived threats to self-worth, Americans move from one horn of this dilemma to the other. Were Americans instead to envision citizenship as involving an entitlement to basic material provision, the welfare debate would likely have been substantially settled by now. But that is not the story so often told of America as a land of opportunity and a place where individuals can rise and fall based largely on their own work. There certainly persists disagreement on just how much homage to pay to the market versus the notion of social citizenship, and to the extent that continues to be so, politicians, experts, and citizens—be they poor or otherwise—can expect another episode of poverty rediscovery and poor-relief reform as Americans continue their struggle with this terribly difficult and important dilemma.

# NOTES

1. Spencer's 1872 *Social Statics* (pp. 352–54), quoted in McCarthy 1963, p. 37.

2. Backer 1993, p. 1016.

3. Jason DeParle, "Lessons Learned: Welfare Reform's First Months," *New York Times,* December 30, 1997, p. A1.

4. Danziger, Haveman, and Plotnick 1981; Masters and Garfinkle 1978.

5. Lampman 1979.

6. Jason DeParle, "Welfare Crucible—A Special Report: Cutting Welfare Rolls but Raising Questions," *New York Times,* May 7, 1997, p. A1.

7. Ibid.

8. Author interview with Joseph Strohl, April 22, 1996, Madison, Wisconsin; see also Corbett 1995.

9. Quoted in Katz 2001, p. 320.

10. Katz 2001, p. 336.

11. Mead 2005, pp. 404–6 (quote on p. 406).

12. Blaug 1963, 1964.

13. SRI International Inc. 1983, especially Part 6, chap. 7.

14. Kearney 2004.

15. Mead 2005.

16. Data from the 2005 American Community Survey, U.S. Census Bureau available online at http://factfinder.census.gov (accessed June 22, 2007).

17. Wulf 2004, pp. 173–78.

18. Sidel 1986, p. 52.

19. Ibid.

20. Ibid., p. 53.

21. Ibid., p. 55.

22. U.S. Census Bureau data, 2005. See Historical Income Tables comparing median annual incomes of female and male full-time workers, including table available online at www.census.gov/hhes/www/income/histinc/p41ar.html (accessed June 22, 2007).

23. Gallagher et al. 1998, p. V-1.

24. Herndon 2004; Hodges 1999.

25. Wisner 1970, p. 23–24; Murray 2004, p. 228.

26. Lieberman 1998, chap. 4.

27. Gilens 1999. As of 2005, 58.5 percent of poor Americans are white (Census Bureau data from the 2005 American Community Survey).

28. Katz 2001, p. 322.

29. Sniderman and Piazza 1993; Edsall and Edsall 1991.

30. Black et al. 2004.

31. Lyndon Johnson's 1964 State of the Union address, *Public Papers of the Presidents of the United States, 1963–64,* bk. 1 of 2, p. 91. Washington, DC: General Services Administration.

32. Hunter 1904, pp. 22–25.

33. Harrington 1962.

34. Relying on data from the U.S. Census Bureau; see Murray 1984 and the Center for Budget and Policy Priorities ("Strengths of the Safety Net," a 1998 report, available online at http://www.cbpp.org (accessed February 10, 2007). For a history of early, unofficial poverty measures, see Fisher 1997.

35. Nash 1979.

36. Census Bureau data, available online at http://www.census.gov/hhes/www/incoem/histinc.ie6.html (accessed February 10, 2007).

37. Census Bureau data, available online at http://www.census.gov/hhes/www/incoem/histinc.ie3.html. (accessed February 10, 2007).

38. Katz 2001, pp. 338–39.

39. U.S. Census Bureau "Net Worth and Asset Ownership of Households: 1998 and 2000" (May 2003; report no. P70-88, p. 12).

# Appendix 1

# Time Line of Significant Developments in American Social Welfare Provision

| | |
|---|---|
| 1601 | English Parliament consolidates its poor laws into what came to be called the Elizabethan Poor Law, which became the basis of the first American poor laws. |
| 1664 | Boston opens its first poorhouse. |
| 1675 | Massachusetts legislature provides relief for frontier settlers who were forced from their homes by King Phillip's War, departing from the principle of exclusive local control of relief. |
| 1732 | Philadelphia opens its first poorhouse. |
| 1735 | Boston begins the practice of *binding out* children of neglectful parents to be raised by other families. |
| 1736 | New York opens its first poorhouse. |
| 1790 | Charleston, South Carolina, opens the Orphan House, the first municipally funded orphanage in the nation. African American children are excluded. |
| 1818 | Congress creates a pension program for veterans of the Revolutionary War. |
| 1824 | The Yates Report in New York State critiques the practice of binding out children to indenture, beginning a gradual elimination of the practice around the country. |
| 1862 | Congress creates pensions for disabled Union veterans of the Civil War. |
| 1865 | Congress creates the Freedmen's Bureau, providing limited relief to former slaves until the early 1870s. |

| | |
|---|---|
| 1889 | Jane Addams founds Hull House in Chicago. |
| 1890 | Photojournalist Jacob Riis publishes *How the Other Half Lives,* an exposé on the poverty in New York's tenements, leading to a greater awareness of urban poverty and to reforms of tenement laws. |
| 1909 | President Theodore Roosevelt hosts a social-work conference at the White House that brings together and encourages proponents of mothers' pensions. |
| 1911 | Illinois becomes the first state to enact a mothers' pension program; Missouri follows later this year. |
| 1912 to 1920 | Thirty-eight other states enact mothers' pension programs. |
| 1933 | Congress creates the Federal Emergency Relief Administration to make grants for unemployment relief. |
| 1935 | At Franklin Roosevelt's urging, Congress creates the Social Security Act. This included retirement pensions as well as Aid to Dependent Children (ADC), the first federally funded welfare program explicitly for the children of poor mothers. |
| 1939 | Congress amends the Social Security Act by creating survivors' benefits, politically isolating nonwidows still on ADC. |
| 1950 | Congress expands grants under ADC to help cover living expenses for children's caretakers. Previously, grants were only intended to cover the children's needs. |
| 1962 | Michael Harrington's *The Other America: Poverty in the United States* galvanizes persistent poverty as an issue during a time of perceived widespread affluence. |
| 1962 | Congress changes ADC into Aid to Families with Dependent Children (AFDC), reflecting the addition of caretaker grants in 1950. The program also expands to cover two-parent families where the primary income earner is unemployed (AFDC-UP). |
| 1962 | Congress passes legislation converting an earlier pilot project into a permanent Food Stamp program. |
| January 1964 | President Lyndon Johnson declares "unconditional war on poverty" in his State of the Union address. |
| May 1964 | President Lyndon Johnson speaks at the University of Michigan and sets forth his vision for the Great Society. |
| August 1964 | At President Lyndon Johnson's urging, Congress creates the Economic Opportunity Act, under which Community Action and various other poverty fighting programs were administered. |

| 1965 | Congress creates Medicare and Medicaid programs. |
|---|---|
| 1967 | Congress creates the Workforce Investment Act (WIN) program that mandates registration for work and training programs among women with children over age 6. |
| 1970 to 1973 | Congress considers but rejects President Richard Nixon's proposed Family Assistance Plan (FAP), which would have granted poor families a guaranteed annual income. |
| 1974 | The Supplemental Security Income program begins operation. |
| 1974 | Congress indexes payments under the Old Age and Survivors' programs to the inflation rate, creating annual cost-of-living adjustments. |
| 1981 | Congress passes the Omnibus Budget Reconciliation Act of 1981, cutting welfare spending by approximately 25 percent. |
| 1984 | Charles Murray's *Losing Ground: American Social Policy, 1950–1980* provides a rationale for conservative welfare reform and helps make the prospect of ending welfare entitlement appear politically possible. |
| 1988 | At the urging of the National Governors' Association and President Ronald Reagan, Congress creates the Family Support Act, which puts in place the first specific targets for placing welfare recipients into jobs. |
| 1992 | As the national welfare caseload reaches 13.6 million individuals, candidate Bill Clinton campaigns for president with a call to "end welfare as we know it." |
| 1996 | At the urging of many groups and President Bill Clinton, Congress creates Temporary Assistance for Needy Families (TANF), abolishing the old AFDC program and with it 60 years of welfare entitlement. |
| 2000 | National welfare enrollment reaches 5.8 million persons, less than half the 14.2 million that used the program in 1994. Welfare reform watchers both celebrate the drop in program use and express concern over the well-being of those who might need public assistance but do not receive it. |
| 2006 | Congress reauthorizes the TANF program, strengthening work requirements for aid recipients and holding states more accountable to meet caseload reduction targets. The national caseload reaches a low point of 4.12 million during December. |

# Appendix 2

# Annotated List of Further Readings

## THE COLONIAL ERA AND EARLY AMERICA

Creech, Margaret. *Three Centuries of Poor Law Administration: A Study of Legislation in Rhode Island.* Chicago: The University of Chicago Press, 1936. A history of poor law and relief in a region that significantly influenced nationwide welfare practices.

Nash, Gary B. *The Urban Crucible: Social Change, Political Consciousness, and the Origins of the American Revolution.* Cambridge, MA: Harvard University Press, 1979. Discusses the economic dislocation, income inequalities, and the resulting urban unrest that preceded the American Revolution.

Smith, Billy G., ed. *Down and Out in Early America.* University Park, PA: Pennsylvania Sate University Press, 2004. A collection of essays on poverty and community responses in the Northeast, the mid-Atlantic, and Charleston, South Carolina, during the eighteenth and early nineteenth centuries.

## THE NINETEENTH CENTURY

Bremner, Robert. *From the Depths: The Discovery of Poverty in the United States.* New York: NY University Press, 1969. Traces the transformation of American thinking about the poor from an anonymous class through to the rise of individualized social work.

Katz, Michael. *In the Shadow of the Poorhouse.* New York, NY: Basic Books, 1986. Documents the poorhouse era and its lasting impact on twentieth-century welfare policy.

Rothman, David. *The Discovery of the Asylum: Social Order and Disorder in the New Republic.* Boston, MA: Little, Brown and Company, 1971. Examines the rise of institutionalization of social deviants in the early to mid-nineteenth century.

## EARLY TO MID-TWENTIETH CENTURY

Abbott, Grace. *From Relief to Social Security.* An account of the transition from early twentieth century mothers' pensions to the passage of the Social Security Act.

Patterson, James. *America's Struggle against Poverty, 1900–1994.* Cambridge, MA: Harvard University Press, 1981. An overview of welfare policy through the twentieth century.

Skocpol, Theda. *Protecting Soldiers and Mothers: The Political Origins of Social Policy in the United States.* Cambridge, MA: Harvard University Press, 1992. A social-political analysis of two early social insurance programs—Civil War pensions and mothers' pensions—and how they fostered the creation of twentieth-century government responses to poverty.

## THE GREAT SOCIETY

Harrington, Michael. *The Other America: Poverty in the United States.* New York, NY: Macmillan Publishers, 1962. Catalyzed Americans to think about persistent poverty in the midst of affluence.

Melnick, R. Shep. *Between the Lines: Interpreting Welfare Rights.* Washington, D.C.: Brookings Institution, 1994. Examines the constitutional and statutory arguments over social welfare provision through the mid- and late-twentieth century.

Piven, Frances Fox and Richard Cloward. *Regulating the Poor: The Functions of Public Welfare.* New York, NY: Random House, 1971. A statement of the placating power of welfare provision over poor people.

## THE 1970S AND 1980S

Edsall, Thomas, and Mary Edsall. *Chain Reaction: The Impact of Race, Rights, and Taxes on American Politics.* New York, NY: W. W. Norton, 1991. An analysis of how overreaching liberalism during the 1960s drove a conservative backlash during the 1970s and 1980s.

Mead, Lawrence. *Beyond Entitlement: The Social Obligations of Citizenship.* New York, NY: The Free Press, 1986. A neoconservative critique of welfare and affirmative action.

Murray, Charles. *Losing Ground: American Social Policy, 1950–1980.* New York, NY: Basic Books, 1984. The quintessential Libertarian critique of the welfare state.

## THE 1990S AND POST-1996 WELFARE DEVELOPMENTS

Blank, Rebecca, and Ron Haskins, eds. *The New World of Welfare.* Washington, D.C.: Brookings Institution, 2001. Essays examine the experiences of current and former welfare recipients following the 1996 end of Aid to Families with Dependent Children (AFDC).

Ellwood, David. *Poor Support: Poverty in the American Family.* New York, NY: Basic Books, 1988. Provided the intellectual core of President Clinton's welfare reform plan.

The Heritage Foundation. http://www.heritage.org. Produces conservative analysis and commentary on welfare and many other issues.

Rockefeller Institute (SUNY Albany). "First Look." http://www.rockinst.org/publications/federalism/first_look/index.html. First Look report of early outcomes under Temporary Assistance for Needy Families (TANF).

The Urban Institute. http://www.urban.org. Has compiled a substantial collection of reports on the welfare since the early 1990s, with a focus on the experiences of states and welfare recipients since 1996.

Weaver, R. Kent. *Ending Welfare As We Know It.* Washington, D.C.: Brookings Institution, 2000. A thorough discussion of the 1996 overhaul of welfare.

# Bibliography

Abbott, Edith. *Public Assistance, Volume 1: American Principles and Policies in Five Parts: With SS Select Documents.* Chicago: University of Chicago Press, 1940.

———. "Public Welfare and Politics." *The Social Service Review* 10 (1936): 395–412.

Abbott, Grace. *The Child and the State.* Chicago: University of Chicago Press, 1938.

———. *From Relief to Social Security: The Development of the New Public Welfare Services and Their Administration.* New York: Russell & Russell, 1966 [1941].

Acs, Gregory, and Pamela Loprest. *Leaving Welfare: Employment and Well-Being of Families That Left Welfare in the Post-Entitlement Era.* Kalamazoo, MI: W. W. Upjohn Institute for Employment Research, 2004.

Alexander, John. "The Functions of Public Welfare in Late-Eighteenth-Century Philadelphia: Regulating the Poor?" In *Social Welfare or Social Control? Some Historical Reflections on Regulating the Poor,* edited by W. Trattner, pp. 15–34. Knoxville: University of Tennessee Press, 1983.

———. *Render Them Submissive: Responses to Poverty in Philadelphia, 1760–1800.* Amherst: University of Massachusetts Press, 1980.

Amenta, Edwin. *Bold Relief: Institutional Politics and the Origins of Modern American Social Policy.* Princeton, NJ: Princeton University Press, 1998.

Auletta, Ken. *The Underclass.* New York: Random House, 1982.

Axinn, June, and Mark Stern. *Social Welfare: A History of the American Response to Need.* 6th ed. New York: Allyn and Bacon, 2005.

Backer, Larry. "Of Handouts and Worthless Promises: Understanding the Conceptual Limits of American Systems of Poor Relief." *Boston College Law Review* 34 (1993): 997–1085.

Bailyn, Bernard. *The Ideological Origins of the American Revolution.* Cambridge, MA: Harvard University Press, 1967.

———. *The Peopling of British North America*. New York: Knopf, 1986.

Bane, Mary Jo. "Welfare as We Might Know It." *American Prospect* 30 (1997): 47–53.

Bane, Mary Jo, and David Ellwood. "Single Mothers and Their Living Arrangements." Unpublished manuscript, John F. Kennedy School of Government, Harvard University, 1984.

Banfield, Edward. *The Unheavenly City: The Nature and Future of Our Urban Crisis.* Boston: Little, Brown and Company, 1968a.

———. *The Unheavenly City Revisited.* Boston: Little, Brown and Company, 1968b.

Bartkowski, John, and Helen Regis. *Charitable Choices: Religion, Race, and Poverty in the Post-Welfare Era.* New York: New York University Press, 2003.

Bell, Winifred. *Aid to Dependent Children.* New York: Columbia University Press, 1965.

Berlin, Isaiah. *The Hedgehog and the Fox: An Essay on Tolstoy's View of History.* New York: Simon and Schuster, 1953.

Black, Amy, Douglas Koopman, and David Ryden. *Of Little Faith: The Politics of George W. Bush's Faith-Based Initiatives.* Washington, DC: Georgetown University Press, 2004.

Blank, Rebecca, and Lucie Schmidt. "Work, Wages, and Welfare." In *The New World of Welfare,* edited by R. Blank and R. Haskins, pp. 70–102. Washington, DC: Brookings Institution Press, 2001.

Blaug, Mark. "The Myth of the Old Poor Law and the Making of the New." *Journal of Economic History* 23 (1963): 151–84.

———. "The Poor Law Report Reexamined." *Journal of Economic History* 24 (1964): 229–45.

Block, Fred, Richard Cloward, Barbara Ehrenreich, and Frances Fox Piven. *The Mean Season: The Attack on the Welfare State.* New York: Pantheon Books, 1987.

Bosanquet, Mrs. Bernard. *Rich and Poor.* New York: Macmillan Company, 1899.

Bourque, Monique. "Poor Relief 'Without Violating the Rights of Humanity': Almshouse Administration in the Philadelphia Region, 1790–1860." In *Down and Out in Early America,* edited by B. Smith, pp. 189–212. University Park, PA: Pennsylvania State University Press, 2004.

Breckinridge, Sophonisba. *Public Welfare Administration in the United States: Select Documents.* Chicago: University of Chicago Press, 1927.

Bremner, Robert. *From the Depths: The Discovery of Poverty in the United States.* New York: New York University Press, 1956.

Brenner, Clifford. "Illegitimacy and Aid to Dependent Children." *Public Welfare* 8 (1950): 174–78.

Bridenbaugh, Carl. *Cities in the Wilderness: The First Century of Urban Life in America, 1625–1742.* New York: Knopf, 1968.

Burke, Vincent, and Vee Burke. *Nixon's Good Deed: Welfare Reform.* New York: Columbia University Press, 1974.

Califano, Joseph, Jr. *Governing America: An Insider's Report from the White House and Cabinet.* New York: Simon and Schuster, 1981.

Caraley, Demetrios. "Washington Abandons the Cities." *Political Science Quarterly* 107 (1992): 1–30.

Caro, Robert. *The Years of Lyndon Johnson: Means of Ascent.* New York: Knopf, 1990.

———. *The Years of Lyndon Johnson: The Path to Power.* New York: Knopf, 1983.

Carper, Laura. "The Negro Family and the Moynihan Report." In *Poverty: Views from the Left,* edited by J. Larner and I. Howe, pp. 196–206. New York, NY: William Morrow and Company, 1968.

Chickering, A. Lawrence. "Can We Do without the Poor?" *National Review* 24 (1972): 392–94.

Congressional Budget Office. *Work Related Programs for Welfare Recipients.* Washington, DC, 1987.

*Congressional Quarterly Almanac.* Washington, DC: Congressional Quarterly Press, Inc. 1964, 1967, 1968, 1996.

Connors, Kathleen. "The Gathering Storm: Welfare in a Depressed Economy." *Public Welfare* 49 (1991): 4–15.

Corbett, Thomas. "Welfare Reform in Wisconsin: The Rhetoric and the Reality." In *The Politics of Welfare Reform,* edited by D. Norris and L. Thompson, pp. 19–54. Thousand Oaks, CA: Sage Publications, 1995.

Creech, Margaret. *Three Centuries of Poor Law Administration: A Study of the Legislation in Rhode Island.* Chicago: University of Chicago Press, 1936.

Danzinger, Sheldon, Robert Haveman, and Robert Plotnick. "How Income Transfer Programs Affect Work, Savings, and the Income Distribution: A Critical Review," *Journal of Economic Literature* 19 (1981): 975–1028.

Davis, Mike. *City of Quartz: Excavating the Future in Los Angeles.* London: Verso, 1990.

Devine, Edward. *The Principles of Relief.* New York: Macmillan, 1914.

Diamond, Jared. *Guns, Germs, and Steel: The Fates of Human Societies.* New York: W. W. Norton and Co., 1997.

Dolgoff, Ralph, and Donald Feldstein. *Understanding Social Welfare.* 6th ed. New York: A. B. Longman, 2003.

Dorrien, Gary. *The Neoconservative Mind: Politics, Culture, and the War of Ideology.* Philadelphia: Temple University Press, 1993.

Drucker, Peter. "Three Unforeseen Jobs for the Coming Administration." *Harper's* 221 (1960): 46–53.

Edelman, Peter. "The Welfare Debate: Getting Past the Bumper Stickers." *Harvard Journal of Law and Public Policy* 27 (2003): 93–100.

———. "The Worst Thing Bill Clinton Has Done." *Atlantic Monthly* 279 (March 1997): 43–50.

Edin, Kathryn. "Surviving the Welfare System: How AFDC Recipients Make Ends Meet in Chicago." *Social Problems* 38 (1991): 462–74.

Edin, Kathryn, and Laura Lein. *Making Ends Meet: How Single Mothers Survive Welfare and Low-Wage Work.* New York: Russell Sage Foundation, 1997.

Edsall, Thomas, and Mary Edsall. *Chain Reaction: The Impact of Race, Rights, and Taxes on American Politics.* New York: W. W. Norton and Company, 1991.

Eisinger, Robert. *The Evolution of Presidential Polling.* New York: Cambridge University Press, 2003.

Ellwood, David. *Poor Support: Poverty in the American Family.* New York: Basic Books, 1988.

Estabrook, Arthur. "Poor Relief in Kentucky." *Social Service Review* 3 (1929): 24–42.

Feder, Leah. *Unemployment Relief in Periods of Depression: A Study of Measures Adopted in Certain American Cities, 1857 through 1922.* New York: Russell Sage Foundation, 1936.

Fisher, Gordon. "From Hunter to Orshansky: An Overview of (Unofficial) Poverty Lines in the United States from 1904 to 1965." Poverty Measurement Working Paper, U.S. Census Bureau, Washington, D.C., 1997.

Folks, Homer. *The Care of Destitute, Neglected, and Delinquent Children.* New York: Arno Press, 1971 (originally published 1900).

Friedman, Milton. *Capitalism and Freedom.* Chicago: University of Chicago Press, 1962.

Gais, Thomas, Richard Nathan, Irene Lurie, and Thomas Kaplan. "Implementation of the Personal Responsibility Act of 1996." In *The New World of Welfare,* edited by R. Blank and R. Haskins, pp. 35–69. Washington, DC: Brookings Institution Press. 2001.

Galbraith, John Kenneth. *The Affluent Society.* New York: New American Library, 1958.

Gallagher, L. Jerone, Megan Gallagher, Kevin Perese, Susan Schreiber, and Keith Watson. "One Year After Federal Welfare Reform: A Description of State Temporary Assistance for Needy Families (TANF) Decisions as of October 1997." Washington, DC: Urban Institute, 1998.

Gallup-Black, Adria. "Federalism, Policy Innovation, and Welfare Reform in the American States." PhD diss., Columbia University, New York, 1997.

Gans, Herbert. *The War against the Poor: The Underclass and Antipoverty Policy.* New York: Basic Books, 1995.

Gelernter, David. "Why Mothers Should Stay Home." *Commentary* 101 (1996): 25–28.

General Accounting Office. *Women's Earnings: Work Patterns Partially Explain Difference between Men's and Women's Earnings.* Report #GAO-04-35. Washington, DC, (October) 2003.

Gilbert, Neil. "The Unfinished Business of Welfare Reform." *Society* 24 (1987): 5–11.

Gilder, George. *Wealth and Poverty.* New York: Basic Books, 1981.

Gilens, Martin. *Why Americans Hate Welfare: Race, Media, and the Politics of Antipoverty Policy.* Chicago: University of Chicago Press, 1999.

Gilliom, John. *Overseers of the Poor: Surveillance, Resistance, and the Limits of Privacy.* Chicago: University of Chicago Press, 2001.

Ginzberg, Eli, and Robert Solow. "An Introduction to This Special Issue." *Public Interest* 34 (1974a): 4–13.

———. "Some Lessons of the 1960's." *Public Interest* 34 (1974b): 211–20.

Glazer, Nathan. *The Limits of Social Policy.* Cambridge, MA: Harvard University Press, 1988.

Gold, Steven. *The Fiscal Crisis of the States: Lessons for the Future.* Washington, DC: Georgetown University Press, 1995.

Gordon, Dianna. "The Welfare Monster." *State Legislatures* 20 (1994): 15–23.

Gordon, Linda. *Pitied but Not Entitled: Single Mothers and the History of Welfare.* New York: Free Press, 1994.

Gueron, Judith. "Work Programs and Welfare Reform." *Public Welfare* 53 (1995): 7–33.

Gueron, Judith, and Edward Pauly. *From Welfare to Work.* New York: Russell Sage Foundation, 1991.

Hall, David, ed. *Puritans in the New World: A Critical Anthology.* Princeton, NJ: Princeton University Press, 2004.

Hamilton, Alexander, John Jay, and James Madison. *The Federalist Papers.* With an introduction by Clinton Rossiter. New York: Penguin, 1961.

Hamilton, Donna Cooper, and Charles Hamilton. *The Dual Agenda: Race and Social Welfare Policies of Civil Rights Organizations.* New York: Columbia University Press, 1997.

Handler, Joel, and Amanda Sheely Babcock. "The Failure of Workfare: Another Reason for a Basic Income Guarantee." *Basic Income Studies* 1 (2006): 1–22.

Harrington, Michael. *The Other America: Poverty in the United States.* New York: Macmillan, 1962.

Hartz, Louis. *The Liberal Tradition in America: An Interpretation of American Political Thought since the Revolution.* New York: Harcourt, Brace, 1955.

Heclo, Hugh. "The Politics of Welfare Reform." In *The New World of Welfare,* edited by R. Blank and R. Haskins, pp. 169–200. Washington, DC: Brookings Institution Press, 2001.

Heisterman, Carl, and Paris Keener. "Further Poor Law Notes." *Social Service Review* 8 (1934): 43–49.

Heller, Walter. "An Economic Prognosis for the 1960's." In *The Social Welfare Forum, 1960,* Proceedings of the 87th Annual Forum of the National Conference on Social Welfare, pp. 79–97. New York: Columbia University Press, 1960.

Herndon, Ruth Wallis. "'Who Died an Expense to This Town,' Poor Relief in Eighteenth-Century Rhode Island." In *Down and Out in Early America,* edited by B. Smith, pp. 135–62. University Park: Pennsylvania State University Press, 2004.

Himmelfarb, Gertrude. *The Idea of Poverty: England in the Early Industrial Age.* New York: Random House, 1983.

Hodges, Graham. *Root and Branch: African Americans in New York and East Jersey, 1613–1863.* Chapel Hill: University of North Carolina Press, 1999.

Hodgson, Godfrey. *America in Our Time.* Garden City, NY: Doubleday, 1976.

Hofstadter, Richard. *The American Political Tradition and the Men Who Made It.* New York: Knopf, 1948.

Howard, Donald. *The WPA and Federal Relief Policy.* New York: Russell Sage Foundation, 1943.

Hunter, Robert. *Poverty.* New York: Macmillan, 1904.

Iceland, John. *Poverty in America: A Handbook.* Berkeley: University of California Press, 2003.

Jacobs, Paul. "America's Schizophrenic View of the Poor." In *Poverty: Views from the Left,* edited by J. Larner and I. Howe, pp. 39–57. New York: William Morrow and Company, 1968.

Jencks, Christopher. "Liberal Lessons from Welfare Reform." *American Prospect,* 13 (2002): A9-A12.

Jencks, Christopher. *Rethinking Social Policy: Race, Poverty, and the Underclass.* New York: Basic Books, 1992.

Jencks, Christopher, and Kathryn Edin. "The Real Welfare Problem." *American Prospect* 1 (1990): 31–50.

Kain, John. "Housing Separation, Negro Employment, and Metropolitan Decentralization." *Quarterly Journal of Economics* 82 (1968): 175–97.

Katz, Michael. *In the Shadow of the Poorhouse: A Social History of Welfare in America.* 10th ed. New York: Basic Books, 1996.

———. *The Price of Citizenship: Redefining the American Welfare State.* New York: Henry Holt and Company, 2001.

———. *The Undeserving Poor: From the War on Poverty to the War on Welfare.* New York: Pantheon Books, 1989.

———. "The Urban 'Underclass' as a Metaphor of Social Transformation." In *The "Underclass" Debate: Views from History,* edited by M. Katz, pp. 3–23. Princeton, NJ: Princeton University Press, 1993.

Katznelson, Ira. "Was the Great Society a Lost Opportunity?" In *The Rise and Fall of the New Deal Order, 1930–1980,* edited by S. Fraser and G. Gerstle, pp. 185–211. Princeton, NJ: Princeton University Press, 1989.

Kaus, Mickey. "The Work Ethic State." *New Republic* (1986): 22–33.

Kearney, Melissa Schettini. "Is There an Effect of Incremental Welfare Benefits on Fertility Behavior? A Look at the Family Cap." *Journal of Human Resources* 39 (2004): 295–325.

Kelso, Robert. *The History of Public Poor Relief in Massachusetts, 1620–1920.* Montclair, NJ: Patterson and Smith, 1969.

———. *Poverty.* New York: Longmans, Green and Company, 1929.

King, Desmond. "Citizenship as Obligation in the United States: Title II of the Family Support Act of 1988." In *The Frontiers of Citizenship,* edited by R. Vogel and M. Moran, pp. 1–31. New York: St. Martin's Press, 1991.

Klebaner, Benjamin. "Pauper Auctions: The 'New England Method' of Public Poor Relief." *Historical Collections* 91 (1955): 195–210.

Klein, Philip. *From Philanthropy to Social Welfare: An American Culture Perspective.* San Francisco: Jossey-Bass Publishers, 1968.

Lakoff, George. *Moral Politics: How Liberals and Conservatives Think.* 2nd ed. Chicago: University of Chicago Press, 2002.

Lampman, Robert. "Work and Welfare: New Directions for Reform," *Focus* (Institute for Research on Poverty, University of Wisconsin, Madison) 4 (no. 1, 1979): 3.

Lane, Chuck. "The Manhattan Project." *New Republic* 224 (March 1985): 14–15.

Lawson, Steven. *Black Ballots: Voting Rights in the South, 1944–1969.* New York: Columbia University Press, 1976.

Lee, Charles. "Public Poor Relief and the Massachusetts Community, 1620–1715." *New England Quarterly* 55 (1982): 564–85.

Leff, Mark. "Consensus for Reform: The Mothers' –Pension Movement in the Progressive Era." *Social Service Review* 47 (1973): 397–417.

Lemann, Nicholas. "The Origins of the Underclass [part 1]." *Atlantic Monthly* 257 (1986a): 31–55.

———. "The Origins of the Underclass [part 2]." *Atlantic Monthly* 258 (1986b): 54–68.

Lemon, James. *The Best Poor Man's Country: A Geographical Study of Early Southeastern Pennsylvania.* Baltimore, MD: Johns Hopkins University Press, 1972.

Lemon, James, and Gary Nash. "The Distribution of Wealth in Eighteenth-Century America: A Century of Change in Chester County, Pennsylvania, 1693–1802." In *Class and Society in Early America,* edited by G. Nash, pp. 166–88. Englewood Cliffs, NJ: Prentice-Hall, 1970.

Lens, Sidney. *Poverty: America's Enduring Paradox: A History of the Richest Nation's Unwon War.* New York, Crowell, 1969.

Lewis, Oscar. *La Vida: A Puerto Rican Family in the Culture of Poverty—San Juan and New York.* New York: Random House, 1965.

Lieberman, Robert. *Shifting the Color Line: Race and the American Welfare State.* Cambridge, MA: Harvard University Press, 1998.

Lieberman, Robert, and Greg Shaw. "Looking Inward, Looking Outward: The Politics of State Welfare Innovation under Devolution." *Political Research Quarterly* 53 (2000): 215–40.

Liebman, Lance. "Social Intervention in a Democracy." *Public Interest* 34 (1974): 14–29.

Low, Seth. "The Problem of Pauperism in the Cities of Brooklyn and New York." In the proceedings of the 6th annual Conference on Charities, New York National Conference on Social Welfare, pp. 200–10., 1879.

Lowell, Josephine Shaw. *Public Relief and Private Charity.* New York: G. P. Putnam's Sons/The Knickerbocker Press, 1884. Reprinted by Arno Press & The New York Times Co., 1971.

Macdonald, Dwight. "Our Invisible Poor." *New Yorker* (1963): 82–132.

Manpower Demonstration Research Corporation. *Evaluating Two Welfare-to-Work Program Approaches: Two-Year Findings on the Labor Force Attachment and Human Capital Development Programs in Three Sites.* New York: Manpower Demonstration Research Corporation, 1997.

Marshall, T. H. *The Right to Welfare, and Other Essays.* New York: Free Press, 1981.

Masters, Stanley, and Irwin Garfinkle. *Estimating the Labor Supply Effects of Income-Maintenance Alternatives.* Madison: Institute for Research on Poverty, University of Wisconsin, 1978.

McCarthy, Eugene. "The Anatomy of Poverty." In *The Social Welfare Forum, 1963.* Proceedings of the 90th Annual Forum of the National Conference on Social Welfare, pp. 36–44. New York: Columbia University Press, 1963.

Mead, Lawrence. *Beyond Entitlement: The Social Obligations of Citizenship.* New York: Free Press, 1986.

———, ed. *The New Paternalism: Supervisory Approaches to Poverty.* Washington, DC: Brookings Institution Press, 1997.

———. *The New Politics of Poverty.* New York: Basic Books, 1992.

———. "The Politics of Conservative Welfare Reform." In *The New World of Welfare,* edited by R. Blank and R. Haskins, pp. 201–22. Washington, DC: Brookings Institution Press, 2001.

———. "Research and Welfare Reform." *Review of Policy Research* 22 (2005): 401–21.

Melnick, R. Shep. *Between the Lines: Interpreting Welfare Rights.* Washington, DC: Brookings Institution Press, 1994.

Miller, S. M., and Pamela Roby. "The War on Poverty Reconsidered." In *Poverty: Views from the Left,* edited by J. Larner and I. Howe, pp. 68–82. New York: William Morrow and Company, 1968.

Mink, Gwendolyn. *The Wages of Motherhood: Inequality in the Welfare State, 1917–1942.* Ithaca, NY: Cornell University Press, 1995.

Mohl, Raymond. "The Abolition of Public Outdoor Relief, 1870–1900: A Critique of the Piven and Cloward Thesis." In *Social Welfare or Social Control? Some Historical Reflections on "Regulating the Poor,"* edited by W. Trattner, pp. 35–50. Knoxville: University of Tennessee Press, 1983.

———. *Poverty in New York, 1783–1825.* New York: Oxford University Press, 1971.

Moynihan, Daniel P. *The Politics of a Guaranteed Income.* New York: Random House, 1973.

———. "Welfare Is Back in the News." *Pubic Welfare* 50 (1992): 6.

Murray, Charles. *Losing Ground: American Social Policy, 1950–1980.* New York: Basic Books, 1984.

———. *What It Means to Be a Libertarian.* New York: Broadway Books, 1997.

Murray, John. "Bound by Charity: The Abandoned Children of Late Eighteenth-Century Charleston." In *Down and Out in Early America,* edited by B. Smith, pp. 213–34. University Park: Pennsylvania State University Press, 2004.

Nash, Gary. "Poverty and Poor Relief in Pre-Revolutionary Philadelphia." *William and Mary Quarterly* 33 (1976a): 3–30.

———. "Social Change and the Growth of Prerevolutionary Urban Radicalism." In *The American Revolution: Explorations in the History of American Radicalism,* edited by A. Young, p. 5–36. DeKalb: Northern Illinois University Press, 1976c.

———. *The Urban Crucible: Social Change, Political Consciousness, and the Origins of the American Revolution.* Cambridge, MA: Harvard University Press, 1979.

———. "Urban Wealth and Poverty in Pre-Revolutionary America." *Journal of Interdisciplinary History* 6 (1976b): 545–84.

Nathan, Richard. "Will the Underclass Always Be with Us?" *Society* 24 (1987): 57–62.

Nathan, Richard, and Thomas Gais. *Implementing the Personal Responsibility Act of 1996: A First Look.* Albany: Rockefeller Institute of Government, State University of New York, Albany, n.d. http:// www.rockinst.org/publications/federalism/first_look.

————. "Is Devolution Working? Federal and State Roles in Welfare." *Brookings Review* 19 (2001): 25–29.

National Association of Social Workers. "Facts and Footnotes for Mr. Moynihan." *Social Service Review* 47 (1973): 418–22.

National Center for Children in Poverty. "Will TANF Reauthorization Help More Vulnerable Families?" *News and Issues* 12 (2002), pp. 5, 8.

National Governors' Association. *Views of the National Governors' Association on Major Legislative Proposals: Hearing before the Committee on Ways and Means, House of Representatives.* 100th Cong., 1st sess., February 24, 1987. Nicholls, George. *A History of the English Poor Law.* London: P. S. King & Son, 1899.

Novak, William. *The People's Welfare: Law and Regulation in Nineteenth-Century America.* Chapel Hill: University of North Carolina Press 1996.

O'Connor, Alice. *Poverty Knowledge: Social Science, Social Policy, and the Poor in Twentieth-Century U.S. History.* Princeton, NJ: Princeton University Press, 2001.

O'Connor, Brendon. *A Political History of the American Welfare System: When Ideas Have Consequences.* New York: Rowman and Littlefield, 2004.

Okin, Susan. *Justice, Gender, and the Family.* New York: Basic Books, 1989.

Olivas, J. Richard. "'God Helps Those Who Help Themselves': Religious Explanations of Poverty in Colonial Massachusetts, 1630–1776." In *Down and Out in Early America,* edited by B. Smith, pp. 262–88. University Park: Pennsylvania State University Press, 2004.

Orchard, Berneice. "The ADC Unmarried Mother." *Public Welfare* 18(1960): 203–8, 216–17.

Ornstein, Norman, Thomas Mann, and Michael Malbin. *Vital Statistics on Congress, 2001–2002.* Washington, DC: American Enterprise Institute, 2002.

Padfield, Harland. "New Industrial Systems and Cultural Concepts of Poverty." *Human Organization* 29 (1970): 29–36.

Patterson, James. *America's Struggle against Poverty, 1900–1994.* Cambridge, MA: Harvard University Press, 1994.

Payne, James. *Overcoming Welfare: Expecting More from the Poor and from Ourselves.* New York: Basic Books, 1998.

PBS Video. "America's War on Poverty: My Brother's Keeper." Arlington, VA: Public Broadcasting Service, 1995.

Pechman, Joseph, and Michale Timpane, eds. *Work Incentives and Income Guarantees: The New Jersey Negative Income Tax Experiment.* Washington, DC: Brookings Institution Press, 1975.

Pearce, Diane. "The Feminization of Poverty: Women, Work and Welfare." *Urban and Social Change Review* 11 (1978): 128–36.

Piven, Frances Fox, and Richard Cloward. "The Historical Sources of the Contemporary Relief Debate." In *The Mean Season: The Attack on the Welfare State,* edited by F. Block, R. Cloward, B. Ehrenreich, and F. Piven, pp. 3–44. New York: Pantheon Books, 1987.

————. *Regulating the Poor: The Functions of Public Welfare.* New York: Random House, 1971.

Podhoretz, Norman. "Neoconservatism: A Eulogy." *Commentary* 101 (1996):19–27.

Pole, J. R. *The Pursuit of Equality in American History.* rev. ed. Berkeley: University of California Press, 1993.

Poynter, John. *Society and Pauperism.* London: Routledge, 1969.

Public Agenda Foundation. "The Values We Live By." New York: Public Agenda Foundation, 1996. http://publicagenda.org.

Quadagno, Jill. *The Color of Welfare: How Racism Undermined the War on Poverty.* New York: Oxford University Press, 1994.

Quincy, Josiah. "Report of the Committee on the Pauper Laws." 1821. Reprinted in *The Almshouse Experience: Collected Reports,* edited by D. Rothman, pp. 1–11. New York: Arno Press & The New York Times Co., 1971.

Rainwater, Lee, and William Yancy. *The Moynihan Report and the Politics of Controversy.* Cambridge, MA: MIT Press, 1967.

Rein, Martin. "Choice and Change in the American Welfare System." In *The Annals of the American Academy of Political and Social Science: Evaluating the War on Poverty,* pp. 89–109. Philadelphia: American Academy of Political and Social Science, 1969.

Rein, Mildred. *Dilemmas of Welfare Policy: Why Work Strategies Haven't Worked.* New York: Praeger, 1982.

Riis, Jacob. *How the Other Half Lives: Studies among the Tenements of New York.* New York: Charles Scribner's Sons, 1890. Reprint, New York: Dover Publications, 1971.

Roosevelt, Theodore. "Address to the First International Congress in America on the Welfare of the Child." 1908. Reprinted in *Welfare: A Documentary History of U.S. Policy and Politics,* edited by G. Mink and R. Solinger, pp. 20–21. New York: New York University Press, 2003.

Rose, Nancy. *Workfare or Fair Work: Women, Welfare, and Government Work Programs.* New Brunswick, NJ: Rutgers University Press, 1995.

Rosenberg, Carroll Smith. *Religion and the Rise of the American City: The New York City Mission Movement, 1812–1870.* Ithaca, NY: Cornell University Press, 1971.

Rothman, David. *The Discovery of the Asylum: Social Order and Disorder in the New Republic.* Boston: Little, Brown and Company, 1971.

Rubin, Lillian. "Maximum Feasible Participation: The Origins, Implication, and Present Status." In *The Annals of the American Academy of Political and Social Science: Evaluating the War on Poverty,* pp. 14–29. Philadelphia: American Academy of Political and Social Science, 1969.

Samuelson, Robert. "One 'Reform' That Worked." *Newsweek* (August 2006): 45.

Sanborn, F. B. "Poor Law Administration in New England." *North American Review* 234 (1872): 1–23.

———. "The Poor Laws of New England." *North American Review* 219 (1868): 484–514. Saunders, Blanche. "ADC—A Good Investment," *Public Welfare* 8 (May 1950): 108–10.

Sawhill, Isabel. "The Underclass: An Overview." *Public Interest* 96 (1989): 3–15.

Schneider, Saundra, and William Jacoby. "Elite Discourse and American Public Opinion: The Case of Welfare Spending." *Political Research Quarterly* 58 (2005): 367–79.

Schorr, Alvin. "Poor Law of 1969." *Social Work* 14 (1969): 2, 108.

Scott, William. *In Pursuit of Happiness: American Conceptions of Property from the Seventeenth to the Twentieth Century.* Bloomington: Indiana University Press, 1977.

Serafini, Marilyn Werber. "Not a Game for Kids." *National Journal* 28 (September 1996): 2011–14.

Shapiro, Isaac, Mark Sheft, Julie Strawn, Laura Summer, Robert Greenstein, and Steven Gold. *The States and the Poor: How Budget Decisions in 1991 Affected Low Income People.* Washington, D.C.: Center on Budget and Policy Priorities, and Center for the Study of the States, 1991.

Shaw, Greg. "The Role of Public Input in State Welfare Policymaking." *Policy Studies Journal* 28 (2000): 707–20.

Shaw, Greg, and Stephanie Reinhart. "Devolution and Confidence in Government." *Public Opinion Quarterly* 65 (2001): 369–88.

Shaw, Greg, and Robert Shapiro. "Poverty and Public Assistance." *Public Opinion Quarterly* 66 (2002): 105–28.

———. "Welfare." In *Polling America: An Encyclopedia of Public Opinion,* edited by S. Best and B. Radcliff, pp. 880–92. Westport, CT: Greenwood Press, 2005.

Sheils, Merrill. "What's up Gidler's Sleeve," *Newsweek* (February 16, 1981): 64.

Sidel, Ruth. *Women and Children Last: The Plight of Poor Women in Affluent America.* New York: Viking Penguin, Inc., 1986.

Skocpol, Theda. *Protecting Soldiers and Mothers: The Political Origins of Social Policy in the United States.* Cambridge, MA: Belknap Press/Harvard University Press, 1992.

Smith, Tom. "That Which We Call Welfare by Any Other Name Would Smell Sweeter: An Analysis of the Impact of Question Wording on Response Patterns." *Public Opinion Quarterly* 51 (1987): 75–83.

Sniderman, Paul, and Thomas Piazza. *The Scar of Race.* Cambridge, MA: Harvard University Press, 1993.

SRI International Inc. *Final Report of the Seattle/Denver Income Maintenance Experiment: Volume I.* Menlo Park, CA: SRI International Inc., 1983.

Stack, Carol. *All Our Kin: Strategies for Survival in a Black Community.* New York: Harper and Row, 1974.

Steiner, Gilbert. "Reform Follows Reality: The Growth of Welfare." *The Public Interest* 34 (1974): 47–65.

———. *Social Insecurity: The Politics of Welfare.* Chicago: Rand McNally and Company, 1966.

Sundquist, James. "Coordinating the War on Poverty." In *The Annals of the American Academy of Political and Social Science: Evaluating the War on Poverty,* pp. 41–49. Philadelphia: American Academy of Political and Social Science, 1969.

Taylor, James. "The Impact of Pauper Settlement, 1691–1834." *Past and Present* 73 (November 1976): 42–74.

Teles, Steven. *Whose Welfare AFDC and Elite Politics.* Lawrence: University Press of Kansas, 1998.

Thanet, Octave. "The Indoor Pauper: A Study." *Atlantic Monthly* 47 (June 1881): 749–64.

Thompson, Tommy. "Welfare Reform's Next Step." *Brookings Review* 19 (2001): 2–3.

Tobin, James. "It Can Be Done! Conquering Poverty in the U.S. by 1976." *New Republic* 156 (June 1967): 14–18.

Trattner, Walter. *From Poor Law to Welfare State.* 6th ed. New York: Free Press, 1999.

Truman, David. *The Governmental Process: Political Interests and Public Opinion.* 2nd ed. New York: Knopf, 1951.

U.S. House of Representatives, Committee on Ways and Means. *Greenbook: Overview of Entitlement Programs.* Washington, DC: Government Printing Office, 1987, 1992, 2000.

van den Haag, Ernest. "Ending the Welfare Mess." *National Review* 20 (December 1968): 1260–64.

van der Zee, John. *Bound Over: Indentured Servitude and American Conscience.* New York: Simon and Schuster, 1985.

Weaver, R. Kent. *Ending Welfare as We Know It.* Washington, DC: Brookings Institution Press, 2000.

Whitman, David. "Welfare." *U.S. News and World Report* 113 (October 1992): 38, 40.

Wilson, William. "Studying Inner-City Social Dislocations: The Challenge of Public Agenda Research." *American Sociological Review* 56 (1991): 1–14.

———. *The Truly Disadvantaged: The Inner City, the Underclass, and Public Policy.* Chicago: University of Chicago Press, 1987.

Wisner, Elizabeth. *Social Welfare in the South: From Colonial Times to World War I.* Baton Rouge: Louisiana State University, 1970.

Wood, Gordon. *The Creation of the American Republic, 1776–1787.* Chapel Hill: University of North Carolina Press, 1969.

Wright, Conrad. *The Transformation of Charity in Postrevolutionary New England.* Boston: Northeastern University Press, 1992.

Wulf, Karin. "Gender and the Political Economy of Poor Relief in Colonial Philadelphia." In *Down and Out in Early America,* edited by B. Smith, pp. 163–88. University Park: Pennsylvania State University Press, 2004.

Yarmolinsky, Adam. "Poverty and Urban Policy: Conference Transcript of 1973 Group Discussion of the Kennedy Administration Urban Poverty Programs and Policies." Kennedy Archive, Harvard University, Cambridge, MA.

Zarefsky, David. *President Johnson's War on Poverty: Rhetoric and History.* Tuscaloosa, AL: University of Alabama Press, 1986.

Zimmerman, Edna. "State Aid for Mothers' Pensions in Illinois." *Social Service Review* 4 (1930): 222–37.

Zimmerman, Joseph. "Federal Preemption under Reagan's New Federalism." *Publius: The Journal of Federalism* 21 (1991): 7–28.

# Index

## About the Author

GREG M. SHAW is an Associate Professor in the Department of Political Science at Illinois Wesleyan University. He has published numerous articles in professional journals such as *Public Opinion Quarterly, Policy Studies Journal,* and *Political Research Quarterly,* chiefly on poverty issues and public opinion analysis.

LIBRARY
ST. LOUIS COMMUNITY COLLEGE
AT FLORISSANT VALLEY